In the Company of Media

Critical Studies in Communication and in the Cultural Industries

Herbert I. Schiller, Series Editor

Forthcoming

In the Company
of
MEDIA

Cultural Constructions of Communication, 1920s–1930s

▼ ▼ ▼

Hanno Hardt

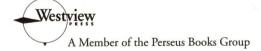
Westview
PRESS
A Member of the Perseus Books Group

Copyright © 2000 by Westview Press, A Member of the Perseus Books Group

Published in 2000 in the United States of America by Westview Press, 5500 Central Avenue, Boulder,
Colorado 80301–2877, and in the United Kingdom by Westview Press, 12 Hid's Copse Road, Cumnor
Hill, Oxford OX2 9JJ

Library of Congress Cataloging-in-Publication Data

Hardt, Hanno.
    In the company of media : cultural constructions of communication,
1920s–1930s / Hanno Hardt.
        p.   cm. — (Critical studies in communication and in the
cultural industries)
    Essays chiefly by the author; includes two essays by Bonnie
Brennen and one essay with Matthew Killmeier as collaborator with
the author.
    Includes bibliographical references and index.
    Contents : Introduction : cultural constructions of communication —
The gaze of the artist : American newspapers in an urban setting —
Revolutionary reportage : constructing the new Soviet journalism —
Negotiated images : the rise of photojournalism in Weimar Germany
— Radio and *kultur* : on the social uses of German broadcasting —
Fictional journalists : news work in American novels / Bonnie Brennen
— Billboards of the dream : Walker Evans on 1930s U.S. advertising
/ Bonnie Brennen — Wireless pleasure : locating radio in the
American home / with Matthew Killmeier — Pierced memories : on the
rhetoric of a bayoneted photograph.
    ISBN 0-8133-1422-4
    1. Mass media and culture. I. Brennen, Bonnie. II. Killmeier,
Matthew. III. Title. IV. Series.
    P94.6.H37 1999
    302.23—dc21
                                                                           99-29461
                                                                                CIP

10   9   8   7   6   5   4   3   2   1

To Vida,
revolucionarka za vedno

Contents

▼ ▼ ▼

Figures

▼ ▼ ▼

Preface and Acknowledgments
▼ ▼ ▼

This book explores the imaginative construction of a cultural history of the media in a series of essays that draw on various artistic and intellectual narratives of Western societies and trace incidental encounters with the means of social communication in different cultural and political settings. By privileging narratives that pertain to the creative definitions of media in the cultural life of a society—and to the emergent media technology during the 1920s and 1930s, in particular—these essays seek to contribute to an understanding of media and their construction in the imagination of artists and writers by reflecting specific attitudes or feelings toward the uses or practices of media.

In fact, the book insists on the proximity of art and everyday life—for the purpose of incorporating the creative into social meanings of media—and suggests that artistic production as social production remains culturally and politically relevant beyond the 1920s and 1930s. The public display of specific artistic constructions of media by artists and, therefore, the creation of specific media realities make works of art important sources of public understandings of media practices. Because of a history of separation of the arts from everyday life by politics and commerce—particularly in the United States—there is much to be done to overcome these traditional barriers. This book is a beginning, and, as such, it is suggestive rather than definitive, selective rather than exhaustive in its treatment of creative and professional narratives concerning media uses and practices.

Since media are not only lived but also remembered, they are found reconstituted in rich and sometimes powerful narratives that challenge the interests of the cultural historian of communication. Such narratives—including the visual arts—are based on reflections or interpretations that are grounded in the real conditions of existence at a specific historical moment. Thus, this book also identifies and describes what Raymond Williams calls structures of feeling, emergent cultural phenomena that manifest themselves in the production of words and images as text.

The book reflects my continuing interest in understanding media through the cultural narratives of uses and practices as elements of a cultural history of communication; thus, Chapters 2, 4, and 5 incorporate earlier discussions that have appeared in *American Journalism, Communication Review,* and the *Journal of*

Communication Inquiry, respectively. Material in Chapter 4 draws on "The Site of Reality: Constructing Photojournalism in Weimar Germany, 1928–33." *Communication Review* 1(3): 373–402, 1996. Material in Chapter 5 draws on "Social Uses of Radio in Germany," *Journal of Communication Inquiry* 6(2): 7–20, and is reprinted by permission of Sage Publications, Inc.

But books are also more often than not collaborative efforts. This one is no exception. I would like to thank my colleagues: Bonnie Brennen, who contributed Chapters 6 and 7; and Matthew Killmeier, who collaborated on Chapter 8. I also wish to thank Derek E. Johnson, who produced an excellent translation for Chapter 3; my research assistant, Liu Xiu, who helped during the final stages of this project; and Katreen Hardt, who assisted with research on New York City artists for Chapter 2. My colleague and director of the School of Journalism and Mass Communication at the University of Iowa, John Soloski, generously provided financial and assistantship support, while graduate students in communication studies and mass communication supplied a congenial intellectual atmosphere for this work.

Book projects need publishers, and I am grateful to Catherine Murphy of Westview Press for her patience during the past years and her guidance through the final process of putting this book together.

Additional institutional support has come from a number of organizations, which have granted permission for the use of images, particularly in Chapters 2, 7, and 8: the ACA Gallery; the Metropolitan Museum and the Whitney Museum of American Art (all in New York); the National Museum of American Art and the Library of Congress Prints and Photographs Division (both in Washington, D.C.); the Butler Institute of American Art (Youngstown, Ohio); Thomson Consumer Electronics, Inc. (Indianapolis, Indiana); and Philips Electronics North America Corporation (Tarrytown, New York).

Hanno Hardt

*Never go forward without going
back first to check the direction.*

—**Bertolt Brecht,** *About the Way to
Construct Enduring Works,
1929–33*

*By now almost nothing that happens benefits storytelling;
almost everything benefits information.*

—**Walter Benjamin,** *The Storyteller, 1936*

Now art is the most effective mode of communication that exists.

—**John Dewey,** *Art as Experience, 1934*

Indeed, literary studies are largely an investigation of ideologies.

—**Leo Löwenthal,** *Zur Literatursoziologie, 1932*

*History concerns itself with changes in the forms of culture, and
aims to discover the real carriers and causes of change in each
particular case.*

—**Georg Simmel,** *Der Konflikt der modernen Kultur, 1918*

1
▼ ▼ ▼

Introduction:
Cultural Constructions
of Communication

This collection of essays focuses on the cultural constructions of public modes of communication in the United States, Germany, and the Soviet Union during the 1920s and 1930s, decades of expansion and transformation of the public sphere in those countries. It was a time when capitalist reconstructions of the media—or socialist transformations, for that matter—combined with literary, artistic, and professional innovations to reshape post–World War I realities.

Knowledge about communication in society arises from the lived experience of individuals, whose encounter with the means of communication defines their uses, and in ways that enhance our understanding of particular cultures. There are several ways of locating media in the course of an epoch. Constitutive texts—such as institutional histories—about the role and function of media in various cultures reveal a good deal about their uses, practices, and ideological foundations. If we move beyond the dominant forms of historical narrative about the institutional media, the focus shifts to issues such as the position of media workers, the idea of work, and class. Visiting ordinary sites of cultural discourse discloses public perceptions and definitions of the uses and practices of media in the routines of everyday life, the media's social, political, and economic context as manifested in individual desires and collective needs. These structures of feeling, as Raymond Williams has called them, provide the framework for the examination of cultural phenomena in this collection of essays.

The rise of modern media institutions is a cultural consequence of technological innovations that reverberate in the social, economic, and political environments.

Indeed, twentieth-century media are the expressions of modernity; by overturning traditional understandings of communication, they create a different sense of community that is both symptom and cause of accelerated demands for change. The latter reflect the political and social volatility arising from the proliferation of new information and enhanced personal mobility—in effect, a crisis of control and stability, at least in Europe. The contemporary press, photography, film, and broadcasting have been central agents of cultural change, engendering timely redefinitions of social communication as they become a central part of the change of the culture in which they operate at a specific historical moment.

The encounter with new media technologies—as part of a process of social and political development—produces a descriptive and explanatory narrative that is the topic of the following essays. Such a narrative also represents a site of struggle over meanings and purposes of media uses and practices of the period, since media technology is always problematic. It is neither a neutral nor a deterministic element of change, but rather part of social discourse, which, when turning political, becomes vulnerable to attacks and open to the potential of transformation.

The articulation of meanings and definitions of media by their various constituencies also provides insights into alienation as time collapses onto itself with the rise of new media like broadcasting, where transmission and reception occur simultaneously with the speed of wireless communication from continent to continent. Distances among individuals increase while opportunities for personal contact decrease dramatically, because technologies of communication, with their incessant demands on time and place, isolate individuals. Even traditional media like newspapers are used by their readers to create distance and separation in the technologically determined environment of urban spaces.

These essays explore a cultural narrative that accompanies the introduction of photography and radio broadcasting during a time of change. It is a narrative that produces and reproduces the meanings of media in an increasingly media-conscious environment whose roots extend into the commerce and political milieu of the times. Such consciousness reflects the centrality of media in constituting and executing the technological rationality of capitalism, which searches for explanations and definitions of media as cultural products. In fact, the realm of culture is the terrain on which technologies of communication are introduced, established, and reinforced; it is also what defines their presence in the public sphere. By concentrating on representation through a critical reading of various contemporary texts, these essays reveal the cultural outlook that directs considerations of media uses and practices.

These texts constitute the cultural constructions of the means of communication by artists, intellectuals, and professionals during the 1920s and 1930s. Their responses, however nontraditional or even critical, nevertheless embrace the dominant explanation of media in society. The latter is set in distinct ideological locations or contexts, ranging from notions of freedom of expression in the

United States to rising democratic principles in Weimar Germany to implementations of socialism in the Soviet Union.

The media are a rich reservoir of a living culture, a kind of public conversation that reveals what moves a nation's social, political, and economic spheres. The media also tell us about themselves. The collective goal of these essays is to present and describe a historically relevant media discourse—albeit in the margins of cultural practices (in art, literature, and journalism)—by treating art and intellectual productions as constitutive material signs of conversations about the media. Although such narratives may be neither politically important nor socially relevant, they nevertheless belong to a venerable tradition of thick descriptions of the relations between media and society in fiction, journalism, and the visual arts. By privileging such cultural constructions of communication, these essays also emphasize the relevance of the incidental or superficial as a surface phenomenon of modern society. In fact, this collection of essays reflects what Siegfried Kracauer (1995, 75) once called the "surface-level expressions" of an era, which "by virtue of their unconscious nature provide unmediated access to the fundamental substance of the state of things" and whose knowledge depends on their interpretation.

Such expressions of an era—manifest in contemporary publications, popular literature, and the visual arts of the 1920s and 1930s—provide the raw material for a critical inquiry into an understanding of media uses and practices at the brink of a technologically driven and politically and commercially exploited demystification of reality. It is a time when new media—and broadcasting, in particular—invade, disrupt, and conquer the private sphere to promote the need for their permanent presence in the lives of individuals. It is also the time when technologies of communication give rise to the spectacle of a mediated existence through the proliferation of pictures, texts, and sounds in the public sphere.

Thus, the 1920s and 1930s are a transformative period of the media in the daily lives of many individuals in the United States, Germany, and the Soviet Union. Such transformations are accompanied by a cultural critique of the media or by alternative definitions of their uses or practices that offer some understanding of the ideological placement of new and old media technologies. The attendant narratives range from exposing the plight of newsworkers in the United States to redefining photography or broadcasting in Weimar Germany to reconstructing the function of the press in the Soviet Union. They include, in every instance, an expansion of a technological rationale, either as an extension of advanced capitalism in the West or as a transition to socialism in the East. The economic dependence of media technology on culture results in a variety of explanations that offer yet another view of media in society. They also challenge the traditional constructions of media histories that have relied more on the strength of institutional sources than on the presence of particular cultural expressions. These essays suggest collectively the importance of reconstructing media history as a story of its users and producers.

Traditional American media history abounds with informative accounts, ranging from comprehensive explanations of the institutional growth of press, magazines, and broadcasting to specialized treatments of individual media practices to the role of particular participants in public communication. Such accounts are typically based on research and writing that focuses on institutional sources and relies on the perpetuation of perspectives that mimic older media (or journalism) histories. Together they provide insights into the workings of media industries and the contributions of publishers or editors, although often without much social or cultural contextualization.

As a result, the historical discourse about media remains isolated from a broader social context and neglects or even disregards understandings of other cultural observers, including artists and writers. In fact, their visions, which focus on the social uses of media, have never entered into a dialogue with traditional producers of media history.

Not even the impact of new ideological perspectives and the rise of cultural studies—which resulted in a new appreciation of social history as an empowering explanation of the present—generated a radically new approach to media history as a form of social knowledge. As I have written elsewhere (1995), media historians have operated under specific social and political conditions; they continued to reproduce compilations of facts—sometimes assisted by a trend toward social-scientific explanations and quantitative history—and to rely on traditional, ideological constructs of media history that reinforced the idea that the history of journalism ought to investigate the institutional power of the press rather than individual participation in the production of media or, more radically speaking, the relationship between the professional practice and private use of media.

The preferred turn to a new understanding of history privileges the realm of culture; it relies on the relationship between culture and history to focus on the significance of discourse, text, and material practice in the renegotiation of historical representations. Its resulting appeal to cultural studies or media studies—and potentially media history—rests on its challenge of conventions and an insistence on the cultural sphere as a central arena of interpretation. In fact, a reconceptualization of media history as a history of media as texts promises to uncover a new awareness of communication in society. The identification and description of interpretive communities and their appropriation of competence—emanating from studying the actual process of media work and its reception by audiences—emerge and constitute the basis for relocating the sense of media power, including the power to define journalism. Such a task would concentrate on notions of accessibility and use, and on how social communication forges definitions of media and society.

However, media history still perpetuates its own ideological position, drawing on the enduring strength of Progressivism, a turn-of-the-century idea that is central to understanding the rise of American journalism to power and influence.

At the end of the 1990s, Progressivism still provides a convenient mindset and a predictable historical narrative for media historians.

The importance of cultural history, as exemplified in the work of Raymond Williams, lies not only in its concentration on the historical potential of the text as product but also in Williams's idea of culture as a "whole way of life." Cultural history should attend to various influences on the construction of texts: the impact of institutional power, the process of work, and more specifically, the intellectual climate of being in the world of journalism.

However, this project proceeds beyond traditional journalism (or media) history or considerations of journalism as social text to consider the cultural construction of the media in the process of creative and intellectual work. Its premise is that media are made not only by individual founders of institutions and realized through the collective commitment of their workers—and subsequently reconstructed in historical treatments of journalism—but are also symbolically reconstructed by the creative labor of various cultural forces in society. They define media by an imagery of their social uses and practices that pervades the discourse of society. Thus, media become part of the cityscapes or rural landscapes of America—or the political environments of the Soviet Union and Germany—where they interact with a range of historical social and cultural practices.

Such an approach suggests that a study of the media is enriched and validated by an awareness of the historical frameworks that provide the media with a cultural identity. The consequence is a cultural history of the media (and journalism) that is based on the importance of cultural practices. It includes the relationship between art and artistic production and society, in particular, since art carries significant cultural weight—especially during the period under examination, when aesthetic discourse moves beyond the private sphere of artists and intellectuals into the public realm, where it typically—but not exclusively—surfaces in an engagement with politics or in the world of commercial illustration and advertising. The presence of images and the process of image making become part of a public narrative in which realism surfaces in the form of reportage and photographic documentation. Texts rival illustrations in their attempts to reconstruct reality, and observation is the key to the acquisition of knowledge. The work of artists and writers contributes to an understanding of a media-centered, urban, and cosmopolitan existence in which technology in the service of democracy becomes an attainable goal (as exemplified by the conditions in the United States) while cultural practices reflect scientific explanations of society.

This book, then, constitutes an exploration of the cultural production of media history. It is driven by curiosity about the potential of culture as a source of historical explanations of media uses and practices and is committed to demonstrating the vitality of cultural perspectives by relying on specific examples of artistic and intellectual labor in the making of media history. Such a project begins with considerations of history and cultural practices and focuses on the representations of media in literature, journalism, and art.

The notion of history has been invariably conditioned by the specificity of the reigning arguments of a particular period, ranging from scientific explanations and the fetishism of facts that preoccupied traditional history to cultural constructions and the centrality of the narrative in contemporary cultural history. In the latter case, linguistic codes constitute social and discursive formations. For instance, Jonathan Culler (1976, 260) once proposed that

> the best way of imaging a relationship between literature and society which could form the basis of a cultural history ... is to think of both literature and the culture of which it forms a part as institutions composed of symbolic systems which enable actions or objects to have meaning, among them literature and genres, whose conventions are devices for the production and organization of meaning.

Similarly, in an earlier turn toward a cultural history, Roland Barthes (1967, 65) wrote, "The narrative of past events, commonly subjected in our culture, since the Greeks, to the approval of historical 'science,' placed under the imperious guarantee of the 'real,' and justified by the principles of 'rational' exposition—does such a narrative really differ from imaginary narrative, such as one finds in the epic, the novel and drama?" Both Culler and Barthes blur the difference between the real and the imagined and confirm the intertextuality of text and context.

But cultural history is understood here as a process of imaginative reconstruction or as a practice of representation that intends to recall the past for purposes of clarifying and/or reinforcing contemporary experiences without obscuring the differences between text and context. It is based on working within an understanding of cultural materialism that recognizes the relationship between the production of meaning and social reality as a meaningful way of distinguishing between text and context. Thus, there is a reciprocal relationship between the discursive and material domains that represents the presence of literature—in the widest sense—as a primary source of insights about media and media practices. Cultural production remains a mode of material production and, therefore, a constituent of social reality. According to Raymond Williams (1977, 99, 165)—who sees "language and signification as indissoluble elements of the material social process itself, involved all the time both in production and reproduction" and who maintains the materiality of writing as activity or practice—language is "a constitutive element of material social practice." The resulting view of cultural history avoids the quagmire of textuality and acknowledges the importance of social, political, and economic contexts; issues of power; and questions of control when the processes of defining media uses and practices become instances of generating social or cultural realities.

As such, these essays constitute an inquiry into an infinite reality that is based on the changing conditions of existence. Since the reasons for historical inquiry change with history itself, however, history must always be partial; there will always be more to tell or see under different social, cultural, or political circumstances and for different intellectual and ideological reasons.

Social and political developments once provided the context for locating the significance of media institutions and their role in society with a strong emphasis on the production of media and their struggle for prominence and influence among other institutions. Notions of competition and survival become important aspects of this story—reminders of the impact of social Darwinism on social thought—and determine the perspective of the historical narrative. The result has been a media-centered approach to journalism history that neglects the context of reception and the formation of a cultural response to the appearance of various media in society. However, beyond distribution (of print media) or installation (of radio sets)—with the intent of cultivating reading and listening habits—they have endured under quite different circumstances. For instance, newspapers and radios have been used by individuals to satisfy specifically private needs—while exceeding their intended purposes—from serving as wrapping paper or body shields to substituting as decorative furniture. Their presence in the lives of people—apart from their specified functions—has been largely neglected, although it is well documented in a variety of cultural records. Likewise, professional (or political) intent has produced definitions of media that reflect the particular interests—or anxieties—of authors caught between progress (the emergence of new technologies or the transformations of older technologies) and their traditional roles as guardians of culture.

The idea of culture is applied here broadly to suggest, along with Williams and others, a context of social existence that contains the experience of communication and the real appearance of media in the daily affairs of people. This perspective indicates that considerations of media history include not only the site of specific details of institutional and professional practices—which constitute one aspect of the historical narrative—but also the verbal and artistic constructions of the encounter with media in everyday life. Media not only create a social and political reality, but they are also used—and reconstructed in their role and function—by individuals for a variety of other purposes. In fact, media history as a cultural production focuses on the practices of cultural workers, their observations about the presence and uses of media in society, and their placement of media within the public and private spheres of society. Their visions provide insights into the place of media and give meanings to artistic or intellectual constructions of media in the world.

When artists or writers describe the social uses of the media during specific historical moments, their efforts provide not only a measure of the significance or importance of media in society, but also demonstrate the pervasiveness of a media culture and its effects on the observer. These essays also explore intellectual and creative expressions that contribute to the making of media in the social and cultural environment of society, where artists and writers have shaped a vision of newspapers, broadcasting, or photography, for instance, as means of communication and integral parts of a technological age. While institutional mandates and professional interests determine questions of meeting informational demands and deciding appropriate forms of communication, artistic and intellectual sources explore the actual existence of media in society with their real or anticipated consequences for individuals. The ensuing observations reinforce the centrality of media in the life of a modern society whose conversations reflect and are reflected in the role of media.

The result is a different media history, steeped in cultural expressions that offer new insights into the relationship between media and society. They range from the rise of definitions and understandings of professional practices to the implementations of communication technologies and the public uses of the media as consumer objects under differing ideological conditions. Running through these essays as a subtext is the realization that while social institutions adapt to media technologies, social, political, and cultural environments also influence the uses of media technologies. Consequently, there is a reciprocal relationship between emerging media technologies and their location within a specific culture at a given historical moment. Even traditional media undergo transformations tied to social conditions. Thus, radio as a communication technology is limited—or freed—by operating within respective cultural contexts; the definition of photography as a powerful visual technology is confined by specific values; and the press, an older technology, is redefined by political institutions or artistic reactions to its pervasiveness. In other words, depending on the prevailing power structure, media technologies develop in various ways to serve the needs of the dominant power structure and reflect the hegemonic order.

Taken together, the following chapters concentrate on the uses of media in Germany, the Soviet Union, and the United States during the 1920s and 1930s, a period of intensive developments in culture and politics. Since they explore the narratives of a specific era, they also provide opportunities for understanding the social and historical currents of the times in various cultural settings and suggest the potential for a cultural history of communication that cuts across political boundaries.

By supplying insights into the observations of differing constituents of cultural experiences in the United States and Europe, the book contributes to a definition of media history that embraces various practices in the name of journalism and communication. Despite similar institutional developments and professional responses to the demands of a modern public, media histories—across different societies—reflect the ideological and political differences in their respective cultural settings. At the same time, however, a recurrent theme of "Americanization" appears in the cultural discourse of Germany and the Soviet Union, for instance. It suggests the pervasive authority of notions of democratic practice and technological advancement that spread from the United States across Europe to engage the imagination of those facing change under difficult political conditions.

Thus, the book becomes an attempt to break down conventional understandings of media history by expanding the search for an intuitive grasp of communication and the role of media and an understanding of media history that includes media uses and the realm of cultural production. The nuanced details of artistic renditions, literary expressions, or intellectual deliberations concerning media and their place in society constitute a series of inquiries into a range of media, from books, newspapers, and magazine advertising to prints, paintings, billboards, and photographs. Collectively they provide an insightful commentary on the importance of media in the discourse of society and advance an analysis of the cultural narrative in pursuit of a cultural history of media.

Chapter 2 focuses on the contributions of American printmakers to the story of newspapers in urban America, with artistic depictions of newspapers in the public and private spheres of the city. Artists are keen observers of society, and their creative or even critical insights constitute yet another form of information about relations between the press and the conditions of the city. Their visual narratives address the uses of metropolitan newspapers as companions in the everyday life of the city dweller, suggesting not only their constant presence in the cityscape but also their importance in the public or private conduct of individuals. The presence of newspapers speaks to the question of communication in an urban society and reveals the paradox of isolation and alienation in a large city. It also emphasizes the transitory nature of the press, whose use value does not reach beyond the end of the day. What emerges from the artistic constructions of the press is a definition of newspapers that supports neither institutional claims nor privileges social nor political significance of the press. Instead, it promotes the idea that the strength of the newspapers may rest in the notion of individual use for purposes that exceed the intent of journalists and publishers.

Chapter 3 shifts to an account of the emerging Soviet newspaper, whose social and political goals differed radically from those of the bourgeois Russian press. This literary and photographic narrative reflects the tempo of gathering information and producing a progressive newspaper for a revolutionary era in which a new form of journalism asserts itself vigorously for the benefit of the people. The essay provides an example of two competing and reinforcing narratives concerning the emergence of a new press. There is the literary construction and language itself that imitate the type and substance of Soviet journalism, and there are the photographs that form yet another essay about the making of a newspaper. Text and photographs reinforce each other, reflecting the intensity of language and the proximity of the visual statements. The juxtaposition of words and pictures merges ideas of progress and constructs a new solidarity of efforts to create an alternative reality for journalism. The essay provides a contemporary example of literature and photography in the service of articulating journalism as a new form of communication in an emerging revolutionary society.

Chapter 4 deals with the invention of photojournalism in Weimar Germany by publishers and photographers under pressure to react against the impact of foreign influences and of intellectuals engaged in an almost immediate critique of photographic practices in the mass circulation press. The rise of picture magazines and the rapidly increasing demands for picture coverage encounter a reluctant, ill-prepared newspaper industry across a vast political spectrum. The process of adaptation becomes a process of negotiation over the uses of photographs as means of communication that pits traditional values against innovative practices and privilege text over image. In addition, existing photographic coverage—mostly in magazines—provides reasons for an immediate assessment of the image as a problematic, even dangerous form of expression, resulting in a uniquely modern critique of the visual as an element of social communication. Thus, photojournalism in Weimar Germany is the story of reluctant change and critical opposition to a particular application of photographic images that strengthen the hegemony of capitalism.

Chapter 5 moves from the realm of literature to journalism as a narrative of contrasting realities. The essay reconstructs the social uses of radio in Weimar Germany through the pages of *The New York Times.* Here journalism as reportorial observation and commentary privileges radio in the cultural context of German society. The narrative consists of a series of short items, or fillers, in the foreign news pages from which radio emerges as a centralized, cultural force with a specific cultural intent that reflects the official German attitude toward the uses of broadcasting in society. The collective effect of these items is the rise of German radio in the service of the state and the realization of distinct, institutional differences between German and U.S. broadcasting as cultural or social institutions. The evolving story of German radio is shaped by news values that stress human interest, timeliness—particularly since radio was a popular pastime in the United States—and social or political differences.

Chapter 6 addresses the rise of the reporter as an active participant in shaping the news through fictional accounts. A number of novels in 1920s America reveal the professional life of reporters and expose the plight of editorial labor in city newsrooms. Bonnie Brennen's essay stresses the potential of fiction as a source of historical insights into 1920s journalism with detailed, relevant information about working conditions and the feelings or attitudes of newsworkers. The discovery of what Georg Lukàcs (1981) once called the reportage novel, with its depiction of reality as an eyewitness account or its impulse to expose the details of the work process, provides the context for contemplating the status of newswork in the United States. The essay focuses on the production of a specific workplace reality whose accuracy or authenticity is confirmed by the response of critical reviews. Journalists exist in subordinate roles, with limited power and unlimited economic hardship. These novels serve similar ideological goals; they identify the process of editorial work and provide an ideological marker in the development of the modern press by articulating a class-conscious critique of the workplace in particular and capitalism in general.

Chapter 7 turns to the rise of billboards as social and cultural context in the documentary photography of Walker Evans. Billboards—as signs of the dominant economic order—preside over people's daily routes during the Depression. They are everywhere—or so it seems—like reminders of hopes for an elusive middle-class affluence. Billboards and homemade signs, as documented by Evans, suggest the pervasiveness of advertising in the America of the 1930s. They offer ideological explanations for an American way of life that creates appearances of prosperity in the face of abject poverty and despair. It is not only an unromantic way of locating American culture but also an engaged argument for photography's value in recording and remembering a historical moment. Evans—like his artist colleagues in New York—notes the presence of yet another medium in the streets of the city and comments on the significance of the visual narrative. The result is a vision of America that must live with the power of images and their effects on the imagination. Advertising in general and billboards in particular reinforce the dominant ideology as they accompany the individual through the streets of the city and into the countryside. Evans exposes this role of advertising in a capitalist society through his revealing photographs; he constructs a reality that lives off appearance and is besieged by the signs of a commercial culture.

Chapter 8 provides insight into the definition of radio as it appears in the living rooms of America in the 1930s, exploring the advertising narratives about radio in family magazines. The rise of broadcasting is accompanied by the manufacture of radio sets and specific commercial appeals to potential buyers. The emerging advertising narrative constructs radio as a raw technology catering to the interests of male customers and at the same time as a household item responding to the role of women. In either case, technology becomes humanized and becomes accessible to the uninitiated, especially with references to middle- and upper-class tastes, the potential of travel, and a general knowledge of the world. Technology is identified with sophistication, and both are attainable through consumption. The construction of radio reveals the era's social, political, and cultural contexts that relate to social mobility, respond to the threat of European politics, and address the physical location of radio sets in the home. Thus, advertisements represent radio as a democratic technology, affordable by most and accessible to all.

Chapter 9 returns more specifically to issues related to the construction of reality, the use of historical evidence, and the role of memory in the assessment of cultural practices that emphasize subjective interpretation. It is a contemplation of the relations between what we see, remember, and know. The use of photographs from the 1920s and 1930s in this case—while emphasizing the attraction of the visual and its prominence as a new public language—also suggests its limitations as evidence. In focusing on the process of interpretation as a subjective and culturally determined practice that involves knowledge and understanding of the conditions of communication, this essay recalls the creative practice of reading a text. It concludes this series of interpretations about the construction of media uses under specific historical situations with a return to subjectivity and the experience of confronting one's own history as well as the importance of community as a source of knowledge. It also serves as a reminder that history is not the expression of a dominant cultural or political order, or a process of identification with an authoritative historical narrative that originates elsewhere, but rather

2

▼ ▼ ▼

The Gaze of the Artist: American Newspapers in an Urban Setting

The documentation of everyday life as a visual experience—beginning with painting and continuing through photography and film—fixes people, objects, and events in time and place and responds to expectations about the image in the discourse of society. In fact, vision occupies a central role in the narratives of Western culture (Jay 1988; Jenks 1995; Debord 1992; Foucault 1977; Merleau-Ponty 1962), and the emphasis on the eye in communication helps to constitute meaning and produce knowledge in the presence of other texts (Calvino 1988). Its importance in constructing social and cultural histories provides the context for this chapter, a visual encounter with artistic representations of newspapers and perceptions of the modern newspaper in an urban environment.

Despite the fact that the study of the press has occupied several academic disciplines for well over a century (Hardt 1979), scholarly inquiries into the physical existence of newspapers and the consequences of their presence in modern society are rare (Fritzsche 1996). Newspapers are portable objects; they penetrate private and public spaces, define real and imagined distances of time and place, and affect human relations with their appearance in people's daily lives. A record of their presence exists in the narratives of society—especially in novels, but also in film, photography, painting, and printmaking—where they make possible an assessment of the memories of a particular era. They are the extensive fragments of a cultural history.

The visual narrative of the arts may contribute profoundly to the construction of a cultural history of the press. Artists, like journalists, transform experience into images of reality that help to explain society. Visual artists and their relations to society offer a rich opportunity for critical observations about the location of media in the social landscape. Engaging the gaze of the artist to explore the presence of newspapers in the social and cultural record of everyday life challenges traditional boundaries of historical inquiry by raising creative thought and artistic expressions to the level of documentary evidence about societal practices; it also legitimizes the role of individual expression in the cultural history of journalism.

As forms of social communication, both history and art—at their best—raise social consciousness; contribute to an appreciation of the discursive in conceptualizing the social, cultural, and political practices of society; and shape the discourse of society by reproducing the tendencies of the times. Like newsworkers, whose experience can be the locus of a reconstructed media history (Hardt and Brennen 1995), artists provide opportunities for challenging dominant interpretations of history. By reconceptualizing traditional visions of newspapers, both journalists and artists—as workers in their respective communities—contribute a diverse perspective on the press as an aspect of urban life.

Recent scholarly works that mine art for insights into historical conditions or disciplinary issues include Peter Paret's *Imagined Battles: Reflections of War in European Art* (1997), Murray Edelman's *From Art to Politics: How Artistic Creations Shape Political Conceptions* (1997), and Maurine Greenwald's "Visualizing Pittsburgh in the 1900s: Art and Photography in the Service of Social Reform" (1997). Whereas Paret and Edelman consider the creative power of artistic expression in historical and political investigations, Greenwald's work focuses on its application to urban social reform. More generally, however, art historians as diverse as Arnold Hauser (1951), Herbert Read (1966), T. J. Clark (1985), and Janet Wolf (1991) have noted the social and cultural conditions for art in Western societies and continue to provide insights into the relation between art and history.

Media historians, on the other hand (and social theorists of culture and communication for that matter) seem unfamiliar with this literature and have ignored the representation of newspapers in the narratives of literature and the arts, where newspapers occupy the public and private spaces of everyday life. Instead, the idea of newspapers—or what constitutes a newspaper—emerges from the institutional press histories that are identified with technological developments, entrepreneurship, and the exercise of First Amendment rights. At best, such accounts reconstruct the presence of the press from traditional evidence and seek to document its institutional practices and their place in social and political history.

The result has been a general neglect of alternative sources that disclose the cultural narrative of society—for example, on the creative responses of literary authors or visual artists to the impact of media on society. Art history has established the specific contexts for American artists and their strong and consistent reactions to social, cultural, political, and economic conditions of the day. Artists constitute yet another intellectual vanguard that challenges traditional conceptions of society and confronts various notions of progress by reflecting on ideological practices and producing critical insights into social existence.

By ignoring the role of visual artists as shapers of visions, purveyors of change, and critics of social conditions, the cultural history of communication overlooks the ways in which paintings, drawings, and prints can creatively evoke the iconology of a period. In fact, cultural histories of communication typically emphasize the emergence of "mass" culture; they adduce the popular—including media practices and their impact on society—and revisit institutional agendas but exclude art as a source of historical evidence. Among recent exceptions are Bonnie Brennen's (1993, 1995) efforts (see Chapter 6) to gain new insights into the relationship between media and society by scrutinizing traditional and revisionist cultural and social histories of the press in light of existing literary treatments about reporters.

An understanding of art and the role of artists is a key to the understanding of society. More specifically, this chapter privileges the artist's gaze and explores its potential contribution to a cultural history of newspapers in 1930s urban America. Frank Luther Mott (1950) called it the era of the "modern newspaper," the aftermath of an economic depression that saw consolidations of media properties and the rise of radio, film, and newsreels as competitive sources of information and entertainment. Since the visual arts of the 1930s were addressing issues of social justice, they are promising sources of social (and political) commentary on the role of newspapers. In fact, they contain critical observations by artists who confronted the popular press (among other institutions), which had become a commercially strong and politically significant cultural establishment supported by millions of daily readers and which faced increasing demands for advertising space.

Another example of the link between a particular set of observations to the totality of social and cultural practices is the emergence of photography, as evidenced in the work of documentary photographers such as Jacob Riis, Lewis Hine, Walker Evans, and Ben Shahn, among others. This trend also signals an understanding of art as an ideological concern that emphasizes the consequences of urbanization. Greenwald (1996, 152), for instance, reports on how the sketches of working-class residents by Joseph Stella and the photographs of Lewis Hine were used to "speak to the eye" in urban reform efforts undertaken in Pittsburgh.

At the same time, visual representations in the form of paintings, prints, or photographs make use of words. They employ texts—in the form of titles or printed and written materials such as books, posters, newspapers, or letters—to confirm or supplement the meaning of the visual and to suggest the relevant relations between word and image in the process of social communication (Butor 1969).

Printmaking—along with documentary photography—became a personal expression of a specific attitude towards the conditions of life. Reproducible and thus easily accessible for large numbers of people, prints ruptured the narrowly defined elitist arena of gallery showings and moved into the mainstream of public life through various modes of publication. For instance, a number of artists joined in the Contemporary Print Group in 1933 to market their prints to close the gap between artists and the public (Flint 1980); the American Artists Congress opened shows throughout the United States in 1936 to increase the accessibility of prints for the public "by making the print relevant to the life of the people, and financially accessible to the person of small means" (*Graphic Works* 1977; *America*

Today 1936). Similar ideas guided the Federal Art Project of the Works Progress Administration (FAP-WPA). Its director, Holger Cahill, oversaw production of more than 200,000 impressions and 11,000 images (Park & Markowitz, 1977); the New York City Graphic Arts Division, established in 1935, advocated prints as a democratic form of art and was responsible for about 50 percent of the FAP-WPA output by 1939 (Kainen 1972).

In addition, the technical potential of reproduction in the form of posters or magazine illustrations also converted art into a public medium whose focus on public issues reduced the distance between art and everyday life. These forms made art socially and politically relevant. For instance, the involvement of artists in Marxist publications like *The Masses* or *The New Masses* demonstrated social concern and political commitment.

The modern newspaper is an urban invention. In fact, Peter Fritzsche (1997, 23) suggests that "the newspaper was inseparable from the modern city, and served as a perfect metonym for the city itself." Identified with the growth of the city and representing its pace, the newspaper invites a process of consumption that is intimately tied to the rhythm of life, moving between haste and leisure, determination and indecision. Read on trains, trams, and buses or perused in the private moments of the day, the newspaper remains the manifestation of a fragmented, decontextualized urban existence. At the same time newspapers appeal to individual readers across class or gender lines; by addressing specific needs, they become an instrument of socialization.

Newspaper content also reinforces values and promotes the power of a shared worldview. On the other hand, content is glossed over and easily forgotten, and newspapers are discarded by necessity and without regret; they mark the daily trail of people moving between places in search of intellectual or emotional gratification; they authenticate urban life. As records of social existence, newspapers locate the reader physically and ideologically and generate various kinds of identities: class, ethnicity, gender, region, or nationality. In his analysis of French society, Richard Terdiman (1985, 120) concludes that the modern newspaper, "in its routinized, quotidian recurrence, in its quintessential prosaicism, in its unrepentant commercialism ... becomes a characteristic metonym for modern life itself."

Newspapers report the noteworthy about the immediate past and are chronicles of specific, ideologically charged constructions of reality whose usefulness ends abruptly, with the purchase of the latest edition. And yet their constant presence in the lives of readers provides a familiar, ideologically consistent, and categorical narrative construction of reality that comforts skeptics and believers alike.

The informal artistic depictions of everyday life not only present objective forms of American life, but they also mark a specific choice of techniques and aesthetic devices in generating social and political appeals. Thus, moving the subject matter from private spaces to public places—streets, public transportation, movie theaters, or parks—acknowledges the importance of the public space in modern life and provides an arena for the critique of its conditions. Consequently, the familiar becomes noteworthy among artists; ordinary circumstances often contain signs of social or political predicaments typically overlooked or disregarded in a society drawn to the spectacular, whereas the main event resides in the ordinary buried in the routines of everyday life. Newspapers constitute part of this environment as ordinary objects of a modern existence; they confer status, dispense information, and provide entertainment, but they are also industrial products whose social uses—as depicted in these works of art—help explain the relations among individuals and with institutions such as the press.

Newspapers are saturated with meanings and representations of social and cultural practices; since any text is read in relationship to others, they are steeped in intertextuality. Roland Barthes (1975) notes the pervasiveness of intertextuality as a hallmark of contemporary culture, in which reality is accessible only in terms of other texts. Thus, the "texts" of 1930s paintings, prints, and lithographs are accessible through newspapers (and their headlines) as representations of public knowledge or institutional power as much as newspapers become plausible requisites of an urban life through the artistic response to the city. The intertextuality of these cultural practices is based on a climate of social and cultural expansion tied to the modern growth of technology and the successful merger of technological advancement and democratic forms. The press and other media of communication participate in transforming the relationship between the individual and nature, promoting the rise of the mechanized landscape (through railroads and automobiles) and reinforcing a general belief in the machine and the notion that change is a desirable social and cultural attribute. The resulting preoccupation with the here and now—accompanied by a loss of history—is the content of the press and the condition of modern existence.

In 1934 the Museum of Modern Art opened "Machine Art," an exhibition of common household and industrial products—ranging from toasters to vacuum cleaners to cash registers—accompanied by its director's suggestion that a way out of the "treacherous wilderness of industrial and commercial civilization [means that] we must assimilate the machine aesthetically as well as economically. Not only must we bind Frankenstein—but we must make him beautiful" (Susman 1973, 5). Indeed, Van Wyck Brooks (1970, 110) argued in his 1917 essay "The Culture of Industrialism" that the United States must rise from the failures of an inherited culture to find its own culture based on everyday experience through the experience of industrialization. The press—with the introduction of telephones, typewriters, rotary presses, and photography—begins to contribute to the construction of a new American culture by merging notions of democracy with a belief in technology to found a modern means of mass communication. Newspapers become the urban representation of modern life with their social and political presence among city dwellers.

As a result of a fast-growing media technology—part of an industrial culture driven in large measure by mass consumption—the American consciousness became technologically informed, filled with images of power and endurance and absorbed by the idea of progress. The critique of technology in America is marginalized in the face of unresolved social and economic problems in urban America and surfaces in traditional yearnings for a return to the pastoral ideal (to echo Leo Marx) or in ideological confrontations between socialist visions of society and the creative genius of late capitalism. Aware of industry's potential, both critiques offer divergent interpretations of the consequences of technological advancement and the specter of a machine in the garden. Newspapers play a major role in the shaping of an American culture as exponents of progress and a better way of life. Their constant presence is a reminder of the collective task of building a better America, where they strengthen capitalism with their knowledge of public tastes and their packaging of information as surveillance and distraction.

The growing presence of media products in the public sphere—beginning with the street sales of magazines and newspapers and culminating in the rise of radio, photography, film, and television—provides artists with a context and focus of their work on the effects of popular culture; visual artists, in particular, are challenged to address the emergence of a visual culture that defied earlier understandings of *Kultur*. Their sense of the ideological in the production of mass entertainment—combined with a desire to comment on the rise of mass culture and a creative need to document the effects of a mechanically reproduced reality—plays a significant role in artistic representations of a modern media culture.

Indeed, American artists occupy a front row in this spectacle of social and cultural change, ready to comment on the experience of a rising media industry that had long abandoned the intellectual artisan tradition of communication for an industrialized process of producing messages for consumption by large and heterogeneous audiences. The reflections of the essayist and pamphleteer had been replaced by the production of public opinion and taste that prized popularity above all other consumption values. American artists continue to face significant changes in the nature of social communication; they benefited from technological change, but they also realized and reflected on the idea of a changing environment seeking to understand the consequences of the machine age.

Artists promptly react to the introduction of new media like movies. Thomas Hart Benton spent time in Hollywood and returned with hundreds of drawings; others—like John Sloan, Reginald Marsh, and Mabel Dwight—also comment in their works on the arrival of movies as yet another replacement of reality (after photography and illustrated magazines) by moving images that challenged society as much as it intrigued artists. Other artists, like Diego Rivera and José Clemente Orozco, respond with an ideological critique that reflects the social and political struggle following the revolutions in Russia and Mexico; since their work is also produced in the United States, it became accessible to American artists—particularly on the East Coast, where it contributes to the tension between European avant-gardism and the growing desire to create a more appropriate American art.

Creative as well as ideological reasons for confronting the presence of media products and their uses in society resulted in a specifically political challenge to the nineteenth century idea of "art for art's sake" as an elitist representation of the role and function of art in society. The economic and political crisis of the 1930s exposes people not only to the myth of progress and equality in capitalist societies like the United States but also energizes artists to address the conflict and encourages the proletariat to take possession of art as a tool of liberation. Artists participate in the surveillance of society, exposing social and economic conditions while sharing their creative insights—not in the prestigious context of galleries or museums, but in the public space of magazines and newspapers, notably in the production of murals as a form of public expression, adapted to the shape and conditions of public spaces and accessible to all segments of society.

At the same time the claims of high culture are challenged by growing demands for low—or popular—culture products, promoted and produced by the media and supported by the relentless developments of various communication technologies like radio, records, film, and photography. The age of "mechanical reproduction"—pronounced by Walter Benjamin at about the same time in Weimar Germany—is one in which the potential of subversion through the mass reproduction and dissemination of art results in a considerable shift in the understanding of culture and the place of artists in particular.

For instance, American artists issue manifestos and join a variety of social and political causes—like the John Reed Club—to promote social justice and the development of a working-class culture. In the context of competing cultural production, movies were considered "a vast corrupt commercial enterprise, turning out infantile entertainment or crude propaganda for the profit of stockholders. Philosophy has become mystical and idealist. Science goes in for godseeking. Painting loses itself in abstractions and trivialities" (Harrison and Wood 1992, 402). When art is conceptualized as a weapon, artists become propagandists in a struggle for equity even when participating in the success of capitalism that was to leave millions of people with nothing but idle hopes and aspirations.

This was also the time when communist and antifascist art begins to appear, mostly in newspapers and magazines of the American left—among them the *Partisan Review* (New York), *Left Front* (Chicago), *John Reed Review* (Washington, D.C.), and the *New Masses* (New York); the last became a major outlet for politically radical graphic artists focused on the rise of Nazi Germany after 1933 (Whiting 1989). Others not directly connected to socialist or communist causes join the attack on Hitler and Mussolini in the early 1940s with the production of paintings, lithographs, and posters in the fight against Nazism and fascism.

However, the major contributions of American intellectuals to Marxism as an alternative ideological position occur in journalism or reportage rather than in the visual arts, notably by writers like Randolph Bourne, John Reed, and John Dos Passos. Granville Hicks and Joseph North have documented the intellectual engagement in cultural-political issues in their collection of writings—*Proletarian Literature in the United States* and *New Masses:. An Anthology of the Rebel Thirties*, respectively (Hicks 1935; North 1969). Also Sidney Finkelstein's *Art and Society*

(1947) is a successful attempt by a Marxist scholar to demonstrate what he called—in reference to Marx—the "humanization of reality." Thus, art becomes a specialized form of creative labor that produces a changed view of reality—a disclosure of the inner world—and not just a recording of the objective world through science, journalism, or photography; art "shows what it means to live at a certain moment, or stage of development, of social life and the conquest of nature. It replaces fact with typicality. It discloses not an actual event but a pattern of outer movement, as a force operating on human hopes and feelings" (Finkelstein 1974, 279).

Similarly, when Meyer Schapiro (1992, 510) identifies the "social bases of art," he argues against the prevailing sentiments of individual freedom for the few at the expense of oppressing the many. He suggests that such freedom "detaches man from nature, history, and society [and cannot] realize those possibilities of individual development which depend on common productive tasks, on responsibilities, on intelligence and cooperation in dealing with the urgent social issues of the moment."

The rise of realism in a social environment dominated by the reality of technological progress results in the portrayal of city life by several printmakers—among them John Sloan, George Bellows, Reginald Marsh, and Edward Hopper—who caught moments of human existence in cityscapes. By the mid–1930s regional artists like Thomas Hart Benton and Grant Wood had begun to focus on the country with black-and-white lithographs of rural life. Social realists also participated in the Federal Art Project of the mid–1930s—among them Ben Shahn, whose militant realism in the tradition of Diego Rivera emerges in his attacks on social injustice. His *The Passion of Sacco and Vanzetti*—unveiled in 1932 in New York—confirms his reputation as a socially and politically committed artist. In this era of technological possibilities, prints are reproduced for mass consumption as posters and illustrations in the press.

The emergence of American printmaking during the first half of the twentieth century marks an extraordinary turn toward people as subjects of a new curiosity: to explore and expose the conditions of life in public places. For instance, in his introduction to a 1936 exhibition catalogue, *America Today*, Alex R. Stavenitz (*Graphic Works*, 1977, 5) suggests that "the exhibition, as a whole, may be characterized as 'socially conscious.'" Accompanied by a rise of realism, the work of these artists is placed in the culture-specific context of concerns for fairness and social justice. The recovery of the realist tradition in artistic expression, however, is also a rediscovery of an imagery of the people at the threshold of an era that would witness their commodification in movie, radio, and television dramas.

In fact, advertising demands a decisive turn to realism, and artists turn to illustration. For instance, the "Art for Advertising" department of the Associated American Artists provided the services of "seventeen highly popular regional painters—including Thomas Hart Benton, John Steuart Curry, and Peter Hurd—to paint pictures for Lucky Strike cigarette advertisements" (Bogart 1997,

234–43). The insistence on realistic renditions of advertising messages coincides with the feeling that realism is a distinctly American art; it parallels the desire of advertisers to appropriate the truth value of art and is indicative of the changing boundaries between the cultural discourse of fine art and the growing power of commercial art. Thus, painters and printmakers face the issue of art and survival in a commodity culture primarily as a question of shifting controls over what had always been a market phenomenon.

The work of Maxfield Parrish best illustrates the artistic response to a public demand for art; it resulted in the production of advertisements, including art prints, accompanied by a creative and intellectual shift from art to illustration and considerable commercial success (Bogart 1997, 234–36). The demands from advertisers and corporate patrons in particular also signify the breakdown between commercial and fine art and suggest the limits of artistic expression with the artists' dependence on big business and the growing influence of commerce and industry on the politics of culture. Not unlike newswork, artwork becomes an indistinguishable production process of advertising and public relations messages. After all, "Art in Advertising must justify itself … in terms of the cash register" (Bogart 1997, 290).

In this atmosphere of cultural transformation, however, some artists continue to confront the conditions of an urban existence, their identity as independent creative workers boosted by government support—like the FAP-WPA—which employed thousands of artists and reinforced the production of American art. In fact, this institutional context encourages the idea of artists as workers in society. With it comes a sense of responsibility to serve the needs of the community with works of art that would stress meaning and content and appeal to a broader public than the traditional, elitist audiences of galleries and museums. Consequently, many artists record the social and cultural practices of modern life in an aesthetically accessible manner to reach a wider general audience.

The result is an art of the American scene created by urban and social realists; the former focus on the city and its people as chroniclers of urban life and without political intent, whereas the latter believe in the role of art in social and political change. For instance, Isabel Bishop argues that she engaged in "observations of fact. I was saying some small thing which was true of American life—apart from politics and economics," whereas Moses Soyer warns artists not to "be misled by the chauvinism of the 'Paint America' slogan.… Do not glorify Main Street. Paint as it is—mean, dirty, avaricious. Self-glorification is artistic suicide. Witness Nazi Germany" (Butler Institute 1996, 75–79).

Beginning with John Sloan's "New York City Life" series of etchings in 1905, printmakers—like George Bellows, Childe Hassam, Edward Hopper, John Marin, and Charles Sheeler, among others—depict the everyday life of people, often in the public thoroughfares of the city. One of them, Fritz Eichenberg (Ekedal and Robinson 1986, 22), a German refugee printmaker, writes about the early 1930s, "I recorded on wood not only what I saw but what I felt, like the Human Comedy on the steps of a brownstone building, and the glitter of Broadway near Times Square, with all its enchanting tinsel, fun and misery. I showed the unemployed warming themselves on the radiators of the Aquarium on Battery Place. And the 'idle rich' feeding the swans on Central Park Lake." And Raphael Soyer (1967, 72) explains, "I always painted what I knew and saw around me. In the 1930s I painted many pictures of unemployed and homeless men, because I saw them everywhere."

Newspapers are very much part of this environment; circulated by the millions every day, their presence on the streets of the city provided an unavoidable encounter not only with a contemporary source of information and entertainment but also with an institutional symbol of continuity and commercial success. Although newspapers were increasingly vulnerable to consolidations and chain ownership during the 1930s, there were still several large daily newspapers in New York City, for instance, where the field had been reduced to four morning and four evening papers by 1940 (Mott 1950, 637). Most of them indulged in the exploitation of working-class practices while inventing imagery that would identify and reinforce a middle-class existence. Newspapers occupy a specific ideological role in the formation of a modern society; by celebrating material success as a social norm, for instance, the press produces middle-class representations that address the life experiences of people. Thus, newspapers in the 1930s cover the running stories of the industrial depression and the beginnings of the New Deal, although the outstanding event of the decade was the 1932 Lindbergh case, resulting in the trial of Bruno Hauptmann and his execution in 1936.

The observations of artists included in this study (see p. 165) reproduce newspapers and their ideological intent in several ways: As part of the cityscape, newspapers represent an interesting cultural aside in the context of other visual representations of an urban lifestyle; as part of an urban existence, readers are located between adaptation and empowerment when newspapers become suppliers of public knowledge and sources of personal comfort. These artists captured a slice of life as people lived it, not unlike the press of the time—including documentary photography—and the realism of contemporary literature. Their American scene is populated by people whose activities are closely observed and reflected in animated images of individuals who make up the life of a city—including working-, middle-, and upper-class representations of the specific relations between individuals and the press. Thus, regardless of whether newspapers appear peripherally or centrally as objects of a visual narrative, their presence reinforces the social or cultural significance of the press across class and gender lines.

Several depictions of newspapers in the representation of urban America offer a particular challenge to cultural historians of the press. This particular selection of images—discussed below—ranging from the early 1900s to the 1940s (although most of the works date from the 1930s) indicate the enduring presence of newspapers in artistic renditions of city life. Unlike later, the press was still a universal medium of information and entertainment during this period. It was present among the working class and, generally speaking, inclusive as a matter of

FIGURE 2.1   *Martin Lewis,* Cathedral Steps, *1931. All rights reserved,* © *The Metropolitan Museum of Art.*

readers' choices rather than exclusive as a marketing strategy (like that of contemporary publishers).

Newspapers assume a number of roles in the depiction of the city as well as the description of individuals. For instance, they are ornaments of an urban environment, discarded objects of a busy life, but also signs of identification, carefully displayed to add prestige and credibility to their owners.

In the prints by Martin Lewis they are carelessly dropped and litter the streets, constituting the defining characteristic of a hectic metropolitan atmosphere. People are on the run; there is movement in both, *Cathedral Steps* (Figure 2.1) and *Subway Steps* (Figure 2.2), with people hurrying past newspapers strewn carelessly over the steps. Although these newspapers are incidental and anonymous objects, they are important in guiding the observer to the motions of individuals who are as indistinguishable as the pages of the newspapers they pass, suggesting not only the rhythm of the city but also the power of anonymity. Newspapers are a fact of urban life, and even in their state of depletion or obsolescence, they are functional signs of an urban culture signaling the presence of an institution that is identified with the social milieu of the city. This work reflects the photographic work of artists around Alfred Stieglitz, in which form diffuses through light and is a reminder of the extensive photographic explorations of the city by many contemporary photographers who documented the details of a prevailing street culture.

FIGURE 2.2   *Martin Lewis,* Subway Steps, *1930. All*

Newspapers are used to evoke the atmosphere of city life in a number of works
by Reginald Marsh, who produced realistic prints of New York City with people in
streets and subways. His observations of subway culture in particular include
newspapers as lost objects, but also—and more significantly—newspapers as the
property of individuals. Here the moment of reading a newspaper isolates individual subway riders from their fellow passengers and draws attention to the
process of reading itself.

For instance, in *Second Avenue El* (Figure 2.3) the viewer faces a middle-aged
man engrossed in reading one section of his newspaper, while *The Daily News,*
with its partially visible front-page headline, "derbilt Elopes,"claims a space on the
seat framed on the other side by a well-dressed woman. To the left a couple is

FIGURE 2.3   *Reginald Marsh,* Second Avenue El, *1929. All rights reserved,* © *The Metropolitan Museum of Art.*

reading a newspaper on the forward seats of the compartment. In fact, the reading of newspapers dominates the image and isolates the lone woman—the non-reader—in an atmosphere of intense preoccupation with the printed word. Similarly, in *Why Not the El* the newspaper has dropped to the floor, the working-class man has fallen asleep, and a middle-aged woman clutching her purse sits next to him, erect, a newspaper partly visible on the other side of the seat. In both prints, newspapers suggest the presence of an outside world in the confined space of the subway; they define the space and dictate the relations of people. Thus newspapers privilege the owner, who is marking his/her space, physically with the help of the unfolded newspaper and intellectually or emotionally by immersing in a study of its content. The result is a distinct separation from the environment and a deliberate retreat into a personal world; the images portray the public as a collection of individuals engaged in their own private activities.

Another image, *Hauptmann Must Die,* is a direct reference to the Lindbergh trial. Here a blond, heavily made-up woman clad in a fur coat sits in the waiting room of a railroad or bus station holding an opened newspaper, *The Daily Mirror,* whose front-page headline screams, "Guilty. Death for Hauptmann" and whose back-page headline reads, "Guilty. Hauptmann Must Die." An obscured

26   *The Gaze of the Artist*

photograph accompanies the headline. Several well-built suitcases at her feet suggest a well-traveled middle-class woman. Behind her, back turned, sits another newspaper reader, whereas other passengers wait passively on the massive benches that dominate the room. At the end of a long and sensational trial, which had occupied the press for weeks, the message goes unnoticed. In fact, as the woman reads the inside of her newspaper, she is oblivious to the story since the headlines are displayed toward the outside; they are for an audience to see—like a public announcement—yet people around the story seem unaffected. Life goes on, the newspaper provides a clear message, but its reach is limited—its significance is circumscribed to a place where people merely pause with other destinations in mind. Headlines offer only brief orientations in time and space. There is great energy in this image, extending from the presence of the newspaper-reading female to the headlines of the newspaper and revealing the decadence and decline of society in a transient environment.

Similarly, in Clement Hauper's *Metro 1st Class* well-dressed individuals, crowded in the confined space of the car, surround the reader, whose newspaper extends outward, pushing against fellow passengers, who are standing face to face without acknowledging one another. The reader is isolated in the ritual of reading on the subway, whereas the faces of his travel companions bear tired, bored, and forlorn expressions that heighten the contrast. Reading the newspaper emerges as a distinctive and meaningful activity that diverts attention from the crowd and suggests an ability to deflect potential intrusion and conflict.

Minna Wright Citron depicts a woman sitting on a box in a subway station, a small stack of newspapers on her lap, her hands in her pocket. She is alone. *An Honest Living* is the portrait of a female news vendor and represents the plight of women in the 1930s. It reflects the strong social conscience of the artist, who was active in the woman's movement. She writes about this image, "there was no model. The woman in this picture is archetypal. She represents the psychology of many women of the day—without training—women who had to reevaluate their thinking and lives.… She had to painfully adjust to the unknown and try to reach for the few opportunities that existed for her" (Ekedal & Robinson 1986, 14). Selling newspapers in the streets of the city required no training and offered no future. Publishers exploited the young and vulnerable—including women—who resorted to selling newspapers in an effort to earn extra money. (Jon Bekken has written extensively about the plight of male and female news vendors [Bekken, 1995, 190–226]).

Aboveground, in the streets of the city, Charles Locke captures the reading of *The Evening Paper*. Whereas the male reader—whose figure fills out the foreground—seems to be more absorbed in his thoughts than in his newspaper, another reader—in the background—is definitely engrossed in his own newspaper. It is an introspective look at life in the city: two men—isolated from the rest of a crowd, leaning against a pillar, perhaps in a subway station—ritually reading the evening paper. This print suggests a physical and emotional isolation of

FIGURE 2.4   *Peggy Bacon,* The Titan, *1929. National Museum of American Art, Smithsonian Institution, gift of Mr. and Mrs. William S. Benedict.*

individuals caught in the process of reading in a crowd. Again, the presence of the newspaper separates rather than unites people, and reading emerges as a thoroughly individual practice.

Similarly, Peggy Bacon's work *Crosspatch* (or *The Titan*) is the detailed study of a newspaper-reading tycoon—a 1920s capitalist, formally dressed in coat, scarf, and hat, standing in a hallway—ready to step out into the public thoroughfare (Figure 2.4). He is perusing a newspaper, and his large frame fills most of the image, implying competence and the power of his social position. The newspaper in his hands becomes a sign of his importance and lends credence to his place in society. But the image also links the newspaper with the influential and powerful and suggests a measure of its own credibility.

In Raphael Soyer's *Window Shoppers* a newspaper is tucked under the arm of a woman who stands on her toes to look over the shoulders of two other women at a window display of a hat shop. Here the newspaper becomes an accessory, like the purse she is holding; but it also signals the identity of an educated and informed individual. The presence of the newspaper suggests intelligence, superior knowledge—if not expertise—and confirms the woman's representation of herself. Thus, the newspaper becomes a cultural code that provides an insight into social standing and that reinforces self-esteem.

Isaac Soyer's *Cafeteria* depicts a coffeehouse scene; the sign on the large window reads, "Ladies Invited." A couple is seated at a small table. The woman looks out over her cup into a pocket mirror, while her male companion holds a newspaper tightly; both are self-absorbed, reading. Mirror and newspaper offer reflections of their being in the world; they invite contemplation and understanding. Although headlines are blurred, photographs of people are visible on the pages of the newspaper, providing evidence and support of the notion that those newspapers are about people but that they are also "daily mirrors." In fact, photographs are mirrors, reflecting reality, albeit in a distorted manner (as does the news); even the actual mirror in the hands of the woman provides merely an approximate image. Mirror and newspaper create and deliver images of the environment; both are equally important for a construction of reality. In fact, a section of the newspaper—visible on the tabletop—reveals yet another photographic image that reinforces the centrality of the image as a modern form of expression and sustains the power of reflection.

Nicolai Cikovsky's *On the East River* depicts two working-class men resting on a pier, looking tired and resigned; it is still daylight and the activities of the harbor occupy the background. The "Daily" tabloid—spread out on the ground in front of them—carries large photographs of men and women which have no relation to these two men; the latter look like Eastern European immigrants, out of place and yet typical of the working-class image of the time. The picture pages in front of them suggest that they may not be able to read more than the photographs themselves. The pictures also demonstrate how the press caters to the demands of an illiterate foreign-born readership. The newspaper is neatly arranged but turned away from them—as if rejected—representing an upside-down world that makes more sense to the artist or observer of the work than to these men. The picture pages depict what they cannot be and cannot understand; thus, the newspaper is yet another foreign space, inviting with its display of faces, whose familiarity becomes deceptive with the absence of textual explanations.

In his 1936 *Street Corner*, Philip Howard Francis Evergood (Figure 2.5) portrays a busy sidewalk packed with individuals whose compression in the limited space creates an emotional as well as aesthetic effect. John Baur (1975, 31) suggests that "it lends itself to a kind of concentrated violence of both feeling and design." Newspapers appear as objects of attention—as one does in the hands of a young male, who is balancing himself on a railing while reading an opened, large-

FIGURE 2.5 *Philip Evergood,* Street Corner, *1936. Courtesy ACA Galleries, New York.*

size newspaper—and neglect, like those littering the street, with parts still readable: The *NY Mirror* leads with "Teen Age Mugger," while the *Daily News* headlines include "Gang War on Baby Face Ride" and "Love Thief Arrested." It is a busy working-class neighborhood with sixteen individuals crowding the narrow sidewalk while moving in both directions. The scene suggests Evergood's concern with social problems engendered by individuals with different ethnic backgrounds occupying the same frame with their diverse activities. The newspaper headlines offer a verbal sketch of the urban environment and suggest the preoccupation of 1930s journalism with violence. They are set against a modest but peaceful setting that implies poverty rather than crime. The presence of these newspapers expresses the complete cycle of their daily appearance in the street life of a city and demonstrates the short distance between usefulness and uselessness and the ease with which the press moves from one to the other.

The company of newspapers in the private spheres of individuals becomes an equally important site for artists to document the pervasiveness of the press in the daily lives of individuals. After all, people share personal space and time with the products of urban journalism.

Evergood's *Still Life* (Figure 2.6) features the breakfast table of a well-to-do upper-class couple. A large vase filled with flowers dominates the table; a folded copy of *The New York Times* with the headline "Japs Bomb Pearl Harbor" is clearly visible on the male's side of the table next to his plate. The couple, unperturbed by the announcement, concentrates on the ritual of breakfast, while the newspaper, with its clarion call of bad news—war, in fact—lies unnoticed on the table. News—however explosive its content—is subordinated to the private

FIGURE 2.6   *Philip Evergood,* Still Life *(no date). Lithograph, 11.5 x 16.25 in. Collection of Whitney Museum of American Art. Gift of Mr. and Mrs. Benjamin Weiss.*

daily rites of their household. Lucy Lippard (Kraeft and Kraeft 1984, xix) writes that this lithograph is

> more vitriolically satirical and more topical.... The figures are seen from a greater distance and more detail is included—most importantly a copy of the *New York Times* with Pearl Harbor blazoned across the headlines. The capitalist couple ... ignore the news, as they pick at their luxurious breakfast, beside the enormous, ironically fertile bouquet.

Here the newspaper constitutes another form of decoration—like the vase with fresh flower, it serves to complement the table setting, and its use value is less obvious than its position on the table.

More than ten years later, in 1949, Evergood portrays *The Forgotten Man*, a double amputee who is slumped in a doorway of a dilapidated house, sitting on a newspaper that protects against a cold and filthy step that is covered with graffiti. Here the public function of a newspaper has been diverted to serve a private need that relates to existence and survival. It attests to the versatility of objects and depicts a functional transformation that confirms individual control and creativity. Once discarded by their readers, newspapers offer yet another opportunity for adaptation and demonstrate their usefulness. As a result, they outlive their one-day life span to remain part of another guise in the cityscape.

FIGURE 2.7   *John Sloan,* Nude and Newspapers, *1927. Etching, 5.5 x 6.75 in. The Butler Institute of American Art, Youngstown, Ohio.*

Allesandro Mastro-Valerio's *Morning Paper* focuses on two nude females sitting on their bed with an opened newspaper between them. It is the newspaper that provides a link to the outside; even in an intimate setting the world is never far away. One of the figures is looking at the pages of the newspaper as they are spread out on the bed, whereas the other one, in a reflective mood, is almost ready to rise. There is a relaxed intensity in this setting, dominated by the reading of the morning paper.

Similarly, three prints by John Sloan offer some insights into the role of newspapers in the daily lives of individuals. In *Nude and Newspapers* (Figure 2.7) a woman rests leisurely on a couch, leaning against the backrest and reading a newspaper with one hand while holding the rest of the large-format paper with her other, ready to continue with the next section. She is totally absorbed in the act of reading, and her nudity provides a stark contrast to the pages of the newspaper. There is an air of confidence and experience in dealing with the outside world, however, which makes the woman comfortable and relaxed. It is still an intimate setting dominated by the reading rather than by the mere presence of the newspaper. According to the artist (Morse 1969, 307), "Nude subjects have so often been treated sensually, sentimentally—or cheaply realistically—that the

FIGURE 2.8   *John Sloan,* The Woman's Page, *1905. All rights reserved, © The Metropolitan Museum of Art.*

American public hesitates to show any interest in a more sincere approach." Here the nude figure becomes the center of an intellectual engagement with the world. She is surrounded by sections of the newspaper; the folded front page next to her reveals part of the title, "Telegram," and suggests the telegram style of the information. The strong black-and-white relationships in the print reflect the black-and-white nature of the newspaper and solidify the image.

In *The Woman's Page* (Figure 2.8) Sloan records his observations of life in the city; a woman, half-dressed in a rocking chair by the window, reads "A Page for Women," while a child plays with a cat on the nearby bed. This is a bedroom scene in which the study of the newspaper provides the reference point for life in a crowded city. The newspaper is a source of her dreams, and the women's page represents a review of unattainable objects and lifestyles that are far removed from the shabbiness of the scene. Yet reading about them is an attractive and powerful distraction; it belongs to the perpetuation of the American dream as evoked through the pages of a metropolitan newspaper: a vicarious yet still affordable experience. Sloan (Morse 1969, 141) comments that he completed his work "with sympathy, but 'no social consciousness'"; he just saw a "woman in this sordid room, sordidly dressed—undressed—with a poor little kid crawling around on a bed—reading the Women's Page, getting hints on fashion and housekeeping."

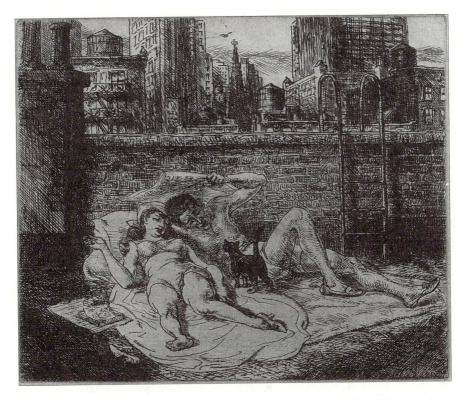

FIGURE 2.9   *John Sloan,* Sunbathers on the Roof, *1941. Etching, 6 x 7 in. Collection of Whitney Museum of American Art. Felicia Meyer Marsh Bequest.*

Finally, *Sunbathers on the Roof* (Figure 2.9) depicts a couple in bathing suits resting comfortably on pillows and blankets. With one arm around the shoulders of the woman and his other arm supporting a large newspaper, the male companion provides protection and security by shielding the couple against the sun. Here the newspaper fulfills yet another improvised function as a screen, this time against nature—its size is more important than its content; the potential of information and entertainment yields to the physical requirement of the moment. This image is another example of Sloan's power of observation, his presence among working people, and his love for detail.

In the style of urban realism, an American reaction to modernism, these images portray the essence of modern life—the city—and comment on the social conditions of its inhabitants. These artists' keen sense of observation created a vision that complements the documentary photography of the time, crafting images with a strongly subjective quality. Prints or paintings—like documentary photographs—can reflect the social and political concerns of their era. But precisely because of their subjective nature and the artists' desire to share the experience of their times, these images can probe even more deeply than photographs into the essence of social conditions.

The presence of newspapers—as icons of personal and institutional power and as components of the public and private practices of individuals—is a commentary on the contradictory nature of an urban existence; newspapers isolate and unite, and they blur the distinction between the useful and the trivial, the partisan and the objective. Nevertheless, people buy and consult the newspaper as a daily routine—and with a mixture of tradition and ingenuity—seeking an instrument of surveillance and a source of information and power. But newspapers not only provide an opportunity to act or offer a social or political identity to their readers. They also reinforce their own power through their very ubiquity and visibility in the lives of urbanites. Newspapers' daily appearance strengthens their position as a social and political institution and reinforces the idea that information and entertainment are indispensable commodities of the modern age. Thus, credibility works both ways when readers and their newspapers reinforce each other's presence. Most important perhaps is the realization that the relationship between the press and its readers is a defining element of urban life before the advent of television in the early 1950s. In fact, the interaction between newspapers and individuals provides specific insights into the social and cultural location of the press during the 1930s.

This selection of prints represents newspapers as a shared site of information and entertainment that encompassed the concerns of the working class and women. At that time newspapers attracted a readership distinguished more by its role in consumption than by class or gender. As a result, the presence of newspapers in these depictions of urban life confirms a common experience, while newspaper reading as a cultural attribute of modernity constitutes a social signifier of participation. Indeed, the visual evidence of 1930s printmaking reinforces an impression of the American press as a pervasive democratizing force in society. This is a widely accepted, liberal-pluralist vision of the press and a traditional argument among press historians. It relies on being in the presence of the press, however, rather than on the intent of the press and the consequences of interactions between content and readers.

As American artists struggled for explanations of an urban life inspired by a shared creative tradition and their own political impulses, they responded to the presence of media as a defining condition of modern culture.

3
▾ ▾ ▾

Revolutionary Reportage: Constructing the New Soviet Journalism

The role of journalism and the press has been an important consideration for revolutionary movements in the twentieth century, beginning with the Russian Revolution. Although various notions about the role of the press can be traced to the socialist movement in Western Europe, especially to the German Social Democratic Party, they surface prominently in Lenin's work, from which they emerged to have a profound influence on the communist world. The subsequent pragmatism of Soviet political leadership continued to recognize the importance of information in general and the role of newspapers in particular in reinforcing and perpetuating revolutionary ideals.

The writings of Lenin address the need for a new press as a political means of uniting dissidents and revolutionaries. The rise of a strong and centralized press in the Soviet Union was rooted in Lenin's ideas, which actually precede the revolution, harking back to the days of illegal, underground activities. In "Where to Begin," Lenin (1961, 5:22) outlines the duties of the press in a socialist society and identifies specific functions of journalism. He suggests, for instance, that a newspaper

is not only a collective propagandist and a collective agitator, it is also a collective organiser. In this last respect it may be likened to the scaffolding round a building under construction, which marks the contours of the structure and facilitates communication between the builders, enabling them to distribute the work and to view the common results achieved by their organised labour. With the aid of the newspaper, and through it, a permanent organisation will naturally take shape.

In fact, Lenin foresees an all-Russian newspaper that would be distributed in large numbers to take advantage of popular discontent and assist in the class struggle.

A generation later, after the defeat of the class enemy, the bourgeoisie, some of these functions are still reflected in Soviet descriptions of the media. Mark Hopkins (1974, 55) notes a "(1) differentiation, to serve various categories of readers, (2) purposefulness of content, especially in discussing problems of socialist development, (3) close association with readers by means of letters and news notes, and (4) organization of public affairs discussions."

These were characteristics of the strong political and ideological roles of the press in the Soviet Union; they also fit Louis Althusser's (1971, 146) description of Ideological State Apparatuses (ISAs), or institutions, which function "massively and predominantly by *ideology*." Althusser adds that "what unifies their diversity is precisely this functioning, insofar as the ideology by which they function is always in fact unified, despite its diversity and its contradictions, *beneath the ruling ideology*, which is the ideology of the 'ruling class.'"

In the case of the Soviet Union, the working class became the ruling class and dominated the process of total transformation. Newspapers remained important for the successful efforts of the proletariat to organize society politically and socially for the revolution, according to Lenin. In "What Is to be Done" (1961, 5:376–516), Lenin insisted on the value of newspapers as political instruments to vitalize the revolutionary movement of the proletariat and as a means of exchanging experiences, materials, and resources; the press was to be open to anyone—a forum for nonjournalist peasants and workers—to participate in the communication of a new society. In this sense the press was to shape and reflect the ruling ideology of a classless society.

But the modern press of the 1920s and 1930s—irrespective of ideological position—is also the expression of the modern period and an integral part of the advancement of society. Nikolai Bukharin (1969, 131), a participant in the revolution, sees a complex situation, "a highly developed technology, a proletariat, a great number of newspapers, and advertising on a tremendous scale," among other issues, as manifestations of modernity, along with the presence of diverse political and economic leaders. Together they constitute the elements of social change, that is, the formation of new relations among individuals and between individuals and institutions. Communication and the press, in particular, provide the means of such changes, and their success inspires others, including observers in Weimar Germany and the United States.

Walter Benjamin—in search of a functional transformation of technology—also addresses the promise of the new Soviet press in light of the rise of a successful, privately owned post–World War I press in Weimar Germany. Since capitalism controls most Western European newspapers, Benjamin anticipates problems for writers who face the technological, political, and existential problems of dependence on commercial decisions. He particularly notes the opportunity, under a Soviet-type press system, to break with traditional capitalist practices by diminishing the distinction between author and public. Under such circumstances, he notes (1986, 225), "The reader is at all times ready to become a writer, that is, a describer, but also a prescriber. As an expert—even if not on a subject but only on the post he occupies—he gains access to authorship. Work itself has its turn to speak."

This is what Bertolt Brecht calls a process of *Umfunktionierung*, a functional transformation of a medium or practice to serve the cause of socialism. Benjamin's own work responds to the rise of new communication technologies such as photography, film, and radio in Weimar Germany and elsewhere in an attempt to seize new technologies—and forms of expression—for the purpose of advancing a different, socialist model of communication. The development of the Soviet press after 1917 offers an example of how to pursue a radical transformation of culture against the interests of capitalism and private media, not only with respect to newspapers but also the broader cultural and political apparatus.

At the same time, in the United States, socialist and communist expressions are channeled through magazines like *Appeal to Reason*, the *International Socialist Review*, *Wilshire's Magazine*, *The Comrade*, and *The Masses*, where intellectuals—and artists in the latter two—found their own venues for mixing socialist ideas with artistic and creative expressions. Despite significantly different political and economic conditions in the United States at this time, the success of the *Appeal to Reason* was quite remarkable. Noting its circulation of almost 1 million, Lenin (1961, 18: 336) suggests that anyone "must acknowledge that a proletarian is powerless when alone but that millions of proletarians are all-powerful." According to Paul Buhle (1987, 90–91), however, there was no "American equivalent to the authoritative *Die Neue Zeit*, much less an *Iskra* to constitute the core of party activism. Rather the public space for Socialism in America was invigorated by the extraordinary diversity of the local Socialist press, publishing in a score of languages."

Meanwhile, in the Soviet Union the press was only one part of a larger and more complex cultural practice—including the arts and literature—that Lenin had appropriated in the interest of the proletariat and the success of the communist cause. After his death in 1924, the cultural scene in the Soviet Union underwent transformations that point toward the preservation of ideological content under formalist principles. Literature, photography, and film remained primary tools for constructing a new socialist society. More specifically, a break with abstract forms provides literature and photography with new contexts—like reportage and photomontage—for revolutionary practices and involves writers and artists who turn from an individualistic perspective to the collective needs of society. Stalin's rise to power, an economic crisis, and the first Five-Year Plan, in 1928, are the sources of a new awareness of the press and the need for communication with the masses of workers and peasants.

Consequently, there appears a considerable amount of writing on photography by Soviet intellectuals, including photographers, during the 1920s, published in *LEF* (1923–35) and *Novy LEF* (1927–28). Futurism, constructivism, and proletcult are in evidence in these attempts to unite artistic and political goals. These and other discussions—involving Osip Brik, Sergei Tretyakov, and Aleksandr Rodchenko, among others—elevate the camera to a versatile and unique instrument of seeing the contemporary world. The photographic practices also made their way to Germany, where the accomplishments of Soviet (documentary/journalistic) photography were translated into new photographic experiences that found a place in the illustrated press, particularly but not exclusively of the left.

Brik (1992, 327) celebrates photography and photomontage, in particular, from a constructivist-productivist position as a total response to the need to embrace the idea of art as a purposeful practice with definite practical goals. Accordingly, "the external appearance of a thing is determined by its economic purpose and not by abstract, aesthetic considerations." In his attack on painting, he suggests that the "photographer captures life and events more cheaply, quickly and precisely than the painter. Herein lies his strength, is enormous social importance. And he is not frightened by any outdated daub." Consequently, he argues (1992, 456) that photographers "must show that it is not just life ordered according to aesthetic laws which is impressive, but also vivid, everyday life itself as it is transfixed in a technically perfect photograph."

Earlier Leon Trotsky (1992, 427–32) had pointed to the importance of photography not only as an educational medium but also as one that would "picture life as it is" and contribute to a new, realistic art. Tretyakov (1992, 460–62) also advocates the use of photography and documentary film in the late 1920s in stressing the social purposes of art like the cinema of fact, for instance. "Soviet reality fixed by the lens of a Soviet camera . . . which finds a place in the pages of an illustrated journal is as important and essential as daily bread" in the context of fighting for an "aggressive, class-active art."

Indeed, the group Oktober declares (1992, 466) that photography, among other arts, was called upon to aid the proletariat in the fields of propaganda and production with a dynamic realism that "reveals life in movement and in action and that discloses systematically the potentials of life ... as opposed to aesthetic, abstract industrialism and unadulterated technicism that passes itself off as revolutionary art."

Rodchenko (Elliott, 1979, 109)—a photographer and prolific writer on his craft at a time when the arts, and painting in particular, struggled with the arrival of photography—proposes to abandon the idea of the portrait as a single work. Cognizant of the disintegration of life, he urges fellow artists to think of the modern portrait in terms of a collection of snapshots executed on different occasions and under different conditions, a form of photo-reportage over time and through different spaces that emphasizes truth and reality and thus the environment in which people exist. In fact, photographic reportage arose against the traditions of art photography to become the documentary or journalistic expression of the time. The result was a struggle between functional and pure photography that is subordinated to the social and political goals of society.

These writings about photography and the concurrent discussions of journalism are constituent elements of the social, political, and cultural context for the following article (below), which constructs a Soviet newspaper in the spirit of a new type of journalism and a new society. Detached from editorial pronouncements, media policies, or political dictates, the article as reportage recreates an atmosphere of journalistic engagement that adds to the historical knowledge of the Soviet press. It is based on the writing of Leonid Saianskii, with photo illustrations by Rodchenko. Both text and photographs effectively produce an image of the new press as an instrument of collective labor and an organizer of public interests. The result is a creative mixture of words and pictures that conveys a particularly strong and positive picture of the role of the press in the making of a new society. This translation (by Derek E. Johnson) provides an insight into the ways in which the history of a revolutionary press was constructed with the support of writers and photographers. It is a verbal painting—charged with productive tension and the creative fervor of a collective practice and accompanied by graphically strong black-and-white photographs—that celebrates the power of realism.

Specifically, Rodchenko's interest in the social and socialist environment of Russia resulted in a photo essay for the magazine *30 Days* to accompany Saianskii's 1928 essay "Newspaper." The photographs illustrate the editorial and mechanical processes of producing a newspaper, ranging from the editorial process of collecting and preparing information to the printing of the newspaper. His commitment to this type of documentary photography is reflected in comments he made on the social meaning of photography and its importance as a means of social communication. At that time Rodchenko proposes that "eighty to ninety percent of any magazine is built on factual material, and neither painting nor drawing can give the sensation of the moment, the actuality of events and their documentary nature; and thus we put our trust in photography, since it shows what happened at a particular place and factually convinces us" (Tupitsyn 1996, 42–43).

30 Days was among the popular magazines of the 1920s. It carried photographs regularly and was devoted to the artistic enlightenment of workers. Rodchenko published another photo essay, "TASS is Speaking," a year later, in 1929. Boris Ignatovich, a fellow photographer, summarizes the position of contemporary photography with his claim that "Soviet photography is different from Western photography: no entertainment, no tricks, no commerce; with the people and for the people; life in all its typical manifestations, with typical people—that is the material Soviet photography uses. Photography is the most contemporary realist art" (Tupitsyn 1996, 47). His remarks confirm the importance of photojournalism in the Soviet press and the role of photographers in the process of shaping the image of society.

Rodchenko's photographs in "Newspaper" concentrate on collective labor, including the role of women in the process of producing a newspaper. Moving his camera in and out of the work environment—with close-ups and portraits—he creates a sense of immediacy and places the reader among newsworkers to become

FIGURE 3.1 *Hour after furious hour, work goes on at the big table and all over the news-room while every telephone rings at the same time....*

a participant in the making of a newspaper. The twenty-four photographs that accompany the text document the making of a newspaper, beginning with an overhead shot of an editorial worker in a smoke-filled room working on a manuscript and ending with an image of a reader sitting at a table, also photographed from above, with a teapot and empty plate next to the newspaper. Work, food, and information appear as equally important ingredients for the success of the revolution. But between these similar images of editor and reader at work reside Rodchenko's photographic observations of the process of editorial labor. He photographs collective work like editing and individual labor like information gathering, as well as objects like incoming mail, old copies of newspapers in the morgue, linotype

метранпажей, веселых наборщиков, тискальщиков, запудренных бумажною пылью экспедиторов, машинистов и линотипистов—настоящая армия, с командирами-журналистами во главе их бригад.

И еще: есть ряды сложных и хитросплетенных из стали и тока машин; драгоценные россыпи гарта (гарт—сплав для набора), крохотных литер—«букашек», шпаций, шпон и марзанов—драгоценные потому, что ни золото всех Клондайков, ни платина и гелий с седого Урала не смогут так вздернуть весь мир на дыбы, как это делает часто простая свинцовая строчка.

Для газеты нет дня, утра или ночи. Но зато у нее есть этапы, по которым она с тяжким, упорным трудом продвигается к своему читателю.

ТЕЛЕФОННАЯ ЖУТЬ

Телефон. Телефон... Теле...
    К аппарату... скорей...
    — Я редакция. Я секретарь...

Такой скромный на вид эриксоновский ящичек, а как он важен и порою невыносим, когда в одной комнате на столах он—сам-третий, а то и четвертый. И как жаль, что наука еще не привесила газетчику третью руку и два лишних уха про запас...

— Алло, редакция. Говорят из Бюро погоды...
— Алло. Говорит Наркомзем...
— Говорит Ленинград... Харьков требует к аппарату...—Дайте, дайте еще десять рук.

Их сейчас уже не хватает, а ведь день только начат огромнейшим городом, и еще не повсюду взялись за работу.

Но вот здесь, в тесной комнате, с планкой над дверью—«Секретариат», уже кипит работа; три стола; три трезвонящих аппарата; десяток напряженных фигур, и уже на столах шелестят блюкноты, и чиркают вечные перья, записывая задания.

— В Наркомпуть к Рудзутаку—беседа о хлебоза...

... готовках — кончает, поняв налету, хроникер, тычет ручку в нагрудный карман и... и нет его в комнате.

— Кафман—клубы! На подступах к революции...—отрывисто бросает секретарь.

Кафмана тоже нет.

— Чекапский... Беседу с Надеждой...
— Константиновной, знаю... О 'долой гра... то бишь неграмотности. Мчусь.

Через четверть часа Кафман — Чекапский—Штих—уже мечутся где-то по коридорам бесчисленных учреждений, ловят завов и начей, убе-

Волны синего дыма плывут над приникшими к рукописям сотрудниками, и в чаду, в тишине, в напряженной горячечной спешке слышен бешеный треск нервных перьев.

ждают курьеров,—«пустить от газеты»,—воробьем присаживаются на подоконник и строчат и строчат—ведь редакция ждет, они глаза ее и уши.

— Кто идет за статьей к Феликсу Кону?
— Кто суд? Кто на пленуме реферирует?
— Я! Я! Я!

Марш-марш... Репортаж весь в разгоне и зав. информацией патетически бьет себя в матую грудь объюсленной чернилами толстовки.

— Больше некого... Всех разогнал... Дайте мне, дайте, умоляю, кого-нибудь... На вокзале встречают сегодня китайских пленников...
— Дать фотографа и заметку сто строк...

50
— Какая сегодня передовая? Тьфу, алло! Ну, я слушаю...

FIGURE 3.2   *Waves of blue smoke float above employees hunched over their writing, and, in the smoke, in the silence, the pressing feverish snap of nervous pens is heard....*

machines, and pieces of lead type. In fact, Rodchenko is fascinated by the printing technology, and several of his photographs describe the essentials of casting type, stereotyping, and printing before he illustrates the sorting and distribution of newspapers. His use of the camera is a celebration of technology, which augments the success of the mass-circulation newspaper as a modern technological achievement in the service of the revolution.

These images appeal to the reader because they not only clearly depict the production of a newspaper, but they also share with the text a creative strength that emanates from their perspective, their graphic qualities, and their layout. The result is a totally modern expression through an application of photography to a

Хроникеры и рецензенты, облепив стол, наперерэи строчат, торопя дано добытую информацию...

Звонит автор: Перепутали, знаете, фразу Искажаете, знаете смысл Проте стую. Дрынь, некогда
Звонит важное учреждение: Поместить речь N и без всяких рэщении Дрынь: ну, еще они, Эх, вот всю газету под речь и дадим!
Звонит модный поэт: Есть норма, обязуете
Дрынь. Извозал! Не до норм
Звонит. звонит. Да кто только не звонит в эти опьяненные дребезгом и треском утренние часы. До тех пор звонят, пока озверевший секретарь не за голову и не завишит, как спрыснутый уголь
Ба-атю-юшки... Ведь наборе ли строчки...
И как будто ответ—самое грозное—дань
из наборного отделения:
А Ма-а... материал. Животишь
Посылаю! Гоню! Баста Налили кровушки, рычит на телефоны секретарь и, рванув ставший тугим воротник с головой ныряет бумажную руду.
На секунду затишье. только бешеный шелест бумаги. Три нагнувшихся головы влили в шапки, ищут лучшее в сотнях рукописей.
Ах, скорей... скорей... наборная ждет
деловитый отрывистый обмен фраз:
Карскую экспедицию Обязательно...
— К...о......ть. Послезавтра Фельетоны за изаны Борьба с пьянкой на тостью страницу... Тут о книгах... Подвалом дадим Лодзь... Где статья о налогах?

Ежедневно пухлые пачки писем со всех концов необъятной страны запромождают столы, и чтением их занят десяток людей

FIGURE 3.3   *Top: News writers and reviewers cluster around the table, racing each other, trying to deal with incoming information....*

Bottom: Every day, thick bundles of letters from all over the country collect on the tables. A dozen people are kept busy reading them....

FIGURE 3.4   *Never looking up from her file box, a busy woman sorts letters, reports, and articles received by topic. She must sort them by department and topic in the information room.*

Лягушачьим на 3   Гро-
теск 28 на 6...

Герольд жирный... Ренато

летят в воздухе упругие,
четкие, лепонатные монострап-
цу в Газете юва клички
шрифтов

Скоро, скоренько... не
торапливает прокуренный Авенир,
завершая первейший этап вели-
кого ипиства—претворения всех
вых слов в густую свинцовую
плоть

А уже прочитал «ночная»
внизу все страницы и горячии,
похожии на паровой молот. пресс
«МАН» загудел результатом. под
магнит   стрелкой манометра и
набирает давление

Сейчас свинцовые полосы
встанут по прессе. на них ляжет
пушистый   толстый картон,
всмятку   другого
ца аппарата выйдет   рица   копия набора   но неп
отольют и размножат металли-
ческие стереотипы. вставят их
на вал, рот   и второй этап
газетных полос кончен

Задыхают размевинными   громадные, с паровоз вышиной, ротационные
машины и начнут тискать газету по 50 тысяч номеров в час.

61

FIGURE 3.5   *Drive shafts groan under the monstrous power of the motors, and six hundred kilometers of newsprint—the distance from Moscow to Leningrad—will run back and forth between the machines' rollers, rustling and sliding. Whistling cutters will slice this ribbon into evenly-sized sheets.*

Это будет не рано. А верней, очень рано—и четыре часа по утру.

Массивные грациозно-неуклюжие, горбатые от валов и надстроек, внизу уже ждут мощные ротационки, печатные машины — последний этап на пути выходящей газеты.

И покорные легким толчкам рычагов, они вдруг зарычат, завздыхают и наполнят грохочущим глухим громом весь двор и все корпуса.

Застонут под чудовищной силой прокатки накрашенные валы, и шестьсот километров бумаги—путь Москва —Ленинград—пробегут меж вращающимися навстречу друг другу валами, шелестя и скользя, а свистящие резаки рассекут эту ленту на ровные уже газетные листы.

Тогда серолицая предрассветная бригада синих рубах подхватит новорожденную Газету, уложит миллион двести тысяч листов в тюки, но местам, адресам и трактам подписки, обвяжет и запакует.

Уже город проснется; откашлявшись сгустками копоти, оживут и задышат заводские трубы и проплачут на Красной куранты свое

Деловитые экспедиторы в синем рассветном полусумраке подсчитают и подберут вкусно пахнущие пачки газет по местам— адресам.

Застонут под чудовищной силой прокатки накрашенные валы, и шестьсот километров бумаги—путь Москва —Ленинград— пробегут меж вращающимися навстречу друг другу валами, шелестя и скользя, а свистящие резаки рассекут эту ленту на ровные уже газетные листы.

медное «доброе утро», когда слезет с мостка, шатаясь от дрожи в ногах машинист, вытрет пот рукавом и, похлопав слонов по горячим бокам, скажет— «баста».

Тут затихнут на время проглотившие сотни пудов бумаги тысячепудовые зверюги, но зато новый грохот разопрет переулок волной звуков. Из чугунных ворот один за другим, осторожно ползивая цепями, выползут двухтонные Делаше —раз—два—три—пять и шесть,—и построятся длинной колонной, чтоб скорее-скорее погрузить тяжелые пачки со свежими адресами:

Пермь, Казань, Одесса, Никольск, Уссурийск...

Ежась от свежего утренника, из подъезда посыпятся дико усталые «ноч- **62**

FIGURE 3.6 *Busy distribution workers in the blue predawn gloom count ink-smelling bundles of paper and sort them by address.*

specific documentary task. Rodchenko demonstrates how to unite creative and journalistic uses of photography for the purposes of illustrating abstract concepts like labor and ideology while providing a visual text or guide for the enlightenment of the reader.

By providing detail, his photographs supplement the text, whose immediacy communicates a similar level of emotional involvement while providing an ideological framework for placing the role of the press in a revolutionary context. For instance, the reader meets the secretary (*sekretar*), one of the principal characters in the story, and much of the action takes place in the secretary's office (*sekretariat*). While the secretary refers to the head of a cell (lowest level of party hierarchy) of the Communist Party organized at the newspaper, the "sekretariat" is the executive committee, which consists of several functionaries. Given that secretaries were primarily responsible for the political correctness of journalists, their presence on the staff of a newspaper invited the reader to consider the press part of a political effort that differed significantly from the traditional bourgeois model of the press.

The immediacy of the text recreates the incredible pace of journalism, which seems to equal the speed of the printing presses and propels the reader into the presence of the complex process of producing a newspaper. The photographs add factual information to an emotionally charged text, which they surround and guard against suggestions of fictional intent. Thus, photographs are placed in the margins of the article, where they contain the text and become reminders of the factual context. At the same time they enhance the text and offer credibility to the literary narrative, which uses direct quotes and colloquial language to suggest proximity and reality.

Together, text and images constitute the insights of a writer and a photographer into the place of journalism, the nature of journalistic labor, and the collective efforts of newswork. Their combined narrative offers an account of the Soviet newspaper that also reflects the aspirations of Lenin and the hopes of those who saw in the press a significant social and political connection to the people of the Soviet Union. It is an insider's report that reflects a specific ideological construction of the socialist press and, therefore, a historical account of the conditions of communication in postrevolutionary Russia. In a way it is a response to Lenin's 1918 admonition to the press (1961, 28:98): "Less political ballyhoo. Fewer highbrow discussions. Closer to life. More attention to the way in which the workers and peasants are actually building the *new* in their everyday work, and more *verification* so as to ascertain the extent to which the new is *communistic*."

"Newspaper" is also an expression of pride and accomplishment that celebrates the production as much as it embraces the human spirit of work. It offers the testimony of an eyewitness whose words are reinforced by the camera. The result is a recreation, through writing and photography as forms of documentary expression, of the everyday reality of Soviet journalism. The notion of documentary is reminiscent of Georg Lukàcs's (1980) writing on reportage and Dziga Vertov

(Michelson 1984), defining the "kino-eye," since the work combines what Lukàcs calls the conceptual (scientific) reproduction of reality with the infallibility of Vertov's perfect mechanical eye. As such, the article is an expression of the power of technology and its contribution to the advancement of a new society.

A short editorial note preceding "Newspaper" (*30 Dnei* 12, 1928, 49–63) declares,

In recent years, the Soviet press has achieved giant successes. Several thousand newspapers are now issued, even in the farthest corners of the USSR. They reveal the life of the country and work indefatigably at the task of building socialism. Several of the capital's newspapers have circulations of half a million and serve millions of working readers. In this article, Leonid Saianskii highlights the newspaper's distinctive everyday life and the boiling revolutionary tempo of its work.

Here is the complete text of the article:

NEWSPAPER

Everything alive in the world—stars, birds, and people, their lives, their dreams, their searchings, their work and leisure—all obey the strict logic of time. Everything is banded by the strict circle of the day and broken into facets called hours by the indifferent hands of time. There are 24 of these facets. That's what nature dictates. But there is one organism, huge and complicated, that works not 8, not 20 hours a day, but as many hours as the unbending will of events requires. Maybe 24, or sometimes 48, because one hour is not like another, and there can be moments in the life of that collective, sleepless organism when an hour is like a year, as in a besieged castle under the blows of a heavy attack.

This organism is called, simply: a newspaper. And this is its story.

Behind the raw, tart and fragrant newsprint of the morning editions of *Pravda*, *Izvestiia*, and *Gudok*, behind their seemingly quiet paragraphs, columns, and articles, lie fierce, worry-saturated flurries of labor and trouble, and many hard, nervous days.

Amid the spicy smells (a mixture of lubricating oil and ink), the rifle-bolt cracks of great battles are heard, as is the drone of distant and important events as reflected on the pages of today's newspaper. There is no country, no map square where newspapers cannot penetrate, because a newspaper doesn't have limited hours for its work. There are only the iron deadlines for typesetting, the rush of proof-sheets.

There is also the work-shirted army with faces pale from eternal sleeplessness, toilers who never see the daylight, cheery typesetters, press operators, shipping agents powdered with paper dust, typists and Linotype operators: the real army, with journalists as commanders at the head of their ranks.

And there are rows of complicated machines made of steel and electric current, precious supplies of type-making alloy, tiny letters, "bugs," leads: all are precious, because neither all the gold in all the gold mines nor platinum nor helium from the gray Urals can make the whole world stand straight up in the air the way a simple leaden line of newspaper type can.

There is no day, morning or night for a newspaper. It has its own schedule, by which it moves laboriously to its reader.

TELEPHONE TERROR. Telephone. Telephone.... Tele.... To the telephone, hurry! "Newsroom." "Secretary."

The giant Ericson boxes[1] are so very important, but they become unbearable when there are three or four of them in one room. It's a pity that science hasn't given man a third arm or one more ear.

"Hello, newsroom? This is the weather forecasting bureau."

"Hello? This is the People's Commissariat for Land."

"Hello? This is Leningrad ... Kharkov calling ... I need ten more hands here.... "

There's a shortage of hands right now, even though the day has only just begun in the big city and not everybody started work yet. But here, in a small room, with a sign reading "Secretary's Office" on the door, the work is boiling; three tables, three ringing telephones, a dozen hardworking figures, and writing tablets are rustling on the tables already, the scratching of fountain pens writing down lists of tasks.

"Go to the People's Commissariat for Roads, to Comrade Rudzutak: ask about bread ... storage," the other finishes, understanding immediately, putting his pen into his shirt pocket and already on his way out the door. "Kafman—clubs! On the coming of the Revolution," interrupts the secretary quickly. Kafman's gone too.

"Chekanskii, talk with Nadezhda ... Konstantinovna,[2] yeah, I know, about the anti-illiteracy campaign: I'm on my way."

In fifteen minutes, Kafman, Chekanskii, and Shtikh are fidgeting in the corridors of numerous offices, catching directors and assistant directors and trying to convince couriers to let them in because they're from the newspaper, sitting on window ledges writing and writing because the newsroom is waiting and they are its ears and eyes.

"Who is going to see Feliks Kon about that article? Who's going to the courthouse? Who's going to report on the plenum?"

"Me ... Me ... Me."

March, march.... The pace is picking up and the assistant manager for information is beating the wrinkled, dirty front of his shirt.

"There's nobody else here ... everybody has a job to do ... give me somebody, the Chinese delegates have to be met at the train station today."

"Give us a photographer and a 100-line article."

"What's on the front page today? *Ptui*, hello? Yes, I'm listening.... "

An author is calling: "You've changed the phrase, you know, you changed the whole sense. I protest!" Riiing! "We don't have time...." Important offices calling. "Put the speech in and don't cut any of it!" Riiing! "Well, fine, I suppose you want us to give you the whole issue for it!" A fashionable poet is calling: "I've got a poem. You'll salivate when you read it." Riiing! "We don't have time ... and we don't need poems."

The telephone rings ... and rings. Is there anybody who isn't calling during these poisoned, clanging morning hours? They call until the frantic secretary claps his hands to his head and hisses like a doused fire. "My God, there isn't one line set in type yet!"

As if in answer, the telephone rings again, threateningly. Then a cry comes from the typesetting department: "Heeey! M-material! The Linotype machines have stopped!" "I'm sending you some! I'm going as fast as I can! That's enough! You've drunk enough of our blood!" the secretary roars into the telephone; ripping his tight collar open, he dives into the pile of paper in front of him.

For a second there is no sound but the rustling of paper. Three bowed heads search for the best bits of material among hundreds of handwritten pieces of paper in the piles. "Hurry up! Hurry up! The typesetting department is waiting!"

There is a confused exchange of phrases: "The Karskii expedition should be covered, obviously." "The cinema stuff can be delayed ... The day after tomorrow ... The feuilletons have been ordered. The anti-alcohol campaign should be on page three ... Here's something about books ... Lodz should be in a footnote ... Where's the article about taxes?"

Riiing! It's the internal telephone. See the editor: it's urgent!

A meeting is called to discuss the issue. Managers of departments, secretaries.... Reports ... hurry up, hurry up!

The secretary's office empties. The telephones ring in an empty room until a self-important courier answers in a powerful, Ukrainian-accented voice: "Everybody's in a meeting. Call back later. Who is this? What should I tell them? Who is that? I'm Polia, the courier."

In the editor's office there's a dusty placard that says "No Smoking"; it's drowning in the blue smoke. Voices hurriedly interrupt each other. "Let's cut it ... closer to the point, comrades! What are we doing for today's issue?"

The newspaper's staff has racked its brains for half an hour, thinking about tomorrow's issue, articles, pictures, and, most importantly, the lead story. Nothing sensational, but an article on some theme with a lot of impact. An article that will grab the reader's attention. Without a lead, there's no issue. But the lead should be sharp and new, and it's the staff's job to sharpen it.

Race of the Quills

"It's interesting how people smoke in American newsrooms," says red-haired Gri, experienced copy editor, pausing in his writing to stretch his back. "It stinks to hell in those 'Heralds' of theirs."

"It's worse than that! They smoke pipes there," interjects his neighbor, bowing over the table. "But the furniture there is better than ours. That's a fact."

They're right: we're too far behind America.

There's nothing to breathe in the small room, lit with two big lamps even during the day and furnished as well with two different-sized tables and squeaking chairs. Almost a dozen staffers are bent over the tables, writing furiously on lined writing paper for their various departments or editing old notes. That's the whole department. Production, party, national—it's all the same.

Their task today, tomorrow, and always, day after day: to choose the best letters from readers and arrange them by topic, read them, and pass them on. In other words, to correct everything: spelling, style, to cut them down, to give them juicy titles, and then send them on to the secretarial office for polishing.

To our dearly beloved newspaper: please print my letter, reads a copy editor in a half-whisper, breaking each phrase into short pieces. *I am Efrim Kondratenko. As a member of the heroic laboring class, I serve as a cutter of hair and make 43 rubles a month. Despite my poor living conditions, I will subscribe to your newspaper by borrowing 100 rubles so that Chamberlain[3] will know about us and not give away our freedom. And please print my pseudonym: Red Eye (or maybe Eagle).*

Make a juicy article out of that letter, so naive yet precious for its open strength and strong-willed style. It needs to be done and it will be done.

The copy editor is a worker himself, a woodworker by trade, and out of a pile of new material he creates an important article for tomorrow: "How the Workers of the USSR Will Build Their Own Factories."

Pens are racing each other, backs are bent: the newsroom is squeaking and murmuring once again, hour after hour. Nobody has time to leave his work and get up to have a sip of stale tea. For the second time today the shadow of Hamlet's father appears through the smoke: the figure of the secretary on duty. He wrinkles his nose and the light flashes off his glasses. He says, "Oh, brother," to no one in particular. "Mmm … yes … the 'Everyday Life' department has brought us lots of copy. Those guys there know how to work. Mmm … yes … "

He says nothing more, just poisons the atmosphere and vanishes. After his words, the pens begin to race one another even faster, the tired copy editors glancing at the door in confusion as they push their pens.

In the typing pool, thirteen typewriters are clattering wildly and copy readers are roaring into the ears of the typists. Files full of finished material are growing fatter and being swallowed one at a time by the silent door of the secretary's office.

Even if the telephones become hoarse from ringing too much, there is no time to chat. Speed is of the essence. Their brains must process 8 to 10 thousand pieces of information important to the reader.…

A car's engine is roaring at the entrance to the building, and a courier with a large package of materials mumbles as he gets into the car. "To the print … and fast … "

The old Opel's engine barks and the car speeds away, sneezing and coughing and belching blue smoke through the streets of Moscow toward the printing plant where the hungry jaws of the printing presses are waiting for food.

The rush grows worse. The drone in the newsroom builds, comprehensible only to those who understand the newsroom din, under which they somehow manage to work, those who labor, write, and create, dozens and hundreds of overburdened, hurried fighters of the newspaper. Running around. Ringing. The clatter of Underwoods. An exchange of hurried words. Orders given on the fly. Hurry, hurry, and hurry some more. And smoke, smoke, smoke.

The bespectacled secretary on duty, running back and forth between departments like a bee, collecting the honey from the lines of text for the soon-to-be-born newspaper. Faster … *Faster* … FASTER …

Very Simple

"The diagram is very simple," says the editor to his foreign guest, walking him to a diagram on the wall. "We Soviet journalists build our newspapers not on sensation, not on the reader's thirst for news. Our paper is written by the reader-worker himself. Its circulation is 500,000 and that means that it's read by not less than a million people every day, avez vous compris?"

"*Oh oui, oui,*" nods the French guest.

"A network of *rabkor*[4] bureaus covers the entire country; *savez vous que ce que c'est le* rabkor? We have thousands of them, and each of them writes about what's happening in his place of work as well as he can: how he lives, what he needs, what he wants. There are lots of letters: into the thousands every day. Some of them get set in type, the rest are investigated with the help of the prosecutor's office and the RKI[5]. Nothing gets lost."

"*Oh, je compris....*"

"Our newspaper," explains the editor in a lecturing tone, "must seek out new phenomena in these letters, pressing questions, and ask questions with the voice of the masses as part of a wider discussion. Or raise them with the proper authorities. A hotline. It's mostly the same in all our newspapers, though a sixteenth of them are in Moscow alone. The departments prepare material from scratch, the secretarial office adds information, inserts it in the text, provides illustrations, chooses the typeface and headlines—that's about it. And we do everything ourselves. We've got our own printing facilities, all the machines and storage space, and even our own transportation pool."

"Workforce?"[6]

"Up to 200 people, that's newsroom and front office. And about 500 in printing and distribution."

"That's wonderful!"

"There's nothing wonderful about it," grins the editor proudly. "We've been on our feet for some time and everything is very simple." He's right.

A colossal apparatus, a working collective bound by a single will— it works like a precision machine 24 hours a day, as if that were simple. But such "simplicity" is possible at only one newspaper in the world: a Soviet newspaper.

In a Living Ring

There are no office hours in a newspaper. Near the secretary's table, a weary man in an old pea coat is trying to give a letter to the secretary.

Grandpa, writes a rabkor in far-away Ukraine who is the old man's pupil and friend, [*there's this man*][7] he's as poor as poor can be; a locomotive broke his ribs and now the doctors are trying to break his nerves. He wants to go to a resort as an invalid but they don't want to give him anything. Help him. I rely on our newspaper, that is to say, on you.

How can we, after reading such a letter, say to this crippled man: "Sorry, comrade, office hours are over; come again tomorrow." There are many such people sitting about here. They come here from thousands of miles away, they stand near the table looking at you with rage, complaint, pain, and hope. They fondle dog-eared, stamped papers from various offices in their calloused hands; in their eyes they've got good, clear, working people's faith in the newspaper and you would have to be a stone idol not to help with an explanation, some information, a hurried note on a piece of paper:

The news staff requests … please review … please expedite the matter.

And not for nothing does the investigations department work 10 hours a day, as more and more people come from the factories, fields, and barracks to the newspaper for help. Unfortunately there is a real scorpion among the readers: the author of a rejected piece. He is always the same man, this author. It doesn't matter what he wears, if he's fat or thin, old or young: he is many-faced but all his faces are talkative, naive, and offended.

"What does N.G. mean? What's N.G.?" he asks, waving his rejected poem.

"You don't know?" answers the literature secretary as quietly as possible. "N.G. means 'No Good.' It's not your first, after all."

"Did you understand it? Listen to this line," the poet howls like a broken gramophone:

> *Farewell for now*
> *My darling*
> *Remember Vanya for a while at least*
> *Let me kiss you now*
> *Let's make our friendship tighter.*

"I can't use it. I've read it," the secretary begs.

"Shhh, just listen to it, brother."

> *Plain light of the sad moon*
> *Lit two backs*
> *And they*
> *Two backs*
> *Sink tenderly*
> *Each into the other's lips.*

"Comrade! Lips don't have backs…. *Pfui*, what am I saying…. Backs don't have lips! Really, I don't have time…."

"You never have time for new poets. I tell you it's … " roars the poet. "Who cares that I live on the street? I'm creating art here! What's your name, anyway? Yes, I demand to know your name!"

The next poet is no easier, though he is more modest. His theme: inflation. Before anyone knows what's happening, he is already reciting in ecstasy:

There's a discount
On shoes and boots again
I'll tell you what
You'll be frozen out
And our big MosSelProm
Will sit on everybody's neck.

The secretary is polite and serious. After listening to the poem he says, "It's not bad, I think, but it's too superficial. Bring in something else."

"Really, really," says the secretary consolingly. "Next, please!"

A tall man with a mustache looms over the table like a tower. "Ah-ah-ah I w-would like to know wh-wh-what are the grounds for your rejection of my story. I can vouch for its id-ideo-ideological soundness."

Bored and silent, the secretary shows the author a marked spot in his manuscript.

With greedy eyes and hands, the lieutenant grabbed Marusha's hips. But still she pushed at the officer's breasts and hit him on the nose.

"We can't accept this, comrade. Officers don't have breasts. And even Whites' noses are masculine nouns, not feminine ones[8]. It just doesn't work."

"I-I-it doesn't w-w-work? But why? Are you a party member?"

"What? Who?"

But an hour has been lost already, sixty precious minutes wasted on purposeless talking. It's a quarter after four, and the last batch of material is ready to be sent out.

Leaving two poets, three people with complaints, and an inventor unheard, the secretary's office is about to be locked up tight. Over the past hour, everything has been checked out one last time. Has anything been forgotten? Will anything interesting be appearing in the other newspapers tomorrow? Because the editor will look at you with silent reproach and say, offended, "Dammit. The other guys got it all, and over here ... you guys were sleeping...."

Forgotten clocks chime: "Siiix." At seven a new shift starts work. "Where's the car? The last shipment ... Where ...? Hurry, hurry ..." Just choke down your lunch, whatever you can find. And back to where everything's waiting.

Where No One Ever Sleeps

A cold blue sunset hangs above the noisy stone labyrinth of evening Moscow. Night hangs above the huge country from Archangel to the Crimea. The villages go to sleep early; the small towns and the suburbs of the big towns are getting quiet, the iron clang of the capital's streets is quieting down, too. Then, in the wet gloom of night, invisible to the naked eye, radio signals grow ever more agitated.

Busy with his microphones, the man who is the ear of the newspaper sits in a room off Shablovka Street where the network's main antenna is located. The man sits penned in by microphones. His lips are pursed, his eyes are motionless. His hand moves like a spring, a pencil above the paper. Static, more static ... the static crackles in his ear. Words, dots, dashes, 25 languages, and snatches of music make up the threads of the radio network in the dark sky. And from all that constant murmuring, important information that will be read tomorrow by millions of readers must be collected.

"This is EKA ... This is EKA ... This is EKA ..." Somebody's sending Morse code signals into the ether from a distant, unknown station. Who is he? An oddly stubborn sender of those three letters; why does he beat the airwaves so persistently?

"This is EKA."

Maybe it's a boat floating somewhere in the Baltic, its hull damaged by a storm, calling from the treacherous mist, repeating those three letters to the owner of the cargo, explaining the reason for its delay. Or maybe it's a trade by an energetic stockbroker from an oak-paneled office in the City of London who's anxious to tell his branch office in Paris about the falling price of diamonds, oil, rubber. Or maybe it's in Kineshma, as far away as the moon itself, poisoned by the waves from homemade radios, unknown but proud, amateur, throwing letters at Europe, trying to reach some part of the family of listeners.

"This is EKA. Kineshma. Frequency 1,000 meters."

"This is EKA. Receiving Berlin from Kineshma."

But the man with the microphone breaks into the airwaves, switching on like a light socket. And he knows: EKA is nothing, forget EKA ... but this is more important: AMZ, AMZ. Amsterdam ... He writes briskly with his pencil: "*Co ... colonies ... court ... Ba ... tavia ... three natives were hanged for attempted rebellion....*" "Enough already! Let's listen to something else. It's obvious what's going on here."

A report is ready and on the table: "*Amsterdam 25. Authorities in Batavia have announced that a colonial court sentenced three natives to death by hanging for attempted rebellion against Dutch rule.*"

"*Da-dee, da-rum-dum-dum!*" The sound of a jazz band from Paris splits the air. "*It's a long waaay, to Tipperaryyy!*" The nasal tones of a bag-pipe emanate from a far-away music hall in Piccadilly. And again, from fox trots to jazz to violin music: "Wa-ar-saw. The textile workers of Lodz ... have been betrayed ... by the PPS...."[9]

"*Rum-tum … ta-rum-dee-dum-dee-dum …*"

"Paris … Syria … a Patrie fighter shot down … killed ; natives …"

"How many? One hundred or two hundred?"

How many tanned, dead bodies are spread across the yellow sands of Syria this evening, fallen to bombs dropped from Patrie fighters? What accounting, what horrible, bloody promissory note will be given to a Paris bank by the hills of bomb-savaged Syria and the bone-strewn deserts of Morocco? But leave that question for another time. For now …

The busy note-taker has picked up India, Lodz, Rome, Samara, Irkutsk, and Spitzbergen. A motorcycle engine is gunned in the night, the bloodshot eye of the rider disappears into the darkness with reports for TASS. For *Izvestiia*, for *Gudok*, for *Pravda*, for *Trud* …

Once again we will finish at four A.M. Call TASS, why aren't we getting any more telegrams? …What … It's been sent … It's here.

Bony and grey from overwork, the telephone operator flicks the handle on the switchboard for the hundredth time to the zero, or to the five, or to the seven—to the Linotype department, to the typesetting department, to the layout department. "Hurry, hurry, give me his proofs … get two machines ready; telegrams are coming in … Abram, I'm begging you, edit as fast as you can, people are waiting …"

"I'm not people …" Snapping, sweating from the furious pace, the night secretary cuts and pastes and straightens pieces. "There will be a lot of pieces, Mikhail Konstantinovich … Macdonald, 300 lines …"

"Cut, cut him," he murmurs viciously. "We don't have any space, the issue is too bloated already … hurry, hurry … the Linotypes are idle …" Yes, they *are* idle. One floor up. Wonderful, clever creatures of metal; pigeon-toed spiders with humming motors.

A busy typesetter has only to punch out a phrase on the keyboard; the Linotype machine takes care of the rest. Match letter to letter, lay it out in four lines, sprinkle it with hot metal, flick the handle, and the finished phrase is through the tube and into the tray. The machine stops itself and sits, clicking: ready for the next one. From the separate pieces of typesetting, new proofs will be created; they will be printed by hand and sent immediately downstairs, where each one is read by lanky Misha, his eyes red from proofreading, writing on the still-wet proofs:

"*4th up—1–2–3–col.*" He yells upstairs: "Hurry, hurry, print!"

At the hard steel tables, flooded with sharp, milk-white light, grubby printers work. "Top of the fourth page, into three columns." Long-nosed, sunken-chested Avenir translates the proofreader's nota-

tions. Avenir is the soul o' this sleepless, buzzing hive. In the mad rush,
he bobs like a buoy on the waves. "Fat Ara" Evstafevich (that's the
friendly name the newsroom has given to its experienced editor) appears from time to time in every department and periodically barks:

"Quickly! ... Faster! Let's have the third one ... No sleeping! ... No
napping! ... Ding-ding-ding ..."

Under the lash of his comments and jokes, the printers' work boils
even harder ...Grey-mustached veteran printers work swiftly with
awls and pens and blades, setting the type into frames, joking and
quarreling among themselves. They pry loose and moisten with
saliva the lines that have dropped off, they lead them and decorate
them with removable lines, they compare typefaces: Assure, Carouse.
"Better?"

"Foggy on 3 ... Grotesque 28 on 6 ..."

"Gerald Thick ... Renato Petite."

Sharp, tight, incomprehensible to the uninitiated: in the newspaper, words (nicknames of typefaces) fly through the air. "Hurry, hurry
..." Avenir, a heavy smoker, pushes everyone along, pushing them to
finish the first step of this great mystery: bringing words to life in a
deep flash of lead ...

The night shift has already read everything, and now the rheostat is
buzzing on a hot M.A.P. press that looks like a steam hammer; the
needle on its pressure gauge flashes and climbs. Now, lines of lead
type are ready in the press. Thick, fuzzy sheets of cardboard lie on top
of them; the machine will click, and from the other side of it matrices
will emerge. Scattered all over the machine are metal stereotypes;
printers will attach them to the drive shaft and the second phase of
the newspaper's birth is complete. It won't be early. It will be very
early: four o'clock in the morning.

Massive, gracefully awkward, hunchbacked where their drive shafts
and superstructures bulge, the powerful printing presses are already
waiting downstairs—the last stage on the road to becoming a newspaper. Obedient, with the flick of a switch they immediately begin
growling and huffing; they fill the whole yard and all the buildings
with the deafening sound of thunder.

Drive shafts groan under the monstrous power of the motors, and
six hundred kilometers of newsprint—the distance from Moscow to
Leningrad—will run back and forth between the machines' rollers,
rustling and sliding. Whistling cutters will slice this ribbon into
evenly-sized sheets. Then, a grey-faced, pre-dawn team of men in blue
work shirts will snatch up the newborn newspaper, put the 1,200,000
sheets into stacks, put each stack in its proper place, under the proper
address, under the subscribers' names, wrap them up and pack them.

The city will be waking up already; coughing out dust, factory smokestacks will be coming to life and taking their first breaths; the clock on Red Square will be crying its coppery "Good Morning!" when the machine operator finishes his shift, and, stumbling from the shaking in his legs and wiping the sweat from his face with his sleeve, slaps his sides and says, "Enough already!"

The ten-ton wild animals that swallowed tons of newsprint will become silent for a little while, but, at the same time, a new clamor will fill the streets with a new wave of noise. From the cast-iron gates, cautiously, one after the other, their chains rattling, two-ton trucks will crawl out—one ... two ... three... five ... now six—in single file, loading as fast as possible, heavy bundles with different addresses:

Perm, Kazan, Odessa, Nikolsk, Ussuriisk ...

Huddled against the raw morning wind, exhausted night workers emerge from the building's entrance; their eyes lovingly follow the trucks carrying to the railway station their baby: the newspaper. The great machine shifts gears one more time. The mad rush moves on to the railway station. But the last tightly-wrapped bundles will not yet have slapped down into the cavernous interiors of the railway cars and trucks with red signs reading "NEWSPAPER" will still be careening back and forth through the city when the telephone begins ringing in the secretary's office, lit with the pale dawn and freshened by the night wind.

Hurriedly, shaking off his coat, his face as yellow as a lemon, his eyes showing his exhaustion, the very same secretary picks up the insistent instrument.

"Hello? Yes, this is the newsroom ..."

Then, dropping into a chair still warm from the night's work, the secretary fumbles in his pockets for a pen, and, looking at the calendar, asks it in a sad voice:

"Well, what should we begin with today? Whom should I call?" But the calendar is silent; perhaps it feels sympathy for him at least. But what's the difference: there's no time to be sick. Or to sleep.

"About the issue ... the issue wasn't bad," says the secretary, the tone of his voice rising, looking through the ink-scented pages. "My God ... well, let's see what they've got in *Pravda*." There is curiosity in his voice, and his face is growing pinker and healthier.

On the other side of the door, reporters' voices make a buzzing sound. The charmed circle is beginning all over again. A new day has crept into the newsroom and the newspaper will not wait.

This reportage constitutes a day in the life of a Soviet newspaper, a creative device frequently used at that time in documentary work—and particularly in photography—to provide a comprehensive picture of daily work routines. Saian-skii reflects on the importance of communication for the success of the revolution and offers an account of newswork in the context of larger social and political goals. The resulting task of the press becomes more important than individual interests and what emerges is an understanding of journalism in the presence of modern technology that emphasizes the collective nature of newswork and emphasizes the role of the Soviet press in public enlightenment. At the same time, reportage as recreation of reality addresses the need to effectively propagandize readers. By recreating the world of Soviet journalism, Saianskii promotes the cause of the revolution and reinforces the role of the press as an organizer of the people. The emerging idea of journalism and the press is consistent with the political goals of the Soviet Union, including the surveillance and control of society through information gathering when enlightenment is reduced to responding to the conditions of a collective life in the spirit of the communist revolution.

NOTES

1. Obscure, probably a reference to telephones (the author frequently refers to machines by their brand names).

2. Probably a reference to Nadezhda Krupskaia, Lenin's widow.

3. A reference to Neville Chamberlain.

4. *Rabochii korrespondent,* "worker-correspondent."

5. Unknown.

6. The French guest speaks Russian, but with a "French" accent.

7. This passage is written in neither Russian nor Ukrainian but in a mixture of the two that is apparently meant to convey a sense of the letter-writer's lack of formal education and/or poor knowledge of written Russian. The old man in the secretary's office is a *rabkor,* as is the letter-writer, who has written to the old man on behalf of a third man. The letter-writer describes this third man as *zaliznichnik,* a word I have been unable to identify.

8. The author of the story declines the word *nose,* a masculine noun in Russian, as if it were feminine.

9. *Polska Partia Socjalistyczna,* the Polish Socialist Party.

4

▼ ▼ ▼

Negotiated Images:
The Rise of Photojournalism
in Weimar Germany

The introduction of a new technology is typically accompanied by a public discourse that reveals the social attitudes and cultural values that shape the climate
of acceptance. Such climate, however, is frequently enough manufactured by
those who organize and control the public sphere, who hold, in effect, what C.
Wright Mills (1956, 117) calls the "power of initiation."

The introduction of press photography in Germany during the late 1920s saw
the emergence of a visual culture that challenged the predominance of the printed
word in public discourse. This chapter focuses on institutional efforts to construct the role of press photography in a climate of social and cultural ferment
that also gave rise to an intellectual response to the emergence of photography as
a new form of journalistic or documentary expression.

At that time individual photographers introduced a new vision of photography
grounded in the aesthetics and political tendencies of the period. They produced
their versions of social reality, while the newspaper press responded with its own
ideological construction of photojournalism amid cultural criticism focused on
the confirmed success of picture magazines. Photographic practices are the product of cultural and political processes at a historical moment when these practices
become the norm for those who share the professional experience of conceptualizing and assigning meanings to photographs and the targets of cultural critique.

Journalistic photography (together with feature and documentary films) in the
1920s offered postwar Germany a glimpse of a changing world, and picture stories involving travel abroad were extremely popular features in German magazines.

But the increasing picture coverage of events abroad satisfied not only the curiosity of readers, it also helped reintegrate a defeated Germany visually into the world community. The publication of foreign images promotes the idea of a liberated and therefore unobstructed gaze of the reader and reinforces a notion of the dominant reader as observer and participant, while the coverage of traditional German social and cultural practices reaffirms the past and validates the power of history. In addition, these editorial routines diverted attention from the social and political crises of everyday life in Weimar Germany by focusing on the exotic and distant.

The potential of photography as a documentary and journalistic tool had been demonstrated with the rise of radical aesthetic and political movements, especially in the Soviet Union and Germany. These movements provide the cultural context for discussions of the relationship between journalism and photography during the latter part of the 1920s. They are guided by the recognition of the factual as a central professional issue and the struggle against distortions of reality with the onset of photographic coverage.

Photography is also recognized as a social and political instrument that allows participation through practice and can be used by large numbers of people. For instance, Anatoly Lunacharsky, Lenin's commissar for education in 1920, once said that "besides his pocket watch, every progressive Soviet citizen must also own a camera" (Günter 1977, 97). More specifically, photography in the Soviet Union gave rise to documentary expression, discussed and implemented first by Dzigo Vertov in his *Kinoglaz* activities, which involved the production of newsreels and the "decoding of life as it is" (Michelson 1984, 49), and by Aleksandr Rodchenko, whose contributions expanded the traditional use of the camera eye. Vertov rejects the Hollywood version of film and insists on the primacy of the documentary approach. His use of the documentary form demonstrates the impact of a social or political theory of revolution on visual expression. Rodchenko also maintains that social transformations must be expressed in a change of form and content and argues for the new possibilities of the photograph not only to describe the world but also to learn how to see it from different viewpoints. He criticizes and confronts the traditional perspective of a "psychology of the navel" with "centuries of authoritarianism behind it" with the rise of the new photography (Khan-Magomedov 1987, 222).

Both men emphasized the importance of producing images based in fact, the documentary values of which would support the goals of the revolution and instill the spirit of socialism in the people. In fact, other Soviet photographers associated with the magazine *Novyj LEF* (*Left Front of the Arts*) recognized that the new challenges of daily life required a new form of representation. They problematized and conceptualized the relationship between the development of new social structures and their visual presentation and decided that the camera represented the best medium for the reproduction of revolutionary matter in a revolutionary manner. As Molderings observes, "The Russian revolution, which liberated all productive forces, also for a time liberated the art of photography" (1978, 91). Technology became the hope of society, and camera technology satisfied the need for documentation. But there were significant differences between bourgeois and proletarian photography; according to Walter Benjamin, the goal of Russian photography—as opposed to photography in capitalist societies—was not "to charm and persuade, but to experiment and instruct" (1977, 63).

Others, particularly Max Alpert and Arkady Shaikhet, who worked for the Soyusfoto agency (founded in 1926), dominated photojournalism in the Soviet Union. They raised the level of professional performance and aroused expectations about the role of photography that pushed beyond formalism to express their commitment to the cause. One result was the creation of serialized images in the form of picture stories, among them, "Twenty-four Hours in the Life of the Filippov Family," which influenced the work of German photographers. A show of about eighty photographs of the typical life of a Russian worker and his family toured Vienna, Prague, and Berlin in 1931, and a photo essay was republished in Willi Münzenberg's weekly picture magazine, *Arbeiter-Illustrierte Zeitung*, a very successful publication of the left (1931, 38). The project inspired a German version, "Die deutschen Filipows," which was produced by a workers collective in Berlin and published in the *Arbeiter-Illustrierte Zeitung* (1931, 48), where its form and function heralded a new and alternative type of photographic practice in the service of political propaganda.

The influence of Soviet photography in Germany, which spread through exhibitions and books, suggests that the rise of a new technology under conditions of development—and under the direction of specific ideological interests—is capable of producing not only powerful visual statements that serve a common cause but also informing the work of others whose aesthetic sensibilities rather than political convictions responded to the challenge of a new photography.

Nevertheless, the uses of photography in Weimar Germany were also part of an ideological/political struggle, when the left, especially the Communist Party, recognized the potential of images as means of propaganda. Thus, the rise of picture magazines results not only in a critique of photography as a technology of reproduction in the hands of bourgeois publishers, but also in an intensive, purposive, and successful exploration of photography as a weapon in the hands of the working class. The function of photography, like the function of art, is politicized, and photographs serve not merely to reproduce the surfaces of everyday life but also to expose the conditions underneath the ordinary and familiar representations of society. The *Arbeiter-Illustrierte Zeitung*, in particular, becomes a forum for a type of photography that identified with the documentary style. The magazine applied photography to construct an alternative reality through combinations of text, photographs, and photomontage. But while it encouraged an ideological perspective and the political engagement of photographers, it also served German bourgeois editors and photographers as a professional guide and creative resource in freeing photographic expression from prewar conventions while still satisfying the specific institutional demands of the middle-class press.

These developments are also part of a more general intellectual and creative exploration of the postwar culture in the journalism of the 1920s. There were increasing demands for facts and objective presentations of the world. Information becomes a central force behind movements in literature and journalism, signaling the end of a social and political era after World War I and emphasizing the power and attraction of the immediacy and actuality of experience as a journalistic event. There was also a new predilection for American press practices of separating fact from opinion, a desirable accommodation of commercial interests and societal responsibilities (Hardt 1989, 7–29).

Photographs cater to the need for facts, reinforcing the professional ideology of objectivity and becoming the site of reality. Editors treated photographic images in their publications as objective representations of people and events. Photographs are assigned the power to establish the real conditions of society, either in the form of middle-class conceptions of tradition and survival or in the provocative style of social criticism, with its attacks on the social and political establishment. They document different truths and different understandings of everyday life and assume an increasingly important role in the conceptualization of news and news coverage. Photographs are products of the camera eye that observes and records pictures everywhere under the most imaginative circumstances. Erich Salomon, for example, sees himself as a neutral observer whose camera intrudes into the social and political gatherings of the ruling elites and reproduces the actuality of the moment.

Thus, photography in Germany is energized by the new social and political conditions in the postwar era and emerges as a "new vision" built on an awareness of the new technology and its aesthetic potential. Magazine photography, in particular, celebrates the new vision under the leadership of editors like Kurt Korff and Stefan Lorant; and photographers like Laslo Moholy-Nagy, Albert Renger-Patzsch, Erich Salomon, and Felix Man help articulate the autonomy of photography vis-à-vis art and its possibilities as a technological means of representation through series of photographic expressions that ranged from the experimental uses of the camera technology to straightforward realism; they address artistic/philosophical issues of space and time as well as the concrete conditions of social change. The glorification of the object was the product of *Neue Sachlichkeit* photography, along with the application of constructivist ideas that emerged from the work of Rodchenko and probe the depth of visual experience to reappear in the documentary and journalistic work of German photographers.

There could be no doubt that photography in all of its forms had become a new and significant structure of social expression and was used to provide social and scientific evidence of the political and natural environment. The press had a particular stake in the discourse concerning facts and the representation of reality since its historical understanding of news or information was seriously challenged by a visual medium that promised to be more direct, more powerful, and quite different in its conceptualization of social reality than traditional textual treatments by reporters. Not since the beginning of the modern press had a new technology threatened to alter the face of newspapers and magazines as radically as photography (the use of full color printing is another such change that occurred much later).

But the introduction of photography requires more than a new outlook on journalistic practices by editors, publishers, or even reporters. It also requires a new form of reception from a potentially large audience; the news is to be seen, not read, and is to provide an immediate encounter with reality. These changes involving aesthetic and material aspects of production and consumption pose questions of culture, including professional expectations and reader satisfaction. Thus, while individual creativity, often channeled through picture agencies, contributes to the popularity of photographic narratives, reader demands or taste cultures are constantly being created and sustained by the press. The goal is to reinforce editorial policies concerning visual presentations and direct the flow of pictures by references to reading habits, cultural preferences, and issues of cultural consumption. In other words, German editors and publishers were deeply involved in the cultural construction of photographs as journalistic expressions. The construction of the image as information by those in control of the uses of photography within the daily press involved more immediate organizational and administrative problems: business arrangements with picture agencies, professional considerations of staffing picture desks and redefining news to accommodate the flow of photographs, dealing with the competitive pressures for more picture coverage, and struggling to comprehend the powerful social and political impact of images and the commercial and political consequences of photojournalism. Beyond these concerns loomed more fundamental questions, however, regarding hegemonic issues of controlling technological change and maintaining political power over the process of defining reality in which the press competes for the supply of visual information about a rapidly changing cultural and political environment.

By 1928 the *Berliner Tageblatt*, for instance, offered its readers several illustrated supplements each week, including *Der Weltspiegel, Illustrierte Film-Zeitung, Photo-Spiegel,* and *Modenspiegel,* to provide a broad spectrum of illustrated information (de Mendelssohn 1959, 248). But picture magazines and movie houses, in particular, had catered for some time to a rising demand for visual information, a demand that threatened conventional forms of public communication. In addition, broadcasting had also come onto the social and political scene in Germany, especially between 1924 and 1930, and offered yet another opportunity for altering traditions of communication in society (see Chapter 5). Its noncommercial nature did not entirely remove the competition for audiences that appears with any emergence of a new media technology with innovative practices. In this case, in particular, theater and concert audiences were attracted to radio listening, although information and education services were equally popular (Hardt 1992).

Thus the newspaper industry of the Weimar Republic confronts the effects of photography on the nature of public communication and extends the process of reception to different and larger audiences. Pictures as reproductions of reality appeal to an audience that can respond to them intuitively or experientially rather than as experts. In fact, the appeal of the photograph—as exemplified by the growing commercial success of picture magazines—also attracts critical responses concerning the adverse effects of the photographic image as a means of exploitation, particularly in the hands of the press.

In the meantime, however, the German press approached photojournalism with predictable trepidation, which was due, at least in part, to the nature of the industry. The lack of a strong national press in Germany was offset by a system of large regional and local newspapers, ranging from district newspapers that relied on syndicated material to a sophisticated urban press in Berlin and Frankfurt, with a relatively large circulation beyond its geographical regions. In addition, the *Generalanzeiger* type of newspaper offers news rather than views. Although Germany boasted more newspapers than any other European country, most were small; the so-called *Heimatpresse* represent the stereotypical notion of local ownership. Oron Hale reports that in the late 1920s 81 percent of the newspapers were family owned and over half of them claimed to be neutral and independent; the press was a business proposition rather than a political calling for many publishers, including those in large metropolitan areas (1964, 3–4), where the encounter with modern photography was strongest because of the publication of national or regional magazines. Many local newspapers were organized in their respective provinces and represented by the Association of German Newspaper Publishers (*Verein der deutschen Zeitungsverleger* or VDZV), the leadership of which, however, was in the hands of the elite press. Only Nazi and Communist publishers remained outside the association. The VDZV was particularly concerned with business and technical aspects of the press, but as Hale observes, "To a greater extent than was customary with trade organizations it was inspired by a sense of high past achievement, of service and obligation to the public and the nation, and of standards that transcended the business balance sheet and the profit and loss statement" (1964, 7–8). These values clearly informed the discussion of the emerging practice of press photography.

The beginnings of press photography in Berlin are accompanied and supported by the rise of press agencies that specialized in photography as early as the beginning of the century. Others followed rapidly before World War I and throughout the period preceding the Weimar Republic. At that time a host of German press agencies begin to compete—mostly with exclusive picture material—for the domestic market, which included the daily press, picture magazines, and, later, the little magazines. The last had been successful in the United States and, by combining novels, reportage, and feature photographs, provided yet another outlet for photographers. In addition, some agencies, among them Dephot and Weltrundschau, initiated work on photo stories rather than on single images to supply magazines with visual narratives. Their contributions, fueled by the creative capabilities of the new photographers and encouraged by the increasing demands for unique story ideas from picture magazines, constituted the raw material of photojournalism, which also affected the style, content, and quantity of visual presentations of daily journalism.

A photographer who worked in the Berlin bureau of Pacific & Atlantic Photos (later Associated Press) recalls the role of agency personnel and how rapidly news photos were distributed to clients around the city and abroad: A typical daily routine consisted of preparing a set of seven to fifteen photographs (subscribers had access to a minimum of seven pictures per day), adding feature photographs—if necessary quotas could not be reached—and producing eighty copies for general shipment and an additional thirty copies for the London, Paris, and New York offices of the Associated Press and for some special customers. German photographers liked working for a foreign agency, and after January 1933 it was also safer for those persecuted by the Nazis than any employment by domestic agencies— although not for long (Kerbs 1983, 26–28).

The introduction of photographs in the German press relies on a variety of foreign picture services; in fact, the frequent use of images made elsewhere and delivered from abroad characterizes the emergence of photojournalism in both newspapers and magazines. The development occurred in the context of two external events, the specific revolutionary discourse in the Soviet Union that inspired specific forms of visual representation and the professional knowledge and practice of photojournalism in the United States, where "the overriding idea came quickly to rule the news photograph: Get a picture fast and print it first" (Hicks 1952, 25). Both events provide the diverse ideological contexts that inform the practice of German photography. They are the cultural arena in which the creative use of Soviet documentary photography confronts the pragmatism of American journalism to produce the creative and professional foundations of 1920s press photography in Germany. Since photographs could deliver powerful statements, they also produced readers and thus guaranteed increasing revenues.

Throughout the late 1920s in Germany, the discussion of photographs in the service of newsrooms is particularly interesting, since at that time most newspaper proprietors were finally becoming convinced that photography was to become a legitimate medium of public communication. According to VDZV estimates, between six hundred and eight hundred newspapers used photographs and texts regularly (*Zeitungs-Verlag* 1928a, 637). Magazine journalism in Germany had already embraced photography as an attractive and powerful way of creating a different visual experience for its readers, but had done so more urgently since magazines had begun to compete successfully for advertisers against a press that had been slow in adopting this new technology.

In fact, the invasion of images during the 1920s and the regular use of photographs by newspapers prompted a series of industrywide responses that reflected the attitudes of publishers concerning the position of the press in the cultural milieu of Weimar Germany and exposed the authoritative claims of publishers over definitions of the press and its relations with readers. These claims also reflect the nature of traditional German journalism, which had functioned more as an ideologically driven dialogue with knowledgeable readers than as an information service for a knowledge-hungry public.

Although financial considerations, unfamiliarity with recent technical advance-ments, and the conditions of producing newspapers—often under collective arrangements and with the help of boilerplate services, for instance—seem to ex-plain the slow adoption of photographs by many newspapers, the major issues were cultural, affecting publishers of magazines and newspapers like Ullstein, who had acted on the realization that readers now preferred photographs to texts. As Kurt Korff, editor of the *Berliner Illustrirte Zeitung*, explains, "Without the picture the things going on in the world were reproduced incompletely, often implausibly; the picture conveyed the strongest and most lasting impression" (1994, 646).

But while the use of photographs by the national magazine press—which was urban and more cosmopolitan than regional or local magazines or the Sunday supplements of larger newspapers—proceeds without much debate, newspaper publishers, who represented the reader interests of a larger section of German so-ciety, move the discussion of photographic images to issues of culture, taste, and the deployment of pictures as expressions of a national culture. In most cases ar-guments against unfamiliar photojournalistic practices are framed by the press in the name of its readers, with frequent references to their high expectations of newspapers. These discussions might have reflected the high cultural standards to which many German newspaper publishers aspired and their desire to remain po-litically neutral. Magazine publishers shared the goal of providing politically non-controversial representations of contemporary conditions. As a result, their mag-azines provided readers with insufficient information about the crises of everyday life during the late 1920s in Weimar Germany while offering a good deal of cover-age of their cultural heritage. For instance, Felix Man, one of the most successful photographers of the era, reports that "scandals, or pictures of nudes were ex-cluded. But short camera-interviews about cultural affairs, art, science, theatre or politics played an important part" (1984).

German newspaper publishers remained particularly sensitive to the significant flow of foreign images into the press and weighed the effects on readers of any uncritical use of such photographic material. They argue for careful editorial choices, expressing their preference for the work of certain picture agencies, par-ticularly those with a firm understanding of what constituted an acceptable pho-tographic image for the German press. Their arguments about picture editing are informed by a narrow, ethnocentric understanding of culture as high culture, and they rely on a traditional notion of *Kultur* to explain reader expectations. As a re-sult, rising public demands for exotic (foreign) images—and therefore potential profits—are met by some German newspaper publishers with resistance on cul-tural grounds.

These debates within the newspaper establishment culminate in a series of arti-cles and letters in the official VDZV publication, *Zeitungs-Verlag*, beginning in March 1928, with a discussion of "the cultural meaning of the newspaper picture" by members of the German publishers association (*Zeitungs-Verlag* 1928a, 637–40). They are an official acknowledgment of the impact of photography on their newspapers, although amid considerable confusion or ambivalence concerning its actual use. Nevertheless, photographs are considered extremely important because they could be easily and effectively understood by more readers, including those who were slow to assimilate the news.

Two reasons emerged for selling their members on the idea that photographic technology and picture-editing competence would be necessary and worthwhile acquisitions: the increasing competition from illustrated magazines and newspaper supplements, particularly in the metropolitan press, and the need to cater to reader interests in photographs. Thus, the incorporation of photographic practices into everyday journalism not only improved the form and content of newspapers but also increased their public appeal and circulation.

After the war the periodical press had already begun to respond to the general hunger for images and the quickening pace of modern existence, but magazines were constrained to deliver mere memories. In fact, Korff suggests that weekly picture magazines should enhance public knowledge by providing the visual version of events that had been verbally recounted in daily newspapers. At the same time it was also the expresssed editorial policy of the magazine that the selection of photographic images should be based not on the importance of the event "but solely on the allure of the photo itself" (1994, 646). On the other hand, only daily newspapers could provide an effective combination of visual immediacy, timeliness, and explanation by supplementing traditional text with photographs.

There was, then, a recognized need for experienced editorial staffs to handle the professional demands for better picture coverage. After all, the news and information value of the photograph—rather than its usefulness as an illustration—and the requirements of accuracy demanded the journalistic expertise of picture editors. The acknowledged autonomy of editorial decision making, however, included the obligation to protect business interests, which are typically couched in terms of readership requests for quality products (*Zeitungs-Verlag* 1928c, 901–904; 1928b, 1617).

Furthermore, discussions among newspaper publishers assign a cultural task and a specific cultural meaning to picture coverage, namely to uphold expectations of *Kulturbewußtsein* (cultural consciousness) and thereby eventually strengthen the influence of the daily press on the public and private spheres of society. At the same time the presence of so-called "destructive" tendencies among sensational newspapers and their mode of visual presentation was considered dangerous; it was certainly rejected by the mainstream press, whose editors were simply expected to act on the importance of the "cultural will" of pictures (*Zeitungs-Verlag* 1928a, 638).

The rhetoric of acceptance by the official organ of Germany's newspaper publishers culminates in the observation that any cultural and technological progress or political action would be spurred by journalistic texts enhanced by explanatory and stimulating pictures (*Zeitungs-Verlag* 1928a, 637). This understanding is a manifestation of two trends: an acquaintance with the power of images and their use or abuse in magazines like the *Berliner Illustrirte Zeitung* or the *Arbeiter-Illustrierte Zeitung,* and a reconsideration of the importance of text in newspapers, a tendency that reinforced fears among writers and reporters that the emergence of a visual culture would result in the demise of the written word.

These editorial developments also suggest to the political right the need to employ photography rather than language and texts for political purposes. However, the Nazi press never appreciated photography as commercial product or social documentation until after 1933, when press photography was regulated and takeovers of the press resulted in a massive exploitation of images for political purposes. Thus, visual/photographic reproductions of social reality were exclusively a result of the ideological perspectives of the bourgeois media and, to the extent to which the left-wing media were successful, their socialist competitors.

More serious, perhaps, was the reigning definition of cultural responsibility that reinforces a conservative argument for the deployment of photographs and reveals the political nature of photographic practices by the press. It was expressed by a German solution to pictorial presentations that sought to counter what was perceived either as creeping propaganda by foreign countries like England or the United States or as a flood of "tasteless" photographs that continued to reach German newspaper offices from these countries. VDZV members seem to meet photographic accounts of social, technological, or political developments from abroad with suspicion; on the other hand, German editors continued to face the fact that about two-thirds of their photographs were supplied by foreign sources (*Zeitungs-Verlag* 1928b, 1617).

In an effort to develop a more patriotic alternative and, therefore, rely on domestic picture sources, editors are called upon to provide pictorial coverage of German accomplishments, like German craftsmanship and the presence of German culture in the lost territories of East Prussia, the Ruhr, and South Tyrol, for instance. This practice already prevailed among weekly picture magazines, which published photographic series celebrating the cultural achievements of the arts and sciences in Germany (*Zeitungs-Verlag* 1928a, 639).

While Korff had hailed the unique contribution of the photograph to the magazine press, which was based on its "impact" rather than its content (1994, 646), daily newspaper editors were admonished to demonstrate that the selection of photographs did not depend on their visual impact or on their usefulness as fillers but rather on their cultural mission. Publishers insist on upholding the tradition of their newspapers as bearers and multipliers of German cultural labor. Thus, editors are reminded of the presence of sensitive readers whose sophisticated knowledge of the value and importance of photographs as representations of German culture would ultimately damage the credibility of those newspapers that might act irresponsibly in their selection and publication of pictures.

This tendentious and chauvinistic perspective on the use of photographs includes a critique of photographers for their general lack of professional expertise. The expressed need to socialize photographers into the professional environment of reporters and editors stands in contrast to magazine work, where photographers and editors cooperated freely and claimed an abundance of professional expertise.

Indeed, the professional image of photographers at that time varies, reflecting the context of work—e.g., newspapers, magazines, and picture agencies—and generational differences. Both are tied to the nature and speed of technological change. For instance, there were those whose technical experience outweighed their education and journalistic skills. They were often newspaper photographers, "who were used as tools in the hands of editors, but they had no standing," according to Fritz Goro, one of Germany's prominent magazine photographers, who later worked in the United States (Smith 1986a, 209). They produced primarily single usable images and represented the early period of German photojournalism, when illustration rather than news and documentation was the guiding principle of visual practices in journalism.

These photographers had been part of what Wilhelm H. Riehl called the "new" proletariat as early as the 1860s. Riehl suggests that to the extent that their "artistic ability defers almost completely to the acquisition of certain manual skills, they may actually have more affinity with the proletariat of factory workers, whose entire livelihood depends on a single set of actions that only retain their value so long as the machinery with which they are working remains in its present state of imperfection" (1990, 239). These practices equal those of their American counterparts, "one-picture" men whose presence at an event and whose capturing of it was more important than the "artistic quality" of their photographs or personal inventiveness (Hicks 1952, 26).

Others approached photography as a technology of communication. They attempt to visualize an event and find a story to tell in photographs. These photographers include highly educated individuals whose discovery of photography as a source of income was at least partially a response to unemployment and the economic crisis of the 1920s and partially a recognition of how to translate bourgeois values into viable picture stories for middle-class readers. They are also individuals who had discovered the practicality of the Leica camera; according to Goro, "Very intelligent people began to take pictures because there was this strange instrument available—the Leica" (Smith 1986a, 209). In fact, there was a tendency to identify the success of modern photojournalism with the availability of the 35-mm Leica camera, and Goro's remarks reflect this common assessment. Interestingly enough, this preoccupation with technological progress among middle-class photographers was missing among those who worked in the traditions of worker photography and Soviet photojournalism. They follow their social and political instincts to confront bourgeois culture with a style of photography that was to reveal the harshness of proletarian life and the corruption of the middle class. Hoernle had called on workers to be the eye of the working class and to produce images that "show class consciousness, mass consciousness, discipline, solidarity, a spirit of aggression and revenge" (1978, 49).

The result is a collective awareness of the new potential of photographic practices that reaches across different ideological territories and is applied effectively in producing commercial and political images while setting professional standards in the field.

Picture agencies at that time typically collected and arranged individual photographs in series on specific topics until professionally independent photographers supplied far more sophisticated documentations. As one of them suggests, "We were the first ones who consciously began to report an event like a story, but in pictures. We learned photojournalism as one learns journalistic writing. A story has a beginning, a main part, minor moments, and an ending" (Kerbs 1983, 185).

Among them was Felix Man, who began working for several Berlin dailies before he joined Simon Guttmann's Dephot (Deutscher Photo-Dienst) and produced a series of remarkable photo essays, including a rare interview with Mussolini in 1931. He often collaborated with a writer and finally negotiated an arrangement with Stefan Lorant and the *Münchner Illustrierte Presse*, which guaranteed him three hundred marks per page plus travel expenses. Man reached the top of his profession quickly and admits in his autobiographical writings that it "was a fabulous amount, and an extraordinary position" (1984).

Another photographer, Alfred Eisenstaedt, felt that "photography was in the air" (1969, 4) after World War I, when he joined the ranks of many amateurs, selling his first photograph in 1925. By 1929 he had discovered that good photographs sold well but that reportage and existing light photography sold better, and he began to work for the Associated Press, which had acquired the Pacific and Atlantic Picture Agency in Berlin and had begun its own News Photo Service in 1927. Eisenstaedt cites Martin Munkacsi and Erich Salomon among the rising stars of early German photojournalism, and he confirmed that "modern photojournalism was invented in Germany by a handful of editors and photographers in the late twenties and early thirties" (1969, 15). He also learned quickly "to search for those aspects of [his] subjects that were visually interesting, that told a story in a strong, pictorial way" (1969, 36). This includes "the power of a single detail to tell a story with great immediacy and impact" (1969, 50).

There were other prolific photojournalists: Wolfgang Weber, Umbo, Neudin, and Tim Gidal. Some of them provided images and texts and belonged to a small group of professionals whose work reflects intellectual and artistic labor. In general, photojournalists worked independently and relied on their contacts to picture agencies or magazines. According to Gidal, each new story was another proof of one's abilities and a new challenge. He argues that spontaneity and originality characterized this earlier work, which occurred under different circumstances than later assignments, particularly in the American context of long-term planning of picture stories (1971, 18–23). Nevertheless, the history of German photojournalism is not the exclusive domain of individuals like Salomon, Man, or Eisenstaedt, but the collective story of dozens of photographers, whose work survives in the pages of German magazines, bearing witness to their many talents (Hardt 1989, 21).

The generation of these photographers shaped the face of photojournalism in Germany and abroad. For instance, the work of Salomon was published in Great Britain, where the phrase "candid camera" was invented for him by the *Graphic* staff, according to Mellor, who feels that Salomon's influence was "vital for the development of photo-reportage" (1978, 122). Many photographers and editors also continued to influence the development of photojournalism after 1933 as emigrants in England and the United States. In fact, the success of *Picture Post* in London and *LIFE* magazine in New York relied on the expertise of émigré editors and photographers like Stefan Lorant (*Münchner Illustrierte Presse*), Kurt Hübschmann (later Hutton), Felix Man, Kurt Korff, Kurt Safranski (*Berliner Illustrirte Zeitung*), Fritz Goro, Andre Kertész, Alfred Eisenstaedt, Fritz Henle, and Martin Munkacsi. Similarly, the Black Star picture agency in New York—founded by another German émigré, Ernest Mayer—contributed heavily to early editions of *LIFE* magazine with the help of German and other foreign photographers (Smith 1986b).

In Germany, however, photographers faced other problems. Newspaper publishers complained that many seemed to know little about journalism, the specific needs of newspaper editors, and the speed of the daily press. Instead of responding to criteria like immediacy and newsworthiness, photographers were accused of submitting seemingly arbitrary and frequently irrelevant selections of feature material, adding to the supply of "ridiculous" and "tasteless" photographs received from England and the United States.

Similar complaints about the lack of photographic quality and the flood of foreign picture material came from an anonymous press photographer, whose explanation reflects the complex problem of working in a highly competitive environment in the 1920s and early 1930s (*Zeitungs-Verlag* 1930, 1182). He suggests that an open market for picture materials had resulted in the overproduction of photographs, particularly with the available supply of images from foreign picture agencies. Newcomers to the field of press photography lacked professional expertise. Their increasing numbers had practically ruined what had been a stable and protected market, depressing the price of published photographs from fifteen to between ten and twelve marks and thus effectively reducing the profit margins that had allowed earlier press photographers to develop stock photographs and archives, and invest time and effort in interesting projects. Instead, photographers now produced only commercially viable images. In addition, most of the large picture agencies, except for Scherl and Atlantic, were in foreign hands. These agencies had arrived from London, Paris, and the United States, with significant capital investments and business methods that allowed them to set lower fees and renegotiate prices for individual pictures (*Zeitungs-Verlag* 1930, 1181). They were also able to react quickly to customer demands and were better acquainted with the news business than competing German photographers. Their domestic clients were typically picture editors with limited budgets and daily deadlines who succumbed to poor taste and thus encouraged German photographers to produce kitsch, which seemed to be marketable as long as editors cared more about the quantity than the quality of the images they were receiving (*Zeitungs-Verlag* 1930, 1182).

The creative insights and commercial instincts of German magazine editors, on the other hand, codetermine the direction and content of photojournalism. After all, institutional support of photographic projects, including the activities of enterprising picture agencies like Dephot or Weltrundschau, relies on the interests and commitments of editors like Korff, Lorant, and Paul Feinhals (*Kölnische Illustrierte*). Although magazines attempt to provide a broad range of images, there is a decidedly strong emphasis on photo stories that typically consisted of four to seven photographs across a couple of pages to deliver a visual narrative in combination with supplementary texts. These stories resemble the story lines of movies and may have been attempts to compete against the visual attraction of film. Editors preferred a wide range of topics; most of them, however, avoided contemporary political issues, or dealt with them retrospectively and concentrated on the broader issues of social and cultural developments, international events of all kinds, sports, and fashion. The result is a celebration of German culture with a broad range of topics: concerts; theatrical performances; the workings of film studios; inside reports from schools, monasteries, and sporting events; travelogues; and expeditions. Photo stories describing unemployment, working conditions, poverty, rearmament, or political extremism were exceedingly rare. Lorant, for instance, claims proudly that he never used a photograph of Hitler before 1933 (1983). The editors of the *Arbeiter-Illustrierte Zeitung*, on the other hand, preferred the confrontational to the inconsequential, featuring documentary photography that exposed social and political problems. Their photographers were workers who were simply identified as worker-photographers.

Photography was used by popular illustrated magazines to construct and reflect a middle-class worldview that often had little to do with the actual conditions of the street. Newspaper publishers must have been well aware of this tendency. Their own discussions of the role and function of press photography reflect the outcome of these professional practices of magazine editors and their cooperation with photographers, whose own projects were successful because of their ideological proximity to the unwritten demands of the industry. Thus, German photojournalism in the 1920s attracts many photographers who produced series of picture essays under the guidance of editors and picture agencies and helped bourgeois magazine journalism succeed commercially. Consequently, photographers produced and published extraordinary photographs of a complete world (*heile Welt*) at the expense of socially and politically critical photographs or photographic series.

Yet public support of critical documentary work appears in the *Arbeiter-Illustrierte Zeitung*, for instance, which embraces a vision of photography as a weapon. Its tenth anniversary edition (in 1931) includes an appraisal of photojournalism by Bertolt Brecht. He suggests that the incredible development of the picture reportage has hardly been a victory for truth about the conditions in the world: photography in the hands of the bourgeoisie has become a cruel weapon against the truth. The immense picture material that is spewn out by the printing presses every day and that seems to have the characteristics of truth, serves, in reality, only to obscure the facts. The camera can lie as well as the linotype machine. The task of the A-I-Z to serve the truth and to restore the facts is of immense importance and is being solved brilliantly, it seems to me" (1975, 125).

There were also letters of solidarity from American readers (for instance, *Der Arbeiter*, the Federated Press (a news service), and the *Daily Worker*, all of New York) and requests for establishing similar magazines in France (*Nos Regards*) and Czechoslovakia (*Svet v obrazech*).

In spite of these developments in photojournalism and their public acceptance, many German publishers—as late as 1931—reject the idea that photographs had enriched the German press, pointing to the editorial inexperience or mismanagement of pictures. The assessment of press photography repeats well-worn references to poor taste and phrases about the unsatisfactory quality of photographs, despite the recent addition of well-paid picture editors (*Zeitungs-Verlag* 1931, 99).

However, it is also acknowledged that editorial staffs should have known better, and they were blamed for acting carelessly, in bad taste, or without political instincts in the course of selecting and treating photographs and texts. Consequently, they were accused of a lack of professional conduct that affected not only the quality of their own newspapers but also endangered the prestige of the German press (*Zeitungs-Verlag* 1931, 99–100).

Indeed, the editors' lack of political instinct in their choice of photographs is noted frequently. For instance, this issue is raised in a letter to the editor of *Zeitungs-Verlag* that complains about the picture coverage of international political meetings and questions whether the press is acting in the national interest. The writer charged that when photographers engaged in candid photography during informal meetings, coffee or lunch breaks, and other equally innocuous events, they ignored their mission to respond to Germany's vital interests. They also misunderstand their professional responsibility towards the interests of readers, who expected meaningful photographs (*Zeitungs-Verlag* 1932, 528).

This letter is an obvious response to Salomon's candid political photographs, which appeared mostly in national picture magazines and frequently in the context of photo essays that had the express purpose of amplifying the political events of the week. The publication of the letter in *Zeitungs-Verlag* merely supports the official opinion of German publishers concerning the quality and status of photographs in the press, reminding readers of the cultural mission of the press, the influence of foreign taste cultures, and traditional journalistic practices. Its appearance is combined with a critique of editorial staffs and their handling of photographs and texts and includes the suggestion that culturally undesirable photographs have been introduced by foreigners and their business practices. Their lack of education (*Bildung*) and their ignorance of German culture and the cultural requirements for supplying appropriate images somehow affected even the editorial selection process (*Zeitungs-Verlag* 1931, 99). Such remarks contain the seeds of contempt and disrespect for anything foreign in a concrete historical situation in which thousands of foreigners contributed effectively and prominently to the cultural life of Berlin and Germany.

Thus, while Berlin had become an important cultural center for intellectual and artistic activities—among them outstanding foreign photographers and picture editors associated primarily with illustrated magazines—the official organization of German publishers confronted inevitable social and cultural change with a great deal of suspicion and hostility. Its position also contradicts the expectations of the public, whose exposure to photographic images through magazine journalism provides a visual context for the experience of foreign cultures. For instance, Germans admired America, in particular, and relied on an encounter with American culture primarily, but not exclusively, through the consumption of images. For instance, Thomas Saunders traces the popularity and criticism of Hollywood films in Weimar Germany (1994) as a form of Americanization, while a contemporary observer, Ernst Lorsy, proposed in 1926 that "chewing gum is the cheapest way to Americanize oneself, and that is why the Germans of today, who harbor an intense yearning for America, have chosen it" (1994, 662).

Under these circumstances, newspaper publishers showed a peculiar reaction to the political and cultural changes in Germany. It is the response of a press establishment that was not only conservative by nature—and therefore inclined to preserve traditional practices—but also particularly responsive to its own historical consciousness and that of its generation—that is, to the aftermath of the war, including Germany's treatment at the hands of it former enemies, to the struggle over the meaning of a democratic society, and, finally, to the specter of modernity.

In fact, the official reaction of German publishers to photographic practices carries the seeds of a totalitarian language that defined national goals and expressed the chauvinism of a narrow, provincial outlook. The closed and antidemocratic language of authority that arises in the 1930s already bespoke a society on the march into a different future. But it is also the conservative voice of commerce that was expressing its fears about a secure place in society. Thus any references to expectations and abilities of readers related to the condition of picture journalism are also expressions of anxiety over the consequences of technological change and cultural diversification for the press. It is the voice of a press that had been prepared for its own demise by industrial interests. These interests, except for Alfred Hugenberg's claims, never completely appropriated the press but did succeed in corrupting the press economically and in discrediting democratic institutions with the aid of newspapers (Koszyk 1972, 169). At stake were major issues of social and political progress and the impact of modernity (with its interest in the visual) on the power of the press to define reality authoritatively and exclusively, not merely narrow concerns over how picture journalism did or did not fit into a preconceived social and cultural role in German society. George Orwell once suggested that language suffers when the political atmosphere is bad; interestingly enough, there are signs of bad times in these official comments about pictures and the press. After all, only a few years later Nazi press laws responded successfully to similar dilemmas in a language that was directed at journalists and spoke officially of the common will, culture, and strength.

These were also conservative expressions of a ruling middle class that raised immediate questions about the role of the Nazi Party during the years leading up to its ascent to power in January 1933. Interestingly enough, the existing Nazi press had not been very effective, particularly in its use of photographic images. It had lacked not only national circulation but also the interest and talent of outstanding photographers and editors, most of whom probably never sympathized with the Nazi cause. According to Gidal, most of the important photojournalists had refused picture agencies permission to offer their work to the Nazi press (1972, 26). In fact, the Nazi press was visually impoverished, "the technical equipment at the disposal of Nazi propaganda was rather primitive," and sophisticated means of communication were absent during the party's rise to power (Zeman 1973, 24). In addition, only 120 of about 4,700 newspapers in Germany with 7.5 percent of the total circulation belonged to the Nazis in 1933; eleven years later 82 percent of the 970 remaining newspapers were owned by them (Wulf 1966, 7). Consequently, the Nazis restricted their propaganda efforts to political meetings and face-to-face encounters, and they celebrated their rhetorical skills; oratory became identified with the success of the Nazi party and was credited for the final victory. As Richard Grunberger suggests succinctly, "In the Nazi beginning was the word—print reinforced it, but in an ancillary capacity" (1971, 391).

Although the party controlled a film production unit and produced a series of documentaries prior to 1933, its use of still photographs was rather restricted. On the other hand, Hitler's popularity had relied on the photographs of Heinrich Hoffmann, and there was an illustrated magazine, the *Illustrierter Beobachter*, which was founded in 1926 by Max Amann and Heinrich Hoffmann. These activities extended the possibilities of visual propaganda for the Nazi party, even in the absence of a strong party press, professionalism, and adequate financial support. Instead, the press was run by party functionaries. It needed advertising revenue and circulated mainly among the party faithful. In addition, journalistic activities were tightly controlled, including the use of picture supplements or the establishment of rival illustrated papers. Even after the 1930 elections, when the Nazis tried to gain control over the bourgeois press through infiltration rather than competition, their success was rather modest. In general, the Nazi press was considered an outcast with its extremist editorial messages and did not fit the German experience of a party press. In contrast, leftist practices of the socialist and communist press, including the *Arbeiter-Illustrierte Zeitung,* enjoyed public acceptance, partly because readers identified with their parties and their press and partly because these parties could offer financial backing to their publications.

By the time of the Nazi victory in 1933, however, the use of photographs for propaganda purposes had become widespread. Several top Nazi officials besides Hitler obtained their own photographers—Hermann Göring (Eitel Lange), Robert Ley (Kurt Boecker), and Joachim von Rippentrop (Helmut Laux) among them (Kerbs 1983, 30). At that time press photography was redefined as a necessary instrument of Nazi propaganda. A Nazi writer argued that its power of representation had popularized and reinforced the idea of race among large numbers of people and had aided the efforts to rally the population around specific causes (Wulf 1966, 126). But, more important, when the control of the German press through state directives becomes a standard practice of the Nazi government, a series of specific and concrete recommendations about the use of photographs, issued on a daily basis or whenever needed, restricted news and documentary photography. The advisories also provided editors with immediate government feedback about photographic practices. Official reactions ranged from reminders that Hitler portraits could be published only with his approval and through registered picture agencies (Wulf 1966, 107) to detailed comments that resembled movie scripts.

For instance, when the propaganda ministry criticized the publication of certain photographs in 1935, the following procedures were requested:

> From now on the reproduction of photographs which depict members of government at dinner tables, in front of batteries of bottles, etc. must be avoided, especially since it is well known that a large number of cabinet members are teetotalers. The ministers participate in social gatherings out of international courtesy or for strictly professional reasons; they consider participation a duty rather than a luxury. Recently the people have gained the completely absurd impression through countless pictures that members of the government overindulge. Photographic coverage must be changed appropriately (Wulf 1966, 95).

This is the beginning of a time when the production and selection of photographic material was governed by the notion of responsibility to people and state, a notion that also defined the nature of journalistic work, including press photography, and controlled access to the profession. In the meantime German publishers struggle against their own demise. But it is too late. They are denounced by Hitler, who accused them of having betrayed his cause. The press law of 1934 is the order of another world, or so it seemed to those who leave Germany for political reasons and to those who remain behind to witness Germany's exit from a history of totalitarian rule twelve years later.

Against a concrete conceptualization of photojournalism by traditional, commercial interests and professional practices stands a critical, intellectual response to the rise of the visual as a cultural force in Weimar Germany; photography raises questions about the authority of the word and challenges conventional forms of social communication.

The rise of photography during the 1920s symbolizes the advent of the contemporary spectator, as visual technologies, freed from the obscurity of artistic and scientific circles, are drawn into the realm of private entrepreneurship, where they helped shape the political and economic vision of postwar society. New communication technologies, including speedy and efficient rotary presses, direct photographic images, film, and radio provide different and revolutionary opportunities for creating a multitude of cultural and political realities. The intensity of visual experiences also raised expectations—and concerns—about the power of the media and the role of public communication in the visual representation of advanced industrial societies.

Throughout this period the discussions of photography reflect the intellectual and political confrontation with the machine age and, perhaps, the arrival of a new intelligence that would control and direct the activities of society.

The production and dissemination of photographs resulted in a new awareness among editors and journalists of the power of visual messages. It was accompanied by a strong suggestion that the essence of photography is its inherent realism, that is, the presentation of the concrete and the realization of material truth. For instance, from the intellectual position of *Neue Sachlichkeit* photography becomes the discoverer and recorder of reality at a time that belonged to a generation of engineers and to the spirit of objectivity. Photography offers opportunities for seeing the world and promises to deliver evidence of its existence. Others find that the emergence of the image is a fitting contribution to an age of extraction and condensation. Photographs represent short, rapid, and precise messages that reflect not only a belief in technology but also a renewed hope that the future would be guided by the rationality of science.

The identification of photography with the fact-finding mission of the postwar generation and its desire for stability offers a suitable political and ideological basis for using photographs in the construction of new social and political realities in Weimar Germany. The resulting employment of photographic evidence in defining and documenting various worldviews and the competition for the eye of the reader are helped significantly by the almost instantaneous popularity of the movies. The establishment of the *Kino* as meeting place and social event—like the traditional social environment of neighborhood pubs or dance halls—concretizes the advancement of a visual culture; it also stimulates the growth of the picture press. The presence of a *Kino* culture offers opportunities for identifying with the features of bourgeois society and encourages fantasies of participation in the exotic, ranging from the customs of foreign cultures to the lifestyles of movie stars. The world comes into sight, names have faces, and recognition breeds familiarity. In fact, this is the beginning of an era in modern journalism in which photography discovers and celebrates the face, which has remained a symbol of its power to dissolve the individualism of people into expressions of class, power, and cultural or political order.

This potential of the visual medium becomes an immediate challenge to a magazine industry, which had already produced its own versions of social reality based upon the use of illustrations and serialized novels. Now picture magazines respond generously to a mass ceremony of viewing with a steady stream of pictures and texts depicting familiar and strange objects and people, including the affairs of the cinema and its stars. Indeed, editors of picture magazines know that their products are extremely accessible, diverse, and offer more durable representations of reality than the movies ever could. They also realize intuitively that they could empower their readers by providing access to images and, therefore, possession of the idols of society, to use Leo Lowenthal's phrase. In fact, the emerging cultural function of "pinups" is a reminder of the success of picture magazines as sources of appropriation for several generations to come.

These remarkable technological and commercial developments in public communication relate to the growth and importance of popular culture in theoretical considerations of the social and political climate in Germany. The critical response to the emergence of photography in Weimar culture by contemporary observers constitutes a rich and exhaustive debate over images and seeing as a form of participation. It had surfaced in the discussions of language and discourse in the Soviet Union and appears frequently as part of a more comprehensive critique of bourgeois media and the commercial uses of photography by illustrated magazines in particular. These comments reflect not only the extent and nature of these concerns but also offer a rather sophisticated theoretical framework for positioning photographs within the cultural practices of society. They are also part of an extensive consideration of the visual culture in conjunction with attempts to theorize film and appeared frequently in discussions of documentary forms of visual expression.

The literature of Soviet filmmaking, for instance, is an important source of first insights and inspired additional reflections in Germany, particularly in the employment of film and photography in social and political causes. There is a commitment to the visual and to the potential of photographs in the service of documenting the social and political reality of society, especially by the left. Thus, discussions of the use of photography are embedded in an authentic political debate about the occupation of the cultural sphere and the struggle over the means of communication and become attacks on the practices of the bourgeois press.

The critique of mass society began in the presence of Marxist orthodoxy in the Soviet Union and the rise of Nazism, fascism, and other forms of authoritarian rule in Germany and elsewhere in Europe. Charismatic leaders had begun to assert their power, posing a threat to postwar societies and their expectations of a democratic future, and communication, culture, and media contributed to the construction and maintenance of such leadership. They become the focus of theoretical writings, especially as the Nazi regime unfolded in Germany, and later in the United States, when similar authoritarian tendencies arose there.

Various writers, among them Frankfurt School members such as Max
Horkheimer, Theodor Adorno, Herbert Marcuse, and Leo Lowenthal, and cultural critics such as Walter Benjamin and Siegfried Kracauer, react against a period of resignation between the two world wars. At that time media offered a false
sense of collectivity, according to Lowenthal (1989, 195), in a reified culture promoting ideological entertainment that fostered inauthenticity and alienation
rather than spontaneity and community. Horkheimer and Adorno (1972, xv)
note the "flood of detailed information and candy-floss entertainment [that] simultaneously instructs and stultifies mankind." The illustrated press during the
1920s—and up to 1933—constitute a specific and relevant example of mass culture, with its generous use of photographs that cater to the production of entertainment and to the promise of escape during particularly difficult economic and
political times. Although their work was not fully known and appreciated until
after 1945, Horkheimer and Adorno already responded to the role of popular culture with their discussions of the culture industry, the commodification of social
life, and the role of the media within the dominant power structure in capitalist
societies. They predict a continuing fragmentation of society through an application of strategies of diversion and the rule of entertainment.

There are also specific reactions to the developments of visual culture in Germany and the effects of photography, in particular, when picture magazines permanently conquered a considerable share of readers fascinated by visual representations of reality and the possibilities of participating in the world through
photographic coverage of people and events. In addition, the daily press also recognized—albeit reluctantly—the potential of photographs as news, adding to the
flood of photographs that reached diverse audiences every day. The strength of
this expansion seemed permanent, aimed primarily against a strong print orientation, and, therefore, against a traditional culture of reading and writing. Such a
development is based on a strategy of producing culture that relies on the predominance of the effect.

Photography as a new communication technology—together with film—represents progress and a specific promise of democracy. But it also symbolizes the
dilemma of modern life, offering a spectacle in return for an audience, while con-
fining individuals to the prescriptions of a mass-produced image world and the
anonymity of consumption.

Thus, when picture magazines propose a new form of participation in the
world, readers become willing accessories as well as victims of a belief that seeing
had actually replaced understanding in the course of contemporary life. The illustrated magazines of those years are instrumental in what Martin Heidegger (1974,
134–64) calls the "conquest of the world as picture." He suggests that pictures
were the products of people. In fact, as early as 1927 he describes, in *Being and
Time,* modern society's obsession with the visual and its privileging of seeing
(*sehen*) over understanding (*verstehen*). In addition, since the picture press—like
newspapers and other media—helped create a "distracted" mode of experience,

social communication emerges as pervasive "chatter" or "idle talk," which reflects the inauthenticity of modern life. Illustrated magazines, with their weekly fare of predictable texts and images, contribute to the ambiguity of everyday communication, since they strengthened what Heidegger calls the neutral and anonymous forces of "they" (*Das Man*), which shift the responsibility of understanding to others.

The prevalent private circulation of photographs and the promotion of photography as a visual encounter with the contemporary world, supplementing (and competing against) the effects of movies, occurs at a time in the political history of Germany when artistic movements interact with the political realities of the Weimar Republic and traditional bourgeois values encounter revolutionary demands for change. In an environment of political unrest and economic uncertainty, conventional social forces struggle with a progressive movement to decide the fate of society.

Picture magazines respond to the social and political problems of Weimar Germany with "chatter" and with the authority of the "they." They engage in what Roland Barthes (1973, 141) later called a form of propaganda in which the "bourgeoisie is constantly absorbing into its ideology a whole section of humanity which does not have its basic status and cannot live up to it except in imagination, that is, at the cost of an immobilization and an impoverishment of consciousness."

In this sense, the bourgeois picture press is a keeper of an ideology that reflects and perpetuates the values of the middle class in Weimar Germany. It engaged in a form of depoliticized speech that, according to Barthes (1973, 141–43), is always "a world without contradictions because it is without depth, a world wide open and wallowing in the evident, it establishes a blissful clarity: things appear to mean something by themselves."

In fact, the primacy of entertainment in structuring media contents and sales strategies has become a meeting ground for a generation of critical investigations of the strategies of popular culture, which range from the use of magazine fiction, dime novels, and comic books to film and television. These media continue to absorb and transform current social, political, and economic problems into attractive, noncontroversial episodes of diversion for a mass market. Most recently, cultural studies have confronted entertainment as political and economic practice in late capitalist societies.

At the time, however, Kracauer (1977/1995) considers entertainment an adequate function of art in capitalist societies, resulting in the production of amusement factories (*Vergnügungsfabriken*) like movies or illustrated magazines. His examination of contemporary society—collected later in *Das Ornament der Masse*—focuses on surface manifestations of popular culture in an effort to locate the position of the masses in history.

The illustrated magazines and photography provide the modern context for a society that is driven by the desire to understand the world through the consumption of photographic images. In fact, Kracauer (1995, 57–58) suggests that their aim is the complete reproduction of the world accessible to the photographic apparatus. They record the spatial impressions of people, conditions, and events from every possible perspective.... Never before has an age been so informed about itself, if being informed means having an image of objects that resembles them in a photographic sense.

At the same time, however, the flood of images destroys individual and collective memories, distorts reality, and breeds ignorance. Kracauer (1995, 58–59) found that "never before has a period known so little about itself. In the hands of the ruling society, the invention of illustrated magazines is one of the most powerful means of organizing a strike against understanding.... The image-idea drives away the idea." The world is equated with the "quintessence of the photographs"; it has become a "photographable present" that has been "entirely eternalized."

Kracauer's critique of the use of photographs in illustrated magazines, especially in America, provides some insights into the place of photography (and film) in the larger cultural critique of society that was part of the intellectual tradition practiced in the feuilleton sections of quality newspapers or highbrow magazines. It speaks to the extent of the critique, the suspicion concerning American culture and its potential influence, and to the level of engagement with new media developments, while offering some insights into the reception of photographs.

Such insights or understandings of popular culture provided the context for a trend toward documentary forms of observation, which include pictures, film, literature, and print journalism, whose direct and descriptive approach leaves little doubt about their intent and created the visual *Gebrauchsliteratur* of picture magazines and movies. The reproduction of observations appeals to the curiosity of the masses, that is, to their hunger for immediate experience, contact with reality, and knowledge of the concrete. Roland Barthes (1981) and Susan Sontag (1977) have written about picture magazines, which provide a knowledge—aided by the evidentiary nature of pictorial presentation—that creates confidence by relying on the scientific basis of photography and the fact-finding quality of modern reporting. But as we have seen elsewhere (Chapter 3), reportage is also a contemporary feature of Soviet journalism, where the move towards realism embraces a broad range of creative and intellectual labor.

Photography—and the critique of the commercial uses of photographs, specifically—responds to the demands of modern life in postwar Germany and emerges in the context of a new realism that attempts to picture life as it is. Photographs suggest proximity to the real conditions of existence, and their use reinforces feelings of participation in the social and political practices of society.

For instance, the art of the photomontage depends on the power of the photographic image as it becomes a means of expressing the contradictions of modern life and renders yet another critique of society. The works of Alice Lex-Nerlinger, Oskar Nerlinger, and John Heartfield illustrate social and political conditions and emphasize the predicament of ordinary people by confronting readers with the brutality and injustice of their own existence. Their photomontages are uniquely modern and highly creative contributions to the social and political discourse in the public sphere; they combine the power of the photograph-as-reality with the political insights of the artist and benefit from the commercial mass-distribution systems of pamphlets, posters, and magazines. They gain effectiveness from a logical extension of the photographic medium and thus are able to share their political and social concerns with millions of people.

The emphasis of the arts, in general, is decidedly upon offering a different vision of the social and political present and restoring the possibilities of a new perspective that reaches beyond the photographic image (Moholy-Nagy) to include music (Bartok to Weill), theater (Piscator), and the new realism of *Neue Sachlichkeit*. The pluralism and diversity of styles in many descriptive, analytical, and critical reactions to Weimar society reflected the extent of artistic and intellectual involvement in questions of change and uncertainty. Writers like Peter Gay (1968) and Walter Laqueur (1974) capture the emergence of a culture shaped by these events, and John Willett (1978) describes the ways in which real human needs were identified and dealt with by the artistic movements of those years.

The natural curiosity of creative minds, social commitment, and, to a lesser extent, political engagement become considerable forces behind the journalism of the 1920s, which burst upon the scene with demands for facts and objective presentations of the world. Information as a literary and artistic form becomes a central concept for contemporary movements in journalism and literature, defining not only a particular stage in the development of a technological society but also conveying the power and attraction of immediacy and the actuality of experience. Leo Lania (1926), for instance, talks about the "social function" of reporting and defines the task of reporters as constructing a commonly held picture of society, while Egon Erwin Kisch (1972/1925) insists that reporters would offer truth and objectivity as exciting and interesting discoveries to their readers.

The general attraction of photography as a mirror of reality, in particular, results also in the appeal of the photo book. The latter becomes a prominent and important source of social and political information and represented a new form of documentary journalism that suggests another construction of photography as a cultural practice beyond pure journalism. Most of the prominent titles grow out of the left-wing literature and journalism of those days and are inspired by a domestic criticism of economic and political conditions.

For instance, Kurt Tucholsky and John Heartfield (1929) collaborated on editing *Deutschland, Deutschland über Alles*. The book attempts to overcome the conventional use of illustrated texts or the ordinary juxtaposition of pictures and descriptions to arouse emotions and stimulate political action. Similarly, Alexander Graf Stenbock-Fermor (1931) documents poverty and exploitation a year later with his illustrated reportage of Germany's working class in *Deutschland von unten. Reisen durch die proletarische Provinz*. There are also different and purely commercial ventures to capture the market for photographic books, works that used a popular thematic approach to collect and publish photographic material. For instance, Ute Eskildsen (1978, 111) suggests that the "title of Renger-Patzsch's book, *Die Welt ist schön* (*The World Is Beautiful*) could serve as a subject heading for a catalogue describing such books."

The confrontation with life as it occurs through reportage provides a journalistic response to the graphic nature of photographs—which themselves contribute to the rise of the reportage—while addressing social and political problems. But the reportage was also a literary practice, and Kisch (1972/1925), in particular, represents this genre of documentary writing with *Der Rasende Reporter,* a series of his own stories that had been rescued from the obscurity of yesterday's newspaper and elevated to the level of contemporary engaged literature. Another outstanding example of the strength and capabilities of the reportage was assembled in *FAZIT: Ein Querschnitt durch die deutsche Publizistik* (1929), which demonstrates its widespread use among conformist, conservative representatives of the bourgeois press as well as among liberal, radical, or revolutionary journalists, whose writings appeared in the publications of commercial publishing houses like Mosse, Scherl and Ullstein, and the leftist publications of Willi Münzenberg.

The birth of pictures as a new way of seeing the world coincides with a crisis of the word. In fact, photography and film emerge as threats to the predominance of the word in the public arena. The impact of photographs and movies, with their intense, evoked visual experience of a modern world, captured the public imagination with bright light, colorful billboards, advertising slogans, and political posters. These visual stimuli mark the commercialization of society and create the conditions under which pictures become ersatz dreams and visual images rather than words occupy an otherwise empty and alienated world. In such a climate the popularity of movies and illustrated magazines at the expense of books and literary magazines, for instance, seems especially problematic, since it reveals and threatens to reinforce dysfunctional breaks in society. Considerations of language as signs of class, authority, or expert knowledge are always suspect until abandoned for the alternative of the image, which seems to offer an open, perhaps even democratic process of communication. For instance, when Hugo von Hoffmannsthal (1921) observes that people are afraid of words, he means that they are alienated from the language of the educated and the semieducated, whose words fail to reach them anyway. Instead, they grasp the concrete, identifiable, and knowable image. Movies and picture magazines fulfilled these desires.

The presence of the visual sparks interest in new forms of writing. For instance, the proximity of reportage to literature, accomplished partly by the practitioners of reportage and partly by the new realism in contemporary literature, raises questions about documentation and reality. Kurt Pinthus exclaims, as early as 1920, that reportage has become literary practice and is an art form (Mörchen 1983). Indeed, the works of novelists whose documentary fiction becomes their literary response to the political and social environment of Weimar Germany are based on research and documentation. Writers like Kurt Tucholsky, Lion Feuchtwanger, and Ernst Glaeser use the press to excavate social facts and to create a critical forum for their relentless attacks on misery and social injustice. They show the ability of photographs to capture the impact of a moment and the capacity of the text to negotiate between past and present.

Leftist authors and journalists, in particular, recognize a special effectiveness of reportage or documentary fiction in their own critique of the bourgeois establishment. The resulting combination of fact and fiction often finds its way into newspapers and magazines as serialized novels or short stories. Such usage blurs the differences between traditional forms of journalism and fictional accounts of the world. Each form creates familiar—or recognizable and thus understandable—realities for those readers who live in and through the visual experience of magazines and movies. Reportage has the potential of rescuing the word, which had seemed to be monopolized, if not *verschleppt*, by cultural and administrative elites. The new forms engage the language of the people, speak the dialects of the street, tell about ordinary life, and restore the power of description. The reportage complements the role of photography as a means of documenting ordinary lives.

Others ignore the image and theorize about the separation of literature and journalism. For instance, Georg Lukàcs (1980, 45–75) considers reportage an appropriate method of disclosure and a most desirable journalistic practice; in "Reportage or Portrayal?" he agrees that the "reportage is an absolutely legitimate and indispensable forum of journalism" as it moves beyond the depiction of facts to "present a connection, disclose causes and propose consequences." But even when the reportage appeals to feelings, it still tries to convince its readers intellectually and thus legitimizes its journalistic function. Since journalism operates with scientific methods, however, the "concreteness of reportage, as of every conceptual [scientific] reproduction of reality, is only achieved with the conceptual disclosure and presentation of causes and inter-connections." Lukàcs recognizes the significance of the reportage-style novel based on observation, like a newspaper report based on eyewitness accounts. But the decisive difference between applying the creative methods of reportage in literature on the one hand and journalism on the other remains the author's ability to account for history. Lukàcs feels that the genuine reportage of literary standing not only permits a "lively, effective and penetrating depiction of a section of reality," but, more important, it would incorporate such crucial insights into history.

The search for relevant or appropriate methods of communication in reconstructing reality in a time of social and political upheavals is also manifested in efforts to transform traditional theater into an instrument of information and to strengthen its participatory role. For instance, Ernst Toller, Erwin Piscator, and Bertolt Brecht depart radically from the idea of a bourgeois theater and its artistic contributions to society. They embrace a notion of theater as a public medium, engaged in the liberation of society by moving the stage into the center of social and political activities. Their theater of the 1920s introduces documentary elements that bridge stage and street and reduce the distance between literature and life.

The theater becomes a public medium that shares specific roles and functions with the emerging picture magazine by depicting conditions, producing information, dispensing explanation, and in its most political guise, delivering instructions and inciting to action.

It is at this intersection of technology, democracy, and art where social and literary critics meet to consider the production of a visual culture and the impact of images on society. Photography becomes a public phenomenon, reinforced by private uses, that dominates the popular discourse of magazines and contributes to the creation of a social and political fiction.

For instance, Kracauer (1977, 34–35) maintains in his discussion of photography, that illustrated magazines had turned against knowledge and had created a wall of ignorance between readers and the world. He concludes that "'pictures-as-ideas' banish ideas, the deluge of photographs reveals the indifference towards what these objects are meant to express. It must not be this way; however, American illustrated magazines, which are often emulated by those in other countries, regard reality as the essence of photographs." The result is a world reduced to pictures by a commercial illustrated press, which continues in its unsuccessful attempt to immortalize the present.

Benjamin (1986, 230) considers the attraction of photographs as "standard evidence" for documenting historical events, but he also observes that the picture press actually projects the consciousness of a media industry that had discovered the seductive power of images. He believes in the continuing importance of the word as an integral part of technological developments, which also lead to a world of pictures. Therefore, picture magazines could merely be "signposts" for their readers, "right ones or wrong ones, no matter." He recognizes the urgency of the textual explanation in a rapidly expanding universe of images by suggesting

> For the first time captions have become obligatory. And it is clear that they have an altogether different character than the title of a painting. The directives which the captions give to those looking at pictures in illustrated magazines soon become even more explicit and more imperative in the film where the meaning of each single picture appears to be prescribed by the sequence of all preceding ones.

Benjamin criticizes, however, the aestheticizing of photography, in particular the photographic efforts of the *Neue Sachlichkeit,* which produced not only a large volume of work on any imaginable subject but also, according to Benjamin, "has succeeded in transforming even abject poverty, by recording it in a fashionably perfect manner, into an object of enjoyment." His critique (1986, 230) also points to the economic function and the political consequences of photography to explain the popular need "to restore to mass consumption, by fashionable adaptation, subjects that had earlier withdrawn themselves from it—springtime, famous people, foreign countries—it is one of the political functions to renew from within—that is, fashionably—the world as it is."

Photography establishes its own credibility as a medium of observation, offering a social reality that was easily accessible, retainable, and ostensibly democratic because it proposes to share observations with those who participate in its consumption. Photography, as a mass-produced ersatz social reality, becomes a powerful source of experience.

The popularity of visual images as objects of curiosity or desire also signals the existence of fundamental problems in society. For instance, the predominantly topical concerns of photojournalism—the arts and sciences, travel and discoveries, the lives of famous people—combined in picture stories or "photo essays" by popular weekly magazines, had their roots in the cultural milieu of a German middle class, which sought an escape from the real conditions of society. Photographic coverage represents opportunities for locating oneself in substantiality, feelings, and dimensions of time and space; photographic images yield a sense of participation, and they brought order into the flow of reality, which was the appeal and attraction of picture magazines.

These are debates about language and images that address the cultural demands of a democracy after a long period of censorship that ended only after the war. At that time demands for news and entertainment spread to new and vast audiences of the socially and economically deprived. And the commercial media respond with a flood of inexpensive reading materials, including serialized novels in existing newspapers and magazines, dime novels, paperbacks, and picture magazines.

The importance of photography is accentuated by a variety of uses and practices. They include its use and dissemination as artistic expression and the critical reaction to its role in art, politics, and everyday life. Photography is also the focus of a much larger general preoccupation, if not admiration, for the potential of technology. Photography, after all, represents a significant scientific and technical achievement that privileges the image as the new language of the modern age. When art is confronted with the arrival of the machine, photography emerges as a new means of production that allowed an instantaneous response to a demanding audience. The promise of an objective reproduction of people or events is a reminder of theoretical discussions about photography that equate the arrival of the new medium in the United States and Europe with an appropriation of realism.

Photography, in its constructivist, surrealist, or *Neue Sachlichkeit* mode, represents the end of a long march from description to interpretation that emerges in the new social and political context of the 1920s, particularly in the Soviet Union and Germany. Photographs become expressions of the state of the world, perspectives on people and events—sometimes disguised as facts and at other times celebrated as opportunities for opinion. Their use value in society preoccupies a number of cultural critics who encounter photographs in the emerging illustrated magazine tradition, in (political) journalism, and in numerous photo books. The last often reflects artistic intent and social concern. Indeed, it was difficult to avoid a confrontation with the potential of photography and ignore its impact on traditional domains of culture and society during the late 1920s in Weimar Germany. Writings about photography were also affected by confidence in technology. The contribution of the machine to the modernist project, beginning with the nineteenth century, continues to have an effect on considerations of photography during the 1920s and 1930s. When photographers finally train their cameras on the accomplishments of a modern industrial society, they are fascinated by the opportunity to observe and document the relationship between new technologies and biology, between industrial design and nature, and to present and represent the structures of human existence in the name of realism.

Their work also incorporates different ways of seeing, leading readers beyond the experience of traditional perspectives to new insights about their living environment as a configuration of images. The world is not only beautiful but also immensely photogenic. In this sense, photography becomes an educator, seeking to arouse an awareness of the extraordinary in the ordinary. At the same time, proliferating photographic images demand attention and become an overwhelming experience for the unsuspecting reader. At this point, theoretical considerations of photography turn into social criticism, and the cultural perspective acquires a political purpose.

Together, photographic practices and critical writings on photography—transgressing political and cultural boundaries—create yet another image of photography in the service of society. While publishers and journalists constructed notions of photojournalism that emerged from cultural and professional agendas of adoption, adaptation, and conventions, critics of popular culture and society convey the conditions of a culture that is mesmerized by the promises of visual technologies. Photography—especially press photography—emerges in 1920s Weimar Germany as a new cultural practice with enormous social and political consequences.

5

▼ ▼ ▼

Radio and *Kultur:* On the Social Uses of German Broadcasting

The cultural history of an epoch is inconceivable without considering social communication: its position in the process of culture and its impact on the relationship between individuals and media institutions. The form and substance of this relationship shape the cultural and political discourse of society.

The history of radio, not as an institutional biography of technological or commercial success or regulatory control, but as a social force in the lives of people, remains a fragmentary project in the United States and in Germany. This chapter is a reminder of the potential for a cultural history of broadcasting and provides an exploratory cultural materialist perspective on the rise of radio and its social uses.

The following narrative is an American view, a thoroughly journalistic gaze, and a contemporary reading of the rise of German radio between 1924 and 1930, when broadcasting burst onto the scene of a society in a fierce political struggle over the discovery and content of democratic forms of participation. This chapter addresses a particular view of radio in Weimar Germany as it was expressed by *The New York Times* in those years. The concern here is not so much the organization and development of the institution of broadcasting, the introduction of new technologies, or the origination of radio stations, but rather the social and political uses of radio: what Germans do with radio, how they perceive it, and how it affects democratic practices in the Weimar Republic.

A cultural inquiry into the rise of radio in Germany suggests a re-examination of the dominant historical discourse by shifting attention to the existence of broadcasting as a social process in the narrative of a foreign culture. Indeed, the discourse about German radio in the *Times* can be mined for significant observations about the uses of early German radio. This essay, then, explores foreign news reporting as mapping of a foreign country. The emerging features of an imaginary

neighborhood on the other side of social, cultural, poltical, or economic boundaries, for instance, may yield ideas for reconstructing social and political meanings
of radio and democracy.

This approach, like Siegfried Kracauer's, suggests that the significance of a historical period can be explored through an analysis of things generally considered
trivial—in this case, the short item or a casual compilation of events presented in
the form of fillers or short items that appear as random remarks about German
radio but nevertheless express the historical conditions of broadcasting. For instance, Kracauer argues in *Mass Ornaments* that "the place which an epoch occupies in the process of history is determined more forcefully from the analysis of its
insignificant superficial manifestations than from the judgments of the epoch
upon itself.... The fundamental substance of an epoch and its ignored impulses
reciprocally illuminate another" (Kracauer 1970, 50). The reportorial surveillance
of radio as a social and technological breakthrough in "mass" communication is
an example of such an analysis.

The flow of information about the social and political uses of radio in Germany begins appearing in *The New York Times* in 1924 and increases steadily over
the years. Discussions of the institution of broadcasting become a regular source
of information about the social, cultural, and political affairs of German society.
Typically hidden in the foreign news section, the information is often brief, consisting of fillers frequently supplied by the Associated Press or the *Chicago Tribune*, whose foreign news desk served a large number of American newspapers,
including the *Times*.

This type of news reporting created in the shadow of important economic and
political events—presented irregularly, yet subject to professional conventions—
forms a contemporary surface phenomenon; it is the product of a newspaper industry and the manifestation of a mass culture, which construct the realities in
and by which individuals existed in the modern world. Its topical narratives and
its silences are designed to meet the expectations of the reader; they are the elements of a cultural history that reveal strategies of distraction and definitions of
the historical situation. But foreign news, especially, not only instructs but also
shares cultural and political biases through the editorial production process. They
appear as forms of "Afghanistanism" in the news columns of the press—that is, in
stories whose consequences rarely affect the daily lives of people but remain journalistic expressions of curiosity, perhaps even astonishment; on occasion, they
may also have served as examples of a desirable and alternative way of organizing
the world—trial balloons, in effect—but without the threat of pending social or
political change.

American radio in the 1920s was becoming a powerful social and political institution whose growth foreshadowed the impact of broadcasting on the definitions of society and democratic practice in the United States. By 1923 more than 2
million homes had radio, and "listening in" had become a national pastime. Many
sets were homemade or home-assembled, and installing one was "a sure way to

become known as a mechanical genius"(*American Review of Reviews* 1923, 52). The development and spread of radio, together with the seemingly uncomplicated application and dissemination of other technologies throughout society—like the telephone and the automobile, which became synonymous with the notion of progress—confirmed among Germans the image of the United States as a thoroughly modern society. Indeed, "*Amerikanismus*" signifies admiration for technology and a way of social (and political) practice that is widespread among German intellectuals in the 1920s.

Germany, on the other hand, was still accommodating this new form of "mass" communication culturally and politically. Its history of broadcasting begins in 1922 with the discussion of the public role of radio and its potential as a medium of social communication, encouraged and controlled by official interests and motivated by the technical developments in the United States and England. In addition, private and frequently clandestine operations of amateur radio enthusiasts are active and engaged; they are already organized in clubs and eager to test the possibilities of broadcasting in an atmosphere of centralized decision-making, including programming. Their experience contrasted with the introduction of radio in the United States only a few years earlier (Lerg 1970, 266–278; 1980, 61–65).

Nevertheless, the accessibility of broadcasting technologies in the 1920s is a shared cultural experience that inspires a cross-cultural fascination with radio's technological potential and the prospects of an age of technology in general. Americans were the perfect audience for information about a social world confronted by the commercial consequences of a quick succession of emerging media such as photography, film, and radio. Extensive newspaper coverage of the advancement of wireless communication elsewhere, including in Germany, satisfies interest in the overall progress of radio, which may be viewed as a quintessentially American invention: loud, invasive, mobile, and technically seductive.

The increased coverage of German broadcasting by *The New York Times* coincides with the popularity of radio among Germans, which was well established by the end of 1924. Between January and December the number of registered listeners had increased from two thousand to five hundred thousand; the *Times* also reveals Hans Bredow's prediction that the "number of new subscribers per month will average about 100,000 for some time to come (*NYT* 1924g, 20). By January 1930, the count increases to over 3 million, and German newspapers are "urging speedy construction of new powerful stations to keep step with the favorable development" (*NYT* 1930a, 6).

Since radio sets located in households are typically used by four to five family members (*NYT* 1929b, 19), the potential radio audience in 1924 is significant enough to gain the attention of the political power structure—political parties, government, and commercial organizations. Radio becomes a site of social and political struggle. Consequently, the emergence of radio in Weimar Germany is treated by American journalism as social, cultural, and political news about domestic or international affairs, while technological developments of radio serve to attract and hold reader attention. Reporting about the adaptation of broadcasting to everyday life in Germany, although incomplete, nevertheless offers an interesting glimpse into how Germans dealt with an emerging communication technology, especially since demands on radio and its applications were rather numerous and varied, and reflects the strength of social, political, and cultural interests in broadcasting.

The 1923 Christmas address by the German chancellor Wilhelm Marx provides an opportunity for the *Times* to reveal the restricted and government-controlled use of radio, a completely foreign idea for American readers, who benefited from access to dozens of radio stations with a variety of programs and who ordinarily did not know or care much about the regulatory process of broadcasting in their own country. The contrasts between developments in the United States and Germany appear even more substantial in the description of the chancellor's broadcast address as "a startling innovation, [which] shows how far this country has lagged behind in radio." In fact, most of the article emphasizes the differences between the United States and Germany in terms of the accessibility of radio to consumers or listeners because of "rigid rules and regulations ... gagging radio enthusiasts." It describes the tedious licensing procedures for the average German, ranging from the annual cost (twenty-five gold marks, or about six dollars) to the need for personal documentation of citizenship and "good moral character." The article also notes how Germans were restricted in their purchase of radio sets; they could only buy sets approved by the Post Office Department and constructed "to receive only those wave lengths specifically permitted by the Government authorities, by which they can hear an evening broadcasting program from the hall of the phonograph company on Potsdamstrasse, a program from the State wireless station at Königswusterhausen and from a couple of other official or semi-official shows." The report goes on to explain that making or assembling sets is illegal, "while sending is absolutely taboo as a capital crime." In contrast, the conditions in the United States are described by Germans as a "wireless anarchy" (*NYT* 1923, 3).

Radio sets become a major sales hit during the 1924 Christmas season in Germany, and the *Times* acknowledges that "radio ... is leading the list of Christmas shoppers. It is dominating the market even to the exclusion of toys." Consequently, "delicatessen, lingerie, leather goods and other stores usually not connected with the radio industry have installed sales departments in anticipation of the popular demands" (*NYT* 1924, 24), undoubtedly to cash in on the popularity of radio listening.

The use of radio, however restricted by government or limited in its programming, emerges from a number of reports as extremely innovative and unique; the introduction of public information services, educational programming, and the formal organization of listener interests surpasses most American measures at that time.

For instance, a Berlin radio station broadcast every morning at 10 o'clock, announcing "the prices of standard foodstuffs ... for the benefit of housekeepers who have been much annoyed by the lack of uniformity in prices throughout Prussia" (*NYT* 1924a, 4). At the same time, advertising increases anger in listeners, who reject commercialism in radio, and results in the formation of an aggressive interest group ready to challenge the activities of advertisers. The *Times* reports, "Spokesmen for the newly organized Radio Protective Association ... hint that the time may come when a radio strike will be declared against the Government. Since each fan pays a license fee of 50 cents a month, such a move would force attention through loss of revenue to the Government" (*NYT* 1926b, 3). Such threats are especially surprising since the time for commercial messages was rather limited. "Out of a total of sixteen hours a day of broadcasting, advertising takes up only about a half hour each day," according to Kurt Magnus, director of the central organization of German broadcasting in 1929 (*NYT* 1929c, 19).

However, there are other, even more innovative developments. In Leipzig, a high school on the air offered regular classes for those wishing to earn diplomas by studying at home. The "Hans-Bredow Volkshochschule" was designed to attract students consisting of

> subscribers of the Leipzig circuit who, at regular evening hours, listen to lectures on scientific, literary, artistic and economic subjects. In the event that technical subjects necessitating diagrams and illustrations are discussed, the pupils receive illustrated booklets in advance, for which they only pay a small fee. The lecturer, at the appointed time, then asks his listeners to turn to page or diagram so-and-so as he elucidates his subject (*NYT* 1924f, 24).

Similarly, the "Staatliche Gymnasium" in Berlin installed thirty-four "radio receiving sets in the class rooms to enable the students of languages to profit by lectures broadcast in other tongues. It is the first German school to be so equipped" (*NYT* 1929a, 22).

To the American readers these experiences are not altogether new, since a certain amount of educational broadcasting was also occurring in the United States; however, the intensity of these examples of civic commitment to radio for education and the implicit quality of the services fit well into the German image of skill, organization, and determination. The primacy of cultural concerns is also suggested in the deployment of broadcasting in the public sphere, an example of alternative applications of radio in a capitalist society.

But the popularity of radio also had negative consequences, ranging from rising trade union concerns about the manufacture of radio sets abroad to the protection of the rights of authors for the presentation of their works and the public's right to information. These concerns illustrate the potential impact on trade barriers of the mass marketing of radio sets—especially the accessibility of an inexpensive technology—and they problematize radio programming by defining and reaffirming the boundaries of private ownership of intellectual and artistic products while recognizing the importance of news dissemination. These concerns also reflect major problems of social and political control over access to specific ideas.

They address notions of property and profits connected with the organization of broadcasting. The American experience with mass production and the export of consumer goods—and, in particular, with managers and producers of radio programs who dealt with the benefits of copyrighted materials as early as 1923—helped make these issues familiar.

The *Times* addresses the problems of applying free-market standards to the sale of radio sets in Germany in a report about press reactions to imports from the United States. The *Deutsche Tageszeitung* is quoted as saying that a request to import American-made radio sets would endanger the German broadcasting industry. The paper charges that in the United States

> the radio industry has developed to such a point that the minute the German market is opened they can flood it with a tremendous amount of apparatus. These may not compare favorably with the German article so far as quality and durability are concerned, but reckless merchants will persuade numberless Germans to buy them before inferiority is found out, and the very fact that they come from America will recommend them to some people (*NYT* 1924c, 15).

The same *Times* article extends its observation about the German reaction to imports by pointing to similar movements against the sale of American Ford cars, which also would be much cheaper than German products (*NYT* 1924c, 15).

The struggle for the protection of copyrighted material reflects the modern consequences of a commodification of the spoken word. The *Times* recounts the stories of two prominent German authors, Gerhart Hauptmann and Hugo von Hoffmannsthal, who objected to having their works broadcast. "Hauptmann has entered objections to broadcasting his winged words by radio concerns at Leipzig and Münster, while von Hoffmannsthal demands from a Berlin concern a royalty on its broadcasting of one of his works" (*NYT* 1925a, 4). A follow-up report a few months later indicates that both authors won their lawsuits and the respective broadcasting companies were ordered to pay damages (*NYT* 1925b, 1). This coverage, by the way, coincides with the first legal test of a copyright issue moving through the U.S. federal courts, decided in October 1925 by the U.S. Supreme Court, which upheld a decision that the broadcasting of copyrighted material was a direct infringement of the law.

On the other hand, the production of news raises different issues: access to information, free flow of news, and the public's need to receive information accurately and speedily. These values are shared by the American press and were supported by legal sentiments in Germany when the Reich's Supreme Court ruled in 1930 that "news broadcast by radio does not enjoy copyright protection." The case was based on the publication of a news story about the return of Graf Zeppelin from America, which had been received from a Stuttgart broadcasting station. According to the *Times*, the court argued that

> while literary works and musical compositions as such might be protected by copyright, topical news is not and its reproduction does not represent any ethical violation

of a third person's labor. It is generally known that daily news may be reproduced from newspapers, the court held, and therefore public opinion would not consider the publication of broadcast news unethical (*NYT* 1930b, 7).

The introduction of broadcasting results not only in a change of personal or familial habits in the organization of leisure but also in keen competition for time and attention from traditional sources of entertainment, particularly theater. The problem also surfaces in the United States, where theater owners find radio to be an economic threat and actors complain that "radio constituted a serious menace to the player's craft." No remedies are offered except competition with better plays; theater operators are countercharged with "obstinacy, avariciousness, ignorance, [and] pig-headedness" by radio-industry interests (Hornblow 1925, 7).

The strategies of German theater management for increasing attendance are more innovative than those of their American counterparts, and the *Times* reports the effort to boost attendance in Germany. After theater managers in Berlin tried unsuccessfully to bar actors from working for broadcasting stations, they offer a free monthly performance to radio subscribers.

> Believing the radio fans would appreciate seeing their favorite artists on the stage as well as hear their voices the producers have proposed to the Government Director of Broadcasting that radio licenses be raised slightly above the present fee of 50 cents monthly and allow the subscribers to attend the theater free of charge at least once a month (*NYT* 1925c, 16).

Radio is not only popular but also effective and—perhaps for the first time—is revealing its potential as an instrument of propaganda. Increasing domestic problems and political tensions abroad lead to an atmosphere of restiveness and anxiety that gnawed at confidence in Germany's economic and political recovery. At this point the *Times* reports the success of a radio drama that anticipated evidence discovered much later in the United States after social-scientific inquiries into Orson Welles's famous *War of the Worlds* broadcast in 1938, a radio play that became the standard example of the powerful impact of broadcasting on listeners. In fact, the conditions in Germany were rather similar to what Herta Herzog found in 1939 in the United States, namely that people were prepared to believe the unusual in times of great uncertainty, especially when the authenticity of program features is successfully combined with the technical realism of performance (Herzog 1955).

For instance, the *Times* reports,

> Several thousand radio listeners were recovering this forenoon from hearing what for a time they thought was a radio report that Foreign Minister Julius Curtius had been assassinated. Actually what they heard was only a radio drama entitled "The Minister is Murdered," in the course of which the radio announcer (the make-believe one in the play) interrupts a concert to announce excitedly that the German Foreign Minister has just been assassinated in the Friedrichstrasse railway station. In view of the

recent Fascist putsch rumours thousands who tuned in just in time to hear the words
of the actor-announcer believed it was a fact. The Minister of the Interior began an
investigation to determine who was responsible for putting such a radio play on the
air at a time of political tension in Germany (*NYT* 1930f, 18).

The fear of the intentional, even conspiratorial use of radio for purposes of political propaganda remains one of the recurring themes in the *Times* coverage of
the development of German radio. The theoretical linkage of media technology
with a powerful effects model of communication seems to evolve at this time. It
becomes a popular strategy for dealing with any introduction of new "mass"
media, particularly radio, photography, film, or, in later years, television.

For instance, the potential effects of radio transmission during political campaigns surfaced as an important public issue in 1924, when the German minister
of the interior was reported as having "strictly forbidden anybody in Germany to
use a wireless broadcasting station for election speeches." Indeed, the decree,
signed by Karl Jarres, states that the "microphone, the most modern of the political allies, is to be reserved for higher things in life and unsullied by political strife"
(*NYT* 1924d, 12). Although government continued to use radio broadcasts to explain its position, the broadcast of Chancellor Hans Luther's remarks on the Locarno treaties and the declared intent of Foreign Minister Gustav Stresemann to
use radio to defend his position at the Locarno meeting caused considerable debate among political parties. As a result, the Nationalists are led to claim "hotly
the privilege of broadcasting their condemnation of the Locarno treaties," since
no decisions had been made at that time whether radio use for political purposes
was a privilege of the government or not (*NYT* 1925d, 2).

Another revealing episode occurs at the end of 1930, amid pessimism and despair about Germany's future and demands that Paul von Hindenburg address
and reassure the German nation. Their appeal to the strength of broadcasting—as
a psychological comfort and/or political support—reinforces the public belief in
the ability of a new technology to make a difference in the attitudes of individuals
toward their own future. The *Times* reports,

"Hindenburg to the microphone" is a cry which bids fair to become one of those
popular demands which will brook no refusal. Reacting against the dark days and
pessimism which hang over the Fatherland now, the nation wants to hear the venerable old Field Marshall's "reassuring and fatherly voice" telling his people their trou-
bles are not unnoticed in the Presidential palace. "Hindenburg's words possess the
faculty of awakening tremendous hope and faith. But he must speak them, not write
them," one paper says. The Reich's President, who has hitherto avoided the microphone as religiously as he stays away from the talkies, is likely to concede a point and
address the nation some evening in the near future (*NYT* 1930g, 3).

Stories like these produce a contrast between political broadcasting in the
United States and the atmosphere of official restriction that hovered over radio in

Germany. Although radio and politics had been well known to each other in the United States since President Calvin Coolidge's historic broadcast address to Congress in December 1923 and the 1924 broadcasts of the national party conventions and election campaigns, American radio is primarily an advertising outlet. It privileges programming designed to entertain rather than to inform and was not intended to provide political education. Thus, the use of radio as a means of participating in the daily routines of the political process in Germany is news to American readers. For instance, a brewing conflict between German government regulations of the political use of radio and rising public pressures to liberate broadcasting becomes news. The *Times* observes that public demands for broadcasting Reichstag debates had become a major issue among German "radio fans," who argued that broadcasting parliamentary sessions would not only be educational but would also satisfy requirements of public debates, even at times when spectators might not be allowed in the chambers. These requests to Reichstag President Paul Loebe were made in the wake of charges by the Communist Party that a settlement between Prussia and the House of Hohenzollern "allotting the ex-ruling family large sums of money, lands and castles" had been reached behind closed doors, when galleries and press benches had to be cleared after tumultuous outbursts (*NYT* 1926a, 6).

The *Times* reports during this period show that radio listening occupied a definite place in Germany's social and political life. Radio is the apparent concern of a variety of groups and organizations, an embattled political territory. The role of radio in democratization is also Albert Einstein's topic at the opening of the seventh German radio exhibition in Berlin on August 22, 1930, when his remarks were broadcast throughout Europe. Einstein admonishes his listeners to shake their apathy towards scientists and to appreciate the potential of technological advancements. He recognized the individuals involved in developing and mass-marketing radio and proposes that "one ought to be ashamed to make use of the wonders of science embodied in a radio set, the while appreciating them as little as a cow appreciates the botanic marvels in the plants she munches." After all, "It was the scientists who first made true democracy possible," Einstein says, "for not only did they lighten our daily tasks but they made the finest works of art and thought, whose enjoyment until recently was the privilege of the favored classes, accessible to all. Thus they awakened the nations from their sluggish dullness." Indeed, Einstein appeals to the power of radio to unite people, suggesting that "until our day people learned to know each other only through the distorting mirror of their own daily press. Radio shows them each other in the liveliest form and, in the main, from their most lovable sides" (*NYT* 1930e, 1).

The positioning of radio in the public realm and the rejection of a commercial system of broadcasting in Germany also provides the *Times* with opportunities for reflecting on the situation at home, where the future of radio was irrevocably tied to commercial sponsorship and advertising revenues instead of public service.

The lengthy *Times* report about the 1930 radio exhibition is dominated by the Einstein address but ends with brief references to technological advances, the declining prices for "middle-distance" receivers, and the fact that "television is being demonstrated but obviously is far from ready for commercial exploitation here" (*NYT* 1930e, 1).

However, Einstein's call for coexistence through broadcasting as an international means of communication remained a utopian vision, perhaps better suited for openings of radio exhibitions than for the realpolitik of international affairs. At the time there were mounting problems with technical interference and unwelcome foreign programming aimed at German audiences.

For instance, relying on German press accounts, the *Times* reports interference with the playing of the German anthem on radio stations in 1924.

> Whenever "Deutschland Ueber [sic] Alles" is broadcast by radio in Germany some one somewhere butts in, according to German newspapers. Whenever the tune is played there is a great stir in the air over Europe, and there is a growing suspicion, the writers say, that the interfering waves "come from somewhere in the direction of the Eiffel Tower in Paris" (*NYT* 1924b, 7).

But while the French may have been determined to respond anonymously to the frequent broadcast of the German national anthem, Soviet sources openly directed propaganda broadcasts from Moscow into Germany and caused considerable official consternation in Berlin.

The *Times* reports the decision of the Communist Party to use its one-hundred-kilowatt station to propagandize its cause in many languages, including German. The initial silence of the German government is attributed to its desire not to draw attention to the broadcasts until effective counterstrategies had been put into place. The Soviet broadcast opens with the words, "Police and soldiers of Germany, remember you are proletarians in uniform: remember in Germany, too, the right way is the October way. Long live the German Soviet Republic." According to the *Times*, the installation of "disturbance" transmitters had been rejected as impractical, since it would have interfered with ship traffic. Instead, it was recommended

> that Berlin should provide the Reich with a talk to follow Moscow's in which the Soviet arguments would be pulled to pieces, but it is feared this would savor of the use of the station for political purposes. Also it has been suggested that an attempt be made to broadcast information in Russian as a counter-activity, but it is feared that Moscow might soon adopt Rumania's system of self-protection (*NYT* 1930c, 10).

A week later the German government protested against the Communist propaganda broadcasts only to be told by Moscow that the "radio talks in German were not intended for Germany, but were meant to give the German colonists in Russia, particularly in the Volga district, the pleasure of hearing their native language once in a while." The *Times* also reports that the task of installing and operating a "disturbance" transmitter, as used by the Rumanians against the Soviet Union, would be the responsibility of the Königswusterhausen radio station. The article mentions the growing suspicion of the government since October 1928, when

"German Communists kidnapped a Socialist editor on his way to a broadcasting station in Berlin and substituted a Communist Deputy, who broadcast his entire speech before the trick was discovered" (*NYT* 1930d, 7).

In pursuit of diverse cultural programming under expanding broadcast technologies, however, Germany sought an exchange with the United States. The *Times* reports the lengthy stay of a German delegation, its visits to several American radio stations, and the announcement of a cooperative arrangement with NBC to transmit programs via shortwave. German experts are particularly interested in "selections such as the negro spirituals, reflecting the typical American entertainment" (*NYT* 1929f, 1). This prompted an editorial response in the *Times,* which offers its own solutions to attaining programming goals while overcoming cultural differences between the countries:

> Americans will read with mixed emotions of the proposal of a group of German radio officials to "exchange" broadcast programs between the United States and Germany. At first the plan sounds attractive. But when the spokesman points out that the German program is likely to include lectures, the charms are less obvious. It is doubtful if a Herr Professor's observations on the introduction of the missing vertebrae in jellyfish would arouse more enthusiasm here than would some of our own lectures in Germany discussing our politics or explaining what trees mean in the life of the average city dweller.
>
> As to the jazz program, here will likewise be differences in opinion. In Germany no jazz is permitted before 10 P.M. This, according to many American listeners, is an innovation devoutly to be wished for. But on the other side are those who wish to see a dead-line on the jazz limit, and who believe that the average citizen is entitled to life, liberty and the pursuit of sleep after midnight without benefit of radio.
>
> It happens that the difference in time between Germany and the United States is such that Germany's post–10 P.M. jazz will reach here in the early afternoon. So also America's choicest (even if driest) lectures are likely to be heard in Germany during the German's jazz hour. Let us hope this will suit all concerned" (*NYT* 1929e, 12).

Fortunately or unfortunately for the editorial writer, the German delegation had already suggested that "special programs will have to be put on because of the differences in time between the two countries" (*NYT* 1929f, 1).

In summary, there is a sense of purpose and direction in the history of early German radio. Its *Kulturanspruch* (cultural claim) seems firmly secured in the expressed rationale for the uses of broadcasting in the public sphere, although the struggle over the boundaries of radio is incomplete, and even inconclusive at this time. Communication technology as context of power relations becomes a useful site for social and political observations, however. Broadcasting also offers a measure of the modern public sphere, whose use varies from society to society, where it is differently defined and assigned. For instance, in the United States, the application of broadcasting technology promotes an understanding of individualism that is identified with choice (of consumption) from a variety of commercially determined sources, while in Germany individualism is implied in opportunities

for cultural advancement offered through a centrally controlled system of broadcasting. These differences signify a different kind of individual activity or personal involvement, and the results are profound; they range from the notion of
commercials as enlightenment to an insistence on the cultural mission of radio,
prioritizing either entertainment or education and information or interpretation.
The idea of entertainment—however central to an understanding of American
radio—is completely absent from the *New York Times* coverage of German broadcasting. In fact, radio in Germany is a serious business, whose societal responsibility is discharged by an authoritative institution rather than by private ownership
and its commercially dictated policies.

Reporting about the affairs of German radio also reflects an increasing ner-
vousness in Germany, ranging from various demands for sharing the power of
broadcasting to the outright use of radio to interfere in the psychological and political spheres of society and the manipulation of the minds of people. The idea
that broadcasting has a powerful effect on individuals and society is implicitly
supported by the *Times*, which finds the consequences of such impact not only
newsworthy, but reacts in what has now become a predictable journalistic response to a belief in media effects by reporting events, including the premeditated
use of selected media by individuals or groups, that reinforce the idea of shaping
public opinion through exposure to media fare. In this historical context, the
Times coverage shifts from cultural to political contexts of radio and discloses an
increasing level of conflict in society.

American readers, involved in their own economic catastrophes of the late
1920s, may have found more worrisome news about Germany in the pages of *The
New York Times*. But the brief reports about German radio, if noticed, certainly
help reinforce the feeling of an impending crisis, in which broadcasting is to play
a major role. The *Times* recognizes the growing political pressures to convert
broadcasting in Germany into a much more inclusive and significantly more responsive medium of social and political communication in a widening conflict
between the domains of *Kultur* and politics. The result is an escalating sensitivity
to a developing social and political struggle over the uses of radio as the Weimar
Republic nears its end.

6

▼ ▼ ▼

Fictional Journalists:
News Work in American Novels

Bonnie Brennen

Journalism allows its readers to witness history: fiction gives its readers an opportunity to live it.

—John Hersey, 1950

Interwar-era novels about newsworkers are examples of the "great reservoir of creative protest against social misery" (Lowenthal 1987, 124) and may offer fundamental insights into the actual working conditions of U.S. journalists during the 1920s and 1930s.

This chapter draws on cultural materialism and considers novels as explicit cultural practices of communication created within a historically specific society and produced under particular social, economic, and political conditions. As tangible embodiments of culture, novels produce meaning and value and may provide useful documentary evidence of representations and misrepresentations of actual lived experience (Williams 1981, 1987). However, each published text is based upon historically determined cultural conventions, forms, and perceptions that guide interpretations and may preclude individuals from reading a novel "in all its freshness as a thing-in-itself" (Jameson 1981, 9). Indeed, novels about newspaper work must not be appropriated uncritically, and their critical reading should include an engagement with the specific material conditions under which texts are produced as well as a consideration of the actual consumption of novels as cultural products.

This chapter explores the publishing history of thirty-five newspaper novels written during the interwar era of 1919–1938. These works, which address the working conditions of U.S. reporters, span a variety of themes and approaches, including adventure stories, mysteries, romances, and career books, as well as social-protest fiction. Some are psychologically introspective, and others are straightforward journalistic accounts of life in newsrooms. In some of these texts the influences of Marx, Freud, and Nietzsche resonate; other narratives are event-oriented and emphasize action over ideas.[1] This chapter also considers the influence on these novels of realism, the dominant popular-culture literary form of the day, along with the background of the authors, their experiences as working journalists, and the strategies they utilize to enhance the realism of their novels. Since the critical assessments of reviewers may reflect an ideological position on what constitutes authentic discourse, this chapter also evaluates their responses through a consideration of scholarly reviews of the novels.

The texts addressed in this chapter are part of the genre commonly designated as newspaper novels; they are commercially produced and extensively distributed books that are geared to popular tastes. Following World War I, public demand for books, particularly fiction, increases dramatically. Novels are considered "bargain" entertainment by publishers and middle-class buyers alike because they cost significantly less than dramatic productions, operas, musicals, and other forms of diversion (Tebbel 1978, 15). Book publishers respond to public sentiment, and during the 1920s the number of new fictional works released grows significantly. Information compiled from *Publishers' Weekly* indicates that in 1920, 1,123 new editions are printed; in 1925, 1,426 novels become available; and in 1929, 2,142. Although there are fewer fictional works published during the 1930s, novels remain popular: in 1930, 2,103 new novels are released; in 1935, 2,039; and in 1939, 1,547 (Tebbel 1978, 683).

Representative of American popular culture during the 1920s and 1930s, the newspaper novels used in this study are generally well received by the public and critics alike, and the popularity of these books may be illustrated by briefly assessing the publishing history of some of these texts. Although only five of the novels, *Manhattan Transfer* (Dos Passos 1925/1953), *Forgive Us Our Trespasses* (Douglas 1932), *An American Tragedy* (Dreiser 1925/1981), *Erik Dorn* (Hecht 1921/1963), and *The Sun Also Rises* (Hemingway 1926/1954), are still in print in the 1990s, the *National Union Catalog* records several editions and/or multiple press runs for most of these novels during the 1920s and 1930s.

For example, six editions of *The Chicken Wagon Family* (Benefield 1925), including an edition for the Armed Services, and five editions of *Trumpet in the Dust* (Fowler 1930) and *The Moon Calf* (Dell 1921) are produced during this era. Four months after its release, in October 1927, the ninth press run of *Splendor*

(Williams 1928) becomes available, while the eighth printing of *The Moon Calf* (Dell 1921) is distributed only five months after its October 1920 debut. Nine press runs of *Peggy Covers the News* (Bugbee 1936/1940) are produced in the first two years of its release, and the success of this novel encourages the release of a series of "Peggy" books, including *Peggy Covers Washington* (Bugbee 1937), *Peggy Covers London* (Bugbee 1939), *Peggy Covers the Clipper, a Story of a Young Newspaper Woman* (Bugbee 1941), and *Peggy Goes Overseas* (Bugbee 1945).

Young Man of Manhattan (Brush 1930), first serialized in the *Saturday Evening Post* and ranked ninth on *Publishers Weekly*'s list of best-sellers for 1930 (Tebbel 1978, 697), sells out its first press run of twenty thousand before its actual publication (*New York World* 1930, 15). In addition, *Forgive Us Our Trespasses* (Douglas 1932) ranked the sixth top selling fictional work for 1933 (Tebbel 1978, 698), and *The Great American Novel* (Davis 1938) is a main selection of the Book-of-the-Month Club for 1938 (Martine 1981, 300). During this era *Manhattan Transfer* (Dos Passos 1925/1953), *The Sun Also Rises* (Hemingway 1926/1954), and *An American Tragedy* (Dreiser 1925/1981) are published internationally, and *Manhattan Transfer* is translated into French, German, Italian, and Spanish.

During the 1920s fictional works generally cost about two dollars, and in the 1930s publishers frequently charge $2.50 for novels by better-known authors.[2] Interest in fiction is widespread, and anywhere from fifty thousand to two hundred thousand copies of popular novels are generally sold; the top novels eventually sell five hundred thousand to a million-plus copies (Tebbel 1978, 32). Given the 15 to 20 percent royalty authors receive during this era, it is not difficult to understand why many newsworkers envision careers as novelists, offering a potential way out of the newsroom. Although all of the journalists whose work is addressed here find at least limited success as novelists, for each newsworker who escapes the newsroom by writing fiction, there are many others who craft books that are never published.

Fundamental to a materialistic explanation of literature is an understanding of the "psychological interaction between artist, artistic creation, and reception" (Lowenthal 1984b, 245). Aligned with Theodor Adorno, Max Horkheimer, and other critical theorists, Leo Lowenthal conceives of "real" art as existing apart from and in opposition to the products of mass culture. From this perspective, art represents an essential means of understanding the relationship between individuals and society; art is thought to impart knowledge, and artists are thought to depict "what is more real than reality itself" (Lowenthal 1984a, x). In contrast, critical theorists maintain that the diversion, distraction, and temporary escape offered by mass culture does not educate but instead manipulates public consciousness.

Horkheimer and Adorno introduce the term "culture industry" to distinguish standardized, profit-driven commodities, the cement of the dominant social order, from autonomous works of art (Adorno 1989, 128–129). The culture industry reduces individuals to "customers" who ultimately become "elements or objects" that help to preserve the status quo (Hardt 1992, 140). However, the conception of mass culture as "unacceptable" or even "nonart" denies the relevance of popular art forms and perpetuates an elitist conception of art based primarily upon aesthetic value. While a cultural materialist theoretical stance addresses conditions of production in the evaluation of all art and is cognizant of issues of standardization and commodification within contemporary capitalist societies, it cautions against value judgments based upon the worth of cultural products. Instead, it regards cultural artifacts as tangible embodiments of culture, produced under specific cultural, historical, and political conditions.

In this chapter the aesthetic value and/or literary merit of the novels is not at issue; instead, the focus is on the intention of these authors and the critical response and public reception to their books as sources of historical evidence. Although the author's intent is never completely transparent (even a direct interview might elicit only equivocation), it is possible to speculate on the motivations and objectives of these writers. While all texts offer potentially useful historical and cultural insights, specific information on the author provides a necessary context for understanding the work. The historian Nelson Blake explains that when novels are used as history, their authors should be judged as witnesses who "testify" about the past. For Blake—whose own study of fiction as history focuses on the biographies of early twentieth-century American authors—it is imperative to obtain some knowledge about the novelists themselves to assess the reliability and validity of specific novels as evidence (Blake 1969, 5).

The authors of these novels are newsworkers and write from firsthand experience as journalists. Before becoming novelists, some writers, such as Ernest Hemingway, John Dos Passos, Meyer Levin, and Katharine Brush, work briefly as newspaper reporters, correspondents, or columnists. Others, including Emma Bugbee, who spends fifty-six years as a reporter on the *New York Herald Tribune*, and Henry Justin Smith, news editor of the *Chicago Daily News* for decades, remain journalists throughout their careers. Authors like Clyde Brion Davis, Royce Brier, and Samuel Hopkins Adams begin fiction writing following extensive experience on newspapers. Until the publication of his first book, Davis was employed for more than twenty years as a reporter or editor on a variety of publications, including the *Denver Post*, the *San Francisco Examiner*, and the *Seattle Post-Intelligencer*. Brier, a Northern California reporter, writes his first novel one year after he wins a Pulitzer Prize for reporting lynchings in San Jose. Adams's investigations of patent medicines, which he wrote while working as a muckraker on the *New York Sun*, helped enact Federal Pure Food and Drug Laws (*The New York Times* 1958, 31). Adams is one of several authors who establish themselves as popular literary figures after lengthy careers as journalists. He becomes a successful novelist, and several of his books, including *It Happened One Night*, are later made into popular movies.

Throughout his sixty-one year career, Clarence Budington Kelland, a former *Detroit News* reporter, estimates that he has written over 10 million words, including sixty novels and two hundred short stories; "Mr. Deeds Goes to Town" is one of several stories by Kelland that also becomes a Hollywood movie (*The New York Times* 1964, 39). Ben Hecht, an erstwhile *Chicago Daily News* reporter perhaps best known for his collaboration with Charles MacArthur on *The Front Page* ("the first classic of the newspaper film genre"), writes more than forty books and sixty-five screenplays, including *Wuthering Heights, Gunga Din,* and *Scarface* (Kaul 1981, 122).

Although all of these newsworkers/authors at one time aspire to culminate their careers as novelists, not all of them remain fiction writers. For example, Gene Fowler, the vagabond reporter who writes for newspapers from Denver to New York, emerges as a well-respected Hollywood biographer; Edward Hungerford, a *New York Herald* and *New York Sun* reporter, becomes an expert on railroad transportation; the former reporter Josef Berger is most frequently remembered as a speechwriter for Franklin Delano Roosevelt, Lyndon Johnson, and Harry Truman; and the one-time reporter Robert Van Gelder is named editor-in-chief of Crown Publishers after serving as editor of *The New York Times Book Review*.

All of these writers are influenced by conventions of the English language, requirements and restrictions of popular literary forms, and societal pressures, which affect "ways of thinking and feeling and writing" (Williams 1990b, 259). Cultural situations, conventions, and forms specific to American society in the 1920s and 1930s significantly affect their writing and therefore should be viewed as a fundamental part of an inseparable social process from which these writers cannot separate themselves.

The novels in this study are published between 1919 and 1938, a period when realist fiction is the dominant popular literary form. It is characterized by a set narrative which leads to closure, illusionism, and a "hierarchy of discourses which establishes the 'truth' of the story" (Belsey 1987, 70). Attempting to capture "reality," realism strives to reproduce, in dialogue, actual speech sounds and rhythms; it carefully analyzes the physical appearance of characters and offers detailed descriptions of settings and events within a specific social environment (Rideout 1992, 209). Yet realism is not simply a matter of form and may derive from every means available to depict reality in a form that people can understand. Realism can discover the "causal complexities of society" (Brecht 1977, 82) as it unmasks the dominant ideological position, and it may also be seen as writing from a class viewpoint, which offers solutions for fundamental social problems.

In their attempts "to get all the facts down," these novelists contribute to what Joseph Beach (1932, 533) refers to as "debunking fever," the prevalent postwar literary attitude of writers disgusted with attempts to mollify American life who instead attempt to realistically depict contemporary material. Three of the authors addressed in this study—Theodore Dreiser, Ernest Hemingway, and John Dos Passos—are assessed by critics as pivotal figures in the development of this narrative tradition.

Designated the "Father of Modern American Realism" (Sherman 1926, 1), Dreiser rejects early twentieth-century literary conventions and offers readers the "unvarnished truth" of contemporary American society (Beach 1932, 327). His "almost literal transcription of an actual murder trial," *An American Tragedy*, released in 1925, is hailed as both "gutter literature" and the "greatest American novel" (*The New York Times* 1945, 14); yet even critics who find value in Dreiser's work often consider his writing style offensive. *The New York Herald Tribune* reviewer Stuart Sherman (1926, 1) explains that although *An American Tragedy* contributes significantly toward a goal of "genuine and adequate realism," the text is also "the worst written great novel in the world."[3] Because of the book's explicit sexual depictions in 1927, it was decried as indecent: It was banned in Boston, and a New York publisher is convicted for selling it.

Reviewers suggest that the release, in 1926, of *The Sun Also Rises* signals the introduction of "Critical Realism," a new method of fictional writing (*Boston Evening Transcript* 1926, 2).[4] Observing that Hemingway's extreme accuracy greatly heightens the intensity of the novel, Lawrence Morris (1926, 142), in a review for *The New Republic*, explains that "between the lines of the hard-boiled narrative quivers an awareness of the unworded, half-grasped incomprehensibles of life." Critics suggest that the novel, which conflates disillusionment with hedonism, articulates the concerns of a "lost generation" and has a profound influence on the youth of America (Nagel 1981, 106).

Following the 1925 release of *Manhattan Transfer*, Sinclair Lewis (1925, 361) determines that more than Dreiser or any other contemporary author, Dos Passos might emerge as "the father of humanized and living fiction … not merely for America but for the world!" Dos Passos, later lauded by Jean-Paul Sartre as the greatest writer of the 1920s and 1930s (Knowles 1981, 218), is assessed in *The New York Times* as "the hardest-boiled of the new-method-ists, the most glittering and devastatingly metallic of the super-realistic" (Stuart 1925, 5).[5]

Although Dreiser, Hemingway, and Dos Passos are recognized during this period for their "authentic" representations of contemporary society, they are not the only authors to employ such literary methods. For example, in *Deadlines*, Henry Justin Smith offers readers "an alibi" for "purloining a bit of atmosphere" of a well-known newsroom in his tale of newsworkers (Smith 1923, i); readers of *Jim of the Press* are apprised that the text "gives a clear, fascinating picture of the place a young man can strive for and attain in a great news-gathering organization. … It is fiction, but it is fact, too" (Dean 1933, i). The publisher of *Copy Boy* insists that "the part each man plays, from copy boy to managing editor, in pressroom or editorial office, is told with fidelity and truth to newspaper publishing practice" (Berger 1938, i), and the entire E. P. Dutton publishing staff endorses the "splendid" depiction of the newspaper world in *Splendor* by Ben Ames Williams, whom they consider one of the "most sensitive interpreters of American Life" (Williams 1928, i).

Traditional disclaimers, which designate novels as imaginary or fictitious, are found in only four novels: *Court House Square* (Anderson 1934), *Though Time Be*

Fleet (Andrus 1937), *Reach for the Moon* (Brier 1934), and *Scoop* (Hart and Byrnes 1930). However, these authors may have utilized disclaimers as a form of legal protection because some of their characters seem strikingly similar to several well-known and influential individuals. Attempts to realistically depict elements of the newspaper business result in legal problems for only one author. Meyer Levin's novel *Reporter* (1929) is withdrawn within weeks of its initial publication, after a prominent newspaperwoman claims that she is identifiable in the text and threatens to sue for libel. In his autobiography, Levin explains that although the newsroom atmosphere is authentic in *Reporter* and that the text includes actual news items (including one from the newswoman who brings the suit), his depiction of "a typically fussy, frippy newspaperwoman, an elderly sobsister who was always dropping pencils, losing bits of paper out of her handbag, and ruining group interviews with 'women's interest' questions," is actually a composite of several newspaperwomen he is familiar with (Levin 1950, 49). Years after the incident Levin questions the decision of his publishers to suppress *Reporter* rather than merely eliminate the "offending passages." He suggests (1950, 50) that his realistic portrayals of sensitive issues and events may have troubled publishing executives, who found the complaint of the newspaperwoman to offer a convenient "solution" to the problem.

In their efforts to enhance the realism of their fiction, these authors often incorporate into their novels discussions of "real" people, actual events, and elements of popular culture. Labor disputes and strikes, presidential elections, the effects of prohibition, kidnapping, thefts, and prominent murders are elements the authors use to supply readers with a historical context for their narratives. Inventions are introduced, intriguing speeches critiqued, and the qualifications of presidential candidates debated; several fictional reporters interview the person they regard as the "greatest living American," William Jennings Bryan, and one newsworker, although honored to actually meet Bryan, experiences a profound sense of inadequacy over the assignment (Davis 1938, 19).

In *Manhattan Transfer* Dos Passos weaves newspaper headlines and stories from the *Wall Street Journal*, *Evening Graphic*, and *The New York Times* into the text to create a montage that offers readers a critique of early twentieth-century capitalist society. Characters actively engage with information found in newspapers; they read and comment upon stories, and they occasionally act upon material found in the daily press. An important story line in the novel begins when an out-of-work attorney peruses the newspaper in search of potential clients and encounters the following information: "Augustus McNiel, 253 W. 4th Street, who drives a milkwagon for the Excelsior Dairy Co. was severely injured early this morning when a freight train backing down the New York Central tracks ... " (Dos Passos 1925/1953, 50). In *Reporter*, actual newspaper headlines such as "Darrow to Defend Evolution," "Loeb Not Crazy, Says Savant," and "Moron Stuffs Girl, 8, in Sewer," appear at the top of each page, offering readers background material that helps to explain the motivations and actions of the central newsworker

(Davis 1938). And, in *American Tragedy*, a local newspaper article delineating the drowning of a young couple, read by the main character, becomes the catalyst for a plan to kill his lover (Dreiser 1925/1981, 438–9).

Contemporary music, current motion pictures, and the work of other popular novelists are also addressed in these texts. In *Buchanan of "The Press"* newswork-ers evoke the name of Samuel Hopkins Adams to justify refusing to cover a partic-ularly distasteful assignment (Bent 1932, 14–15), while the writing of Sherwood Anderson, Hemingway, Thomas Wolfe, and others is evaluated by other journal-ists. For example, in *The Great American Novel*, Dreiser is judged a "magnificent reporter" who should, however, be "required to phone all his books to a good rewrite man" (Davis 1938, 238). The interjection of actual news stories and ele-ments of popular culture into the narratives not only help to authenticate the novels as realistic representations of the newspaper world but also further blur traditional distinctions between fact and fiction.

These novels also discuss perceived differences between factual and fictional rep-resentations. Although a few of the texts adopt the simplistic, idealistic position that newspapers always publish the "truth," most find reporting the truth a difficult and costly goal. Preferring to limit their discussions to the pursuit of facts, they address factors that influence the creation and production of news. Blurring the distinctions between fact and fiction, their ultimate concern is making the news, and in these novels reporters often fabricate stories to get bylines, make additional money, or to keep their jobs. They suppress information to suit advertisers, invent stories for cir-culation drives, and shade their reports according to newspaper policy and editorial direction. Following publication of a particularly creative fabrication, one reporter is told by his city editor, "I've been in the newspaper game for twenty years, my boy, and you're the biggest liar I have ever known" (Douglas 1932, 124). Justifying writ-ing a story he knows is false, another reporter explains, "You see, I had to write it that way.... It was such damn good copy" (Levin 1929, 176). Most of the novels admit that facts are "hard to arrive at. And when you get them they are usually dis-gusting" (Lewis 1924, 21). Facts are thought to mean little without interpretation and context, especially in contemporary capitalist society, where people are consid-ered numbed by the excess of "cold facts." Bombarded with incidents of death and destruction, they become desensitized to the "cruel realities" of urban life.

In these novels, the writing style employed by the authors, as well as their choice of material, resonate more closely with autobiography than with fictional writing. In fact, some of the authors' biographers explicitly address the autobio-graphical nature of these novels. For example, the hero of *The Moon Calf* by Floyd Dell is a small-town boy who, like the book's author, leaves home and travels to Chicago to pursue a literary career. In addition, Hecht's experiences as a newspa-per reporter at the *Chicago Daily News* from 1910 until 1924, where he specializes in crime news, are generally thought to have provided the background for all of his novels, including *Erik Dorn;* Ben A. Williams's book *Splendor* is most likely a chronicle of his own experiences as a young newsworker.[6]

In their attempts to authentically depict the work environment of journalists, these authors frequently recreate their own experiences as newsworkers. In one sense these novels are an outlet in which the authors express their fears, frustrations, concerns, and dreams. And if, in these novels, their dreams sometimes seem naive utopian fantasies, other newsworkers do not seem to mind, for as one reporter in *The Chicken Wagon Family* explains, a "log house in the deep silent woods by the softly flowing stream" is a recurrent "dream home" of the majority of urban newsworkers during this period (Benefield 1925, 152). In these novels newsworkers frequently dream that their newspaper work will eventually lead them to a literary career. An experienced journalist in *Splendor* echoes the perceptions of many other fictional newsworkers when he suggests, "There's no future for a man in the newspaper business. Nothing but a lot of work, and a sanitarium when your nerves play out. Late hours, long hours, dull scratching at things. But a writer is always a writer. If a man can write, he's free; he can get out, away from the paper when he wants. A free man" (Williams 1928, 205).

At least one reporter in each novel is currently working on a novel, or is planning, considering, or dreaming about writing one. Journalists link their ability to write with their personal freedom; they believe that becoming novelists will allow them to eventually quit the news room and lead more fulfilling lives. In the novels newsworkers discuss plans to write books on a diverse assortment of sports figures, politicians, and business leaders. *The Great American Novel* is actually a diary of the thoughts, impressions, and experiences of the plans of one journalist for an "all-inclusive" novel.

In *Lords of the Press*, George Seldes demarcates the class of newsworkers, whom he terms "working newspapermen," from publishers, editors, correspondents, and columnists, the elite "trained seals" of the press. He finds that reporters, blinded by egotism, are usually unable to stand up for their own interests and are therefore exploited and treated as "the lowliest of animals" (Seldes 1938, 370). Novelists, for the most part, agree with Seldes's caustic assessment of reporters, and in these books newsworkers perceive themselves as outcasts, tainted by their reporting tasks. They thus prefer the "clumsy, misfit term" *newspaperman* to *journalist* or *reporter* (Adams 1921, 219). In novels such as *Peggy Covers the News* (Bugbee 1936/1940), *The Girl Reporter* (Claudy 1930), *Private Props* (Mallette 1937), and *Though Time Be Fleet*, when the newsworker is a woman, being told "you're a good newspaperman" is considered the highest compliment a female journalist can receive (Andrus 1937, 247). As rank-and-file reporters, these writers may have been treated as expendable commodities who could not voice the oppressive and dehumanizing conditions that they endured. Yet in their novels, these authors are finally afforded the opportunity to articulate the material realities of their existence.

Although many book reviewers during the 1920s and 1930s merely provide plot summaries of the novels, others critically engage the texts. The scholarly response to these novels primarily involves the perceptions of reviewers regarding the authors' proximity to realistic depictions of journalists within the newsroom environment; critics also address the qualifications of these writers for commenting on the lives of newsworkers. Reviewers frequently comment on the "authenticity," "truthfulness," and "accuracy" of these texts, and some critics focus their assessments completely on the concept of realism.[7] For example, according to *The New York Times*'s reviewer, the treatment of the newsroom in *Erik Dorn* (Hecht 1921/1963) is "a series of word pictures of amazing strength and realism" (*The New York Times Book Review and Magazine* 1921a, 18),[8] while other reviewers comment that the story of *Young Man of Manhattan* (Brush 1930) was told "with such skill and such reality" that it may be seen as "the only authentic story of a young man of the Manhattan press" (Butcher 1930, 11).[9] *Buchanan of the Press* author Silas Bent is referred to as "the reporter of the reporter's job" who performs his task "without the embellishments of romantic rewrite. He pictures the routine as alternately feverish and stupid, hours of high-pressure labor followed by days of drudgery" (*New York Herald Tribune Books* 1932, 9). And one reviewer of *Sallie's Newspaper* (Lewis 1924) explains that while individuals may hope that the novel is fiction, the text which incorporates current news and commentary must be seen as fact (*The New York Times Book Review* 1924, 9).

The judgments of reviewers reflect an ideological conception of what constitutes "authentic" journalistic practices in the United States during the early twentieth century.[10] The critics consider first-hand knowledge of the newsroom essential; the *Boston Evening Transcript*'s assessment of *Deadlines*, which suggests that "no one but a newspaper man could have given this graphic account of 'the Quaint, the Amusing, the Tragic Memoirs of a News-Room'" (*Boston Evening Transcript* 1923, 4), reflects a view shared by many other critics. Reviewers frequently contrast the depictions of newsworkers in the novels with the author's own journalistic experience—and impressive credentials generally translate into positive reviews. Most notably, the journalistic achievements of Pulitzer Prize winner Brier are cited by critics to validate his first novel, *Reach for the Moon*. Heralding the book as an example of "brilliant retrospective reporting," *The New York Times* reviewer explains that in the novel, Brier's "journalistic proficiency stands out conspicuously" (*The New York Times Book Review* 1934c, 26).[11]

Critics cite Emile Gauvreau's experience as the editor of two New York tabloids to authenticate his novel about tabloid journalism, *Hot News*; one reviewer describes the novel as "a sad commentary on the present state of newspapering written with authority by one 'in the know'" (*Boston Evening Transcript* 1931, 2).[12] Evaluating Gene Fowler as "one of New York's ablest reporters," the *New York Herald Tribune Books* suggests that the realistic depiction of the journalism profession in *Trumpet in the Dust* is fundamentally due to Fowler's extensive newspaper experience (Flexner 1930, 23).[13] In one instance *The New York Times* somewhat incestuously claims that because Robert Van Gelder writes from "first-hand experience" as one of their own staff reporters, "there is a real smell of printer's ink" in *Front Page Story* (*The New York Times Book Review* 1937b, 12). Ethical dilemmas aside, the fundamental issue is the evaluation of fictional works based on the employment background of their authors. Reviewers repeatedly emphasize journalistic experience in their appraisals of the credibility and value of newspaper novels, and they consistently maintain that newsworkers are most adept at accurately portraying the newspaper industry.[14]

Realistic depictions of the newspaper environment are frequently cited by critics in support of the authenticity of these texts. For example, in *Peggy Covers the News* the "outstanding" newspaperwoman Bugbee is thought to offer young women who dream of newspaper careers an excellent description of the demands placed on female newsworkers. According to one critic, the novel, which addresses the organizational structure of one New York metropolitan newspaper, is written in "fictional terms" that are not "too rosy for reality" (*The New York Times Book Review* 1936, 14).[15] Reviewers of *Deadlines* maintain that Smith accurately portrays the "reality" of the newspaper office. *The New York Times* finds that although its form is "fictional," Smith's work "in spirit is accurate truth" (*The New York Times Book Review* 1923, 17), while the *Springfield Republican* suggests that "the basis of fact is apparent and the naturalism (we should say 'accuracy' or 'realism') of the telling makes the truth" of *Deadlines* "striking" (*Springfield Republican* 1923, 7a).[16]

The Unconscious Crusader (Williams 1920) is said to offer readers "a glimpse of the inside workings of a newspaper office" (*The New York Times Book Review* 1920a, 329),[17] and *The Copy Shop* (Hungerford 1925) is praised for the "veristic nature" of its depiction of the news room (*New York Herald Tribune Books* 1925, 11).[18] In a *Saturday Review of Literature* essay, Iowa State journalism professor Mitchel V. Charnley determines that because of the authenticity of the newspaper background, *Jim of the Press* (Dean 1933) may be considered "semi-fact" (Charnley 1933, 342), while *The New York Times* suggests that *Round Trip* (Tracy 1934) "depicts journalism in its lowlier aspects, with a truer semblance of reality than is generally the case in novels of the press" (*The New York Times Book Review* 1934a, 18).[19]

Reviewers also focus on the authentic representations of newsworkers in connection with larger issues of early twentieth-century American society. The "superbly accurate" chronicle of newsworker Homer Zigler in *The Great American Novel* (Davis 1938) is also considered a diary of the United States from 1906 to 1937; according to one reviewer, it may be "the only genuine novel ever written about a newspaper man" (Morley 1938, 5). The *Christian Science Monitor* maintains that this novel offers young men and women a warning to "pause before they hasten to enroll in journalism classes," along with an indictment of newspaper publishers "who have not been in the forefront of providing improved working conditions" (*Christian Science Monitor* 1938, 11).[20] Sinclair Lewis (1925, 361), writing in the *Saturday Review of Literature*, finds that in *Manhattan Transfer* John Dos Passos "presents the panorama, the sense, the smell, the sound, the soul, of New York. ... The book covers some twenty-five years of the growth and decay of not only the hundred or more characters, but of the whole mass of the city—

the other millions of characters whom you feel hauntingly behind the persons named and chronicled."

Critical assessments of *Splendor* agree that in this "story of all life," the significant changes in American society are well illustrated by Williams (*The New York Times Book Review* 1927, 6) and that his depiction of the life of one newsworker is also the story of millions of "plodders inside and outside the press" (Bent 1928, 20).[21] The *Saturday Review of Literature* finds that in *Hot News* (Gauvreau 1931) the actual newspapers and newsworkers involved in tabloid journalism, along with "the wretched personalities exploited in news stories are so little disguised that even a tabloid reader can identify them" (*Saturday Review of Literature* 1931, 57); *The New York Times* finds that in *Two Loves* (Arnold 1934), the experiences of the reporter in the newsroom, a "victim" of the depression, are "uncomfortably and convincingly pictured" (*The New York Times Book Review* 1934b, 7).

A few reviewers equate realistic depictions of journalism with the aesthetic value of the texts. For example, *The New York Times Book Review* finds that *The Great American Novel* (Davis 1938) "is presented with such completeness and with so much accuracy that the result is a work of art" (Van Gelder 1938, 6); the *New York Tribune* determines that in *Deadlines,* Smith's experience as a newsworker blends with his artistic imagination to create "an entertaining and informative series of accurate stories of newspaper life" (Rascoe 1923, 17).

Yet other reviewers who link the authenticity of these novels to the professional experience of their authors question the ability of journalists to craft "good" literature. While one critic finds that the representation of twentieth-century journalism in *Erik Dorn* (Hecht 1921) attests to the "fundamental artistic sincerity and significance of the work" (Goldberg 1921, 6), another reviewer insists that because Hecht's reportorial style is "untouched with emotion or philosophy," the book cannot be considered literature but instead "first-class journalism" (Colum 1921, 282). In addition, the *Boston Evening Transcript* reviewer finds that in *Reach for the Moon,* the acclaimed journalist Brier lacks the "elasticity of imagination" necessary to bridge the gap between news writing and fiction and that while Brier "can perpetuate with faultless artistry" the actions of his characters, he is unable to articulate their significance (*Boston Evening Transcript* 1934, 3). A *New York Times* reviewer suggests that the established reporting techniques that Silas Bent relies on to craft *Buchanan of the Press* detract from the success of the novel; the characters are thought to often reflect "the startling outlines of a good job done with the ticking of a deadline clock," and the novel ultimately lacks "the subtler qualities that make for rounded characterization" (*The New York Times Book Review* 1932, 7).

Critics consider only two of the thirty-five novels to offer unrealistic representations of the newsroom environment. *The New York Times* admonishes John Mellett for his depiction of the field of journalism in *Ink*, which left "practically everything to be desired" (*The New York Times Book Review* 1930a, 21); the *Boston Evening Transcript* concludes that "as a picture of newspaper life it has all the variety of a patent medicine endorsement" (*Boston Evening Transcript* 1930b, 2). Reviewers consider *Success* by Adams distorted and misleading; it is thought to depict only the scandal and sensationalism and to ignore the "honorable" side of journalism (*Outlook* 1921, 486). *The New York Times* describes the novel as a "tour de force of unreality" that is "painted entirely in scarlet and saffron" (*The New York Times Book Review* 1921b, 30).[22] In contrast, however, the *Literary Review* critic finds that Adams does a credible job depicting the "concessions" and "concealments and silences" that newsworkers are forced to commit in order to keep their jobs (Gavit 1921, 115). The descriptions of working conditions of journalists in these two novels are actually quite consistent with those depicted in other texts. The presentation of the material, however, is different. In *Ink* and *Success* the tone is considerably more hostile, and little attempt is made to veil the bitterness that these two authors obviously feel toward the newspaper industry.

The critical response to these novels offers additional evidence to support their use as evidence in reconstructing a history of newsworkers. Reviewers find these texts entertaining and educational; they laud the vast majority of these newspaper novels for their realistic and authentic depictions of the newsroom milieu. And they maintain that as former (or current) journalists, these writers knowledgeably address the working conditions of rank-and-file newsworkers. While somewhat surprising from a 1990s perspective, the depictions of the interwar newspaper world may actually have reinforced elements of the status quo. The descriptions of newsworkers are not substantially different from the contemporary labor conditions that many other workers endure in early twentieth-century American society.[23]

In these novels there are no calls for rebellion, revolution, or change, no strategies for challenging the capitalist appropriation of the media. Resigned to the prevailing working conditions, expectations, and demands, the newsworkers in these novels merely fantasize about personal freedom, dream of escaping the bureaucratic system, and hope for a better tomorrow. Although the depictions of the newspaper world offered by these authors inform and educate the public, these novels are also well received and critically acclaimed because they amuse, divert, and entertain Americans during the 1920s and 1930s.

NOTES

1. A number of finding aids were extremely helpful in compiling novels from this period. In addition to assorted fiction guides, including *A Guide to the Best Fiction* (Baker and Packman 1967) and the *Fiction Catalog* (Cook and Monro 1942; Yaakov and Greenfelt 1991), Steve Weinberg's (1991) data on novels with journalists as characters were useful, as was Thomas Berry's *The Newspaper in the American Novel* (1970).

The following novels are addressed in this chapter: Samuel H. Adams (1921), *Success*; Phil L. Anderson (1934), *Court House Square*; Louise Andrus (1937), *Though Time Be Fleet*; Elliott Arnold (1934), *Two Loves*; Barry Benefield (1925), *The Chicken Wagon Family*; Silas

Bent (1932), *Buchanan of "The Press"*; Josef Berger (1938), *Copy Boy*; Royce Brier (1934), *Reach for the Moon*; Katharine Brush (1930), *Young Man of Manhattan*; Emma Bugbee (1936/1940), *Peggy Covers the News*; Carl Claudy (1930), *The Girl Reporter*; Clyde Brion Davis (1938), *The Great American Novel*; Graham Dean (1933), *Jim of the Press*; Floyd Dell (1921), *The Moon Calf*; John Dos Passos (1925), *Manhattan Transfer*; Lloyd C. Douglas (1932), *Forgive Us Our Tresspasses*; Theodore Dreiser (1925), *An American Tragedy*; Gene Fowler (1930), *Trumpet in the Dust*; Emile Henry Gauvreau (1931), *Hot News*; Hugh V. Haddock (1937), *City Desk*; James S. Hart, and Garrett D. Byrnes (1930), *Scoop*; Ben Hecht (1921/1963), *Erik Dorn*; Ernest Hemingway (1926), *The Sun Also Rises*; Edward Hungerford (1925), *The Copy Shop*; Clarence Budington Kelland (1923), *Contraband*; Meyer Levin (1929), *Reporter*; Edwin Herbert Lewis (1924), *Sallie's Newspaper*; Gertrude Ethel Mallette (1937), *Private Props*; John C. Mellett (1930), *Ink*; Henry Justin Smith (1923), *Deadlines*; Henry Justin Smith (1933), *Young Phillips, Reporter*; Don Tracy (1934), *Round Trip*; Robert Van Gelder (1937/1946), *Front Page Story*; Ben Ames Williams (1928), *Splendor*; Sidney Williams (1920), *An Unconscious Crusader*.

2. The original cost of novels is in line with popular fiction of the era: twenty-two are first released at $2, eight at $2.50, four "bargain" books—*Jim of the Press* (Dean 1933), *Deadlines* (Smith 1923), *Young Phillips, Reporter* (Smith 1933), and *An Unconscious Crusader* (Williams 1920)—cost only $1.75, while Theodore Dreiser's (1925) two-volume *An American Tragedy* is initially priced at $5.

3. Reviews in *The New York Times Book Review* (Duffus 1926) and the *New York World* (Crawford 1926) also reflect this judgment. In contrast, *Saturday Review of Literature* (Anderson 1926) finds exceptional value in Dreiser's novel, while the *Boston Evening Transcript* considers it meritless (Edgett, 1926).

4. Additional reviews that address the realism of *The Sun Also Rises* include *The Dial* (1937), *The Nation* (Tate 1926), *The New York Times Book Review* (1926), *New York World* (Gorman 1926), *Saturday Review of Literature* (Chase 1926), and *Springfield Republican* (1926). Reviews in *The Independent* (Boyd 1926) and *New York Herald Tribune Books* (Aiken 1926) also emphasize Hemingway's "brilliant" use of dialogue to establish the authenticity of the novel.

5. Other reviews in the *Boston Evening Transcript* (1925b), *Literary Review of the New York Evening Post* (Brickell 1925), *The New Republic* (Harper 1925), and *New York Herald Tribune Books* (Ross 1925) concur with the assessment made in *The New York Times*.

6. For example, see biographical information on Ben Hecht (Kaul 1981) and obituaries of Floyd Dell (Whitman 1969) and Ben Ames Williams in *The New York Times* (1953).

7. For example, see reviews of *The Moon Calf* (Dell 1921) in *The Bookman* (Benchley 1921), *Boston Evening Transcript* (1920b), *The Nation* (1920), *The New Republic* (1920), *The New York Times Book Review* (1920b), and *Publishers' Weekly* (Hopkins 1920); the critique of *The Chicken Wagon Family* (Benefield 1925) in *The Bookman* (1925); the appraisal of *Reach for the Moon* (Brier 1934) in *Boston Evening Transcript* (1934); the assessment of *Though Time Be Fleet* (Andrus 1937) in *New York Herald Tribune Books* (Bell, 1937); and the commentary on *Trumpet in the Dust* (Fowler 1930) in *New York World* (Joel 1930).

8. Other reviews also focus on the realism in *Erik Dorn*; see *The Bookman* (Rascoe 1921), *Boston Evening Transcript* (Goldberg 1921), *The Dial* (Seldes 1921), *The Freeman* (Colum 1921), *Literary Review of the New York Evening Post* (Macy 1921), and *The New Republic* (Hackett 1921).

9. Additional critiques that address this novel's realism include *Boston Evening Transcript* (Schriftgiesser 1929), *Portland Evening News* (Cail 1930), and *New York Herald Tribune Books* (Ross 1930).

10. Although many reviews of the novels are not signed or are written by staff book reviewers, some assessments are written by established novelists such as Sinclair Lewis (1925), Conrad Aiken (1926), and Alfred Kazin (1938); two authors, Silas Bent (1928) and Robert Van Gelder (1938), whose own novels are considered in this study, also critique other newspaper novels.

11. Other reviews that equate Brier's journalistic ability with the validity of his novel include *Boston Evening Transcript* (1934) and *New York Herald Tribune Books* (Irwin 1934).

12. See additional reviews that stress Gauvreau's professional experience in *The Bookman* (1931), *The New Republic* (1931), *New York Herald Tribune Books* (Geller 1931), *The New York Times Book Review* (1931), and *Saturday Review of Literature* (1931).

13. See other analogous reviews in *The Bookman* (1930), *New York Times Book Review* (1930b), and *New York World* (1930).

14. Additional discussion linking literary achievement with the authors' newspaper careers is found in reviews of *Scoop* (Hart and Byrnes 1930), in *Atlantic Monthly* (M. Ross 1930), *Boston Evening Transcript* (1930a), and in *The New York Times Book Review* (1937a) of *Though Time Be Fleet* (Andrus 1937).

15. Reviews in the *New York Herald Tribune Books* (Becker 1936a; 1936b) agree with this assessment.

16. Additional reviews in *New York Tribune* (Rascoe 1923) and *Boston Evening Transcript* (1923) laud the newsroom realism in *Deadlines*.

17. See other comparable reviews in the *Boston Evening Transcript* (1920a) and the *Springfield Republican* (1920).

18. Additional reviews in the *Boston Evening Transcript* (1925a), *The New York Times Book Review* (1925), and *Springfield Republican* (1925) also focus on the authentic picture of a newspaper office in the *Copy Shop*.

19. The realistic depiction of the newspaper environment is also addressed in reviews of *Scoop* (Hart and Byrnes 1930) and in *Boston Evening Transcript* (1930a); critiques of *Buchanan of The Press* (Bent 1932) in *New York Herald Tribune Books* (1932) and *The New York Times Book Review* (1932); the assessment of *Front Page Story* (Van Gelder 1937) in *New York Herald Tribune Books* (1937); and the appraisal of *Copy Boy* (Berger 1938) in *New York Herald Tribune Books* (Walker 1938).

20. Other critics find the story of one newsworker in *The Great American Novel* to accurately reflect conditions of contemporary American society; see reviews in *The New Republic* (Powell 1938), *The New Yorker* (Fadiman 1938), *New York Herald Tribune Books* (Kazin 1938), and *New York Times Book Review* (Van Gelder 1938).

21. Similar reviews are found in *The Bookman* (Field 1928), *Boston Evening Transcript* (1927), and *Outlook* (1927).

22. Additional commentary that focuses on the unrealistic aspects of *Success* is located in *Boston Evening Transcript* (Edgett 1921) and *Springfield Republican* (1921).

23. For example, see discussions of labor conditions in *Tragic America* (Dreiser 1931), *Brother Can You Spare a Dime? The Great Depression 1929–1933* (Meltzer 1969), and *The Critical Communications Review*, Volume 1: *Labor, the Working Class, and the Media* (Mosco and Wasko 1983).

7

▼ ▼ ▼

Billboards of the Dream: Walker Evans on 1930s U.S. Advertising

Bonnie Brennen

Evans's photography has colored all of our memories so that we can no longer separate our fact from his fiction, or vice versa.

—A. D. Coleman, 1971

Considered one of the greatest twentieth-century artists, Walker Evans captured American culture within its specific historical context and brought an ethical sophistication to documentary photography. This quintessential American photographer shunned both artistic pretension and commercial acceptance, favoring instead clear, direct, simple, straightforward representations of industrial society that often illuminated the ironic potential of the American Dream.

Preferring the sharp focus and exceptional detail of large-format cameras, Evans used an 8 x 10–view camera set at a small aperture for much of his seminal work in the 1930s. He shot his subjects straight on, without sentimentality or commentary; it was a camera technique that matched the stark realism of his own way of seeing. "Sublimely simple, resonant, and profound" (Purvis 1993, 52), the

images of the most influential of the Farm Security Administration (FSA) photographers changed the way generations of people perceived the United States.
Evans was unwilling to create images to support the propaganda of a particular
political or governmental perspective; distancing himself from his subject matter,
he adopted a reflective, anonymous, almost disinterested stance, providing a historical record of what "any present time will look like as the past" (1982, 151). To
this day the purity and transparency of Evans's seemingly effortless pictures, created without pretense or artifice, ensure their place as a primary sourcebook for
depression-era American history.

Scholars suggest that while Evans's individual photographs offer timeless depictions of American society, when the images are arranged sequentially, the jux-
tapositions of these pictures create a variety of new relationships and meanings.
In fact, the continued republication of much of Evans's 1930s work, including the
reissuing of two of his collections of photographs, *American Photographs* and *Let
Us Now Praise Famous Men*, has introduced new generations to his photography
and has prompted considerable scholarly attention. The fiftieth anniversary edition
of *American Photographs*, published in 1988, continues the 1962 (second-edition)
tradition of dedicating the book to future generations, not only as a formative example of photographic art but also as historical evidence.

Assessing the unity and coherence of *American Photographs* as a "remarkable
achievement," Alan Trachtenberg (1989, 235) suggests that Evans struggles to define an alternative role for photography against prevailing artistic norms of the
1930s. J. A. Ward (1985) situates Evans's significant artifacts, characters, and experiences within the historical specificities of the southern region of the United
States, whereas Lew Andrews (1994) reinforces the importance of reading *American Photographs* as a sequence of images rather than as a pictorial collection. Although Evans's photographs for *Let Us Now Praise Famous Men*, the text of which
was written by James Agee, were taken in Hale County, Alabama, in 1936, Ken
Takata (1989) emphasizes their continued ability, some fifty years later, to speak
to audiences regarding fundamental issues in society. More recently, Paula Rabinowitz assesses (1992) the images and Depression-era reportage of the text to in-
terrogate sexual, class, and racial positions in bourgeois society; Miles Orvell
(1993) suggests that the documentary model Evans and Agee created still provides insights for future investigations of American culture.

While assessments of individual book projects certainly reinforce Evans's position as a creative genius, this chapter focuses on the advertising images Evans creates during the Depression, a period generally considered his "most creative"
(Trachtenberg 1989, 245), when he works as an information specialist for the Division of Information for the Resettlement Administration (later known as the
FSA). Unlike other FSA photographers who, at the request of the United States
government, are willing to evoke hope, heroism, and other humanistic concerns,
Evans keeps his emotional distance from his subject matter and produces plain,
uncompromising representations of Depression-era culture. In a spring 1935

handwritten draft memorandum to the FSA, Evans (1982, 112) insists that he must never be asked to create propaganda to support any governmental policy and explains that the value of his photographs "lies in the record itself which in the long run will prove an intelligent and farsighted thing to have done. NO POLITICS whatever."

In photographing a myriad of printed and hand-made signs, billboards, and posters, Evans suggests the ironic presence of advertising in twentieth-century industrial society, particularly in his comparison of the actual living conditions with "public symbols of material power" (Ward 1985, 119). His emphasis on signs remains a constant theme throughout all of his photography, and, in later years, Evans extends his interest to the actual collecting of logos, signs, billboards, and other advertising ephemera. While these advertising images certainly offer a critique of industrial capitalism, this chapter suggests that they may also illustrate a "structure of feeling," a way of experiencing and understanding American culture in the 1930s, particularly as it relates to the development of advertising in contemporary society.

Raymond Williams (1961, 63) conceives of structure of feeling as an attempt to distinguish practical, evolving, lived experiences within the hegemonic process from the more formal fixed concept of ideology. In one sense, structure of feeling represents the culture of a period, the actual "living result" of a particular class or society, which corresponds to the dominant social character; yet it also illustrates expressions of interactions between other nondominant groups. A structure of feeling incorporates "meanings and values as they are actively lived and felt," particularly as they interact with and react against selected formal beliefs (Williams 1977/1988, 132). It describes the tension between the lived and the articulated, and methodologically it provides a cultural hypothesis that attempts to understand particular material elements of a specific generation, at a distinct historical time, within a complex hegemonic process. Williams (1961, 49) suggests that when a culture's structure of feeling can no longer be addressed by its members, it can be approximated from a consideration of the society's "documentary culture," which includes all types of recorded culture, including photographs, novels, poems, films, buildings, and fashions.

The artist's imagination, in Williams's view, transforms specific ideologies and produces a specific response to a particular social order and an understanding that can be more "real" than ordinarily observable. For Williams (1983, 264–265), this sense of imagination allows a synthesis between the personal and the social that creates and judges a whole way of life in terms of individual qualities: "It is a formation, an active formation, that you feel your way into, feel informing you, so that in general and in detail it is not very like the usual idea of imagination ... but seems more like a kind of recognition, a connection with something fully knowable but not yet known." Evans's understanding of the actual role he plays in the creation of his own photography is similar to Williams's understanding of the artistic imagination. Finding his choice of subject matter less a conscious preference than a magical "irresistible tug from inside," Evans explains, "It's as though there's a wonderful secret in a certain place and I can capture it. Only I, at this moment, can capture it, and only this moment and only me" (Evans in Rathbone 1995, 116).

It is not surprising that advertising images constitute an important component of Evans's photography. The son of an advertising executive, Evans learns the persuasive pull of advertising from his father, who worked at Lord and Thomas as a copywriter for Albert Lasker, the dominant advertising personality early in the twentieth century and one of the first individuals to use mass psychology in advertising. In her biography of Evans, Belinda Rathbone (1995, 20) notes that his home life was unhappy: "As far as Walker could see, the American dream of a happy family life, one of the targets at which his father had learned to aim his subliminal advertising persuasions, was neither pure nor true." Perhaps Flaubert's description (quoted in Rathbone 1995, 30) of advertising people as "noisy competitors with souls as flat as billboards" may also have encouraged Evans's critique of the handmaiden of material culture.

While the history of the dissemination of persuasive information can be traced back thousands of years, scholars generally agree that the formation of modern advertising emerges from specific characteristics and needs of corporate industrial capitalism, including a system of market control, an advanced distribution organization, and the development of consumer credit. From 1880 to 1930, such changes in industrial capitalism helped to engineer the advancement of an organized system of persuasion and commercial information. By the end of World War I, straightforward business announcements and crudely designed advertisements begin to give way to psychologically sophisticated campaigns created by advertising specialists promoting specific products and helping to foster consumerism. Not surprisingly, by the 1930s advertising has become "capitalism's way of saying 'I love you' to itself" (Schudson 1986, 232).

In modern advertising it is never enough to sell a product; the acquisition of merchandise is associated with social and personal values and meanings. In one sense advertising acts "as an agency of social control" (Carey 1989, 23), encouraging individuals to follow prescribed social "norms" and consume products appropriate to current economic and social conditions. Yet it also "magically" convinces people that social needs and desires such as love and companionship are attainable through the acquisition of commodities so that, for instance, by brushing with a particular toothpaste, an individual will ultimately be rewarded with true love. As Williams (1980, 188–189) explains,

> If the consumption of individual goods leaves the whole area of human need unsatisfied, the attempt is made, by magic, to associate this consumption with human desires to which it has no real reference. You do not only buy an object: you buy social respect, discrimination, health, beauty, success, power to control your environment.

Stuart Ewen (1976, 31) finds that modern advertising creates the "fancied need" that requires consumers to buy, not to quench their own needs but to satisfy the "real needs of the capitalist machinery." During the 1930s advertisements begin to focus on "social insecurity" to sell products and the overall idea of consumerism; and, Ewen suggests (1976, 38), advertisements encourage self-conscious anxieties among people who are made to feel emotionally uneasy and uncomfortable.

An emphasis on "social insecurity" is the hard-sell tactic favored by advertisers during the Depression as advertising revenues begin to fall from a high of $3.4 billion in 1929 to a low of $1.3 billion in 1933 (Fox 1997, 118–119). In an effort to keep costs down, advertisers limit the use of illustrations and color, and appeal to consumers' personal insecurities through the use of sensationalized and threatening slice-of-life stories, gross exaggerations, extensive body copy, loud headlines, contests, prizes, and two-for-one promotions. Advertising appeals often focus on consumers' fear, guilt, and shame, violating prevailing standards of decency in their preoccupation with body odors, personal flaws, and job insecurity. During the 1930s advertisers capitalize on widespread unemployment, favoring scare campaigns in their attempts to connect job security with the use of their brand of razor blades, toothpaste, mouthwash, stockings, and so on. Advertisers also focus on parental guilt to sell such items as breakfast cereal, pencils, toilet tissue, and light bulbs. In 1934 the advertising executive Bruce Barton (quoted in Fox 1997, 120) suggests that "ideals have been abandoned, standards have been sunk," and he warns that the proliferation of "silly advertisements, dishonest advertisements, disgusting advertisements" now discredit the business and put its practitioners on the defensive.

Convinced that the hard-sell approach encourages consumers to purchase products during troubled economic times, advertisers increasingly seek new outlets for their messages. Farm Security Administration photographs, including many taken by Walker Evans, document the intrusion of billboards and advertising signs on the social landscape of 1930s America. For example, local advertising agents offer, at no cost, to paint three sides of a barn any color requested by the farmer if the agent can advertise his or her product on the side of the barn facing the road. At the height of the Depression, barns glorifying "Clabber Girl," the "Gold Dust Twins," and "Bull Durham" are found in every state (Goodrum and Dalrymple 1990, 42).

Evans's photographic documentation of Depression-era society often addresses the appropriation of consumer culture and suggests the ironies of depicting "a society of pleasure that is inseparable from the consumer society which gave it birth" (Mora and Hill 1993, 34). Rejecting the commercialism, "slick technique," and saccharine romanticism of most American photographers, Evans (1980, 185) offers the work of Eugene Atget, specifically his "lyrical understanding of the street, trained observation of it, special feeling for patina, eye for revealing detail," as an example of what photography should encompass. Overall, the key to Evans's photographic style is his ability to disappear into his work, to view American culture without appearing to comment on it. Preferring the term "documentary style" to "documentary photographer," he (1982, 216) explains that "documentary is police photography of a scene and murder. ... That's a real document. You see art is really useless, and a document has use. And therefore art is never a document, but it can adopt that style. I do it."

His antiromantic way of situating American culture within its specific historical moment, as well as his emphasis on visual and literary satire and illusion, resonates with the philosophies of two of his early influences, Baudelaire and Flaubert. From Baudelaire Evans gains an understanding of the role of photography as a memory aid for the historical record—as a "record-keeper of whomsoever needs absolute material accuracy for professional reasons" (Baudelaire 1980, 88). Always cognizant of Flaubert's strict adherence to realism and his insistence on the objective treatment of his subjects, Evans (1982, 70) maintains that he incorporates, "almost unconsciously," an understanding of the "non-appearance of the author. The non-subjectivity that is literally applicable to the way I want to use the camera and do." Trachtenberg (1989, 240) suggests that Flaubert also helps Evans to break from prevailing traditions and expectations, to see himself as an artistic rebel who would do for photography what Flaubert did for the novel: "With his eye for signifying detail, for the accidental revelations in juxtaposed objects, including written signs, and with his wit in laying one picture next to another, Evans set out to prove that apparently documentary photographs could be as complex as a fine piece of writing, as difficult and rewarding in their demands."

Trachtenberg (1989, 241) emphasizes the literariness of Evans's photography and suggests that he evaluates his images based on the literary techniques of "eloquence, wit, grace, and economy," as well as "structure and coherence, paradox and play and oxymoron." For Evans photography does not mimic literature—it is itself a language, the "most literary of the graphic arts"(quoted in Ware 1993, 147).

Aware of the contradictions inherent in technological society, much of Evans's work emphasizes the exploitation of individuals by machines and the influence of mass-produced goods and services on the quality of life for members of the working class. There is pessimism as well as humor in his depictions of technological progress, particularly when seen in the context of the actual living and working conditions of millions of Americans during this era. For example, in his photographs of the homes of miners in West Virginia, Evans contrasts the poverty and lack of material comfort with the opulence of advertising posters with which they decorate their living environments. While commercial images of Santa Claus and Coca-Cola logos provide the predominant decorating touches, commenting obliquely upon the residents' inability to purchase the consumer goods that tempt them in these advertisements, they also represent the creative energy of these individuals. Echoing Williams's (1980, 184) dictum that, "Advertising is the official art of modern capitalist society: We put it up in our streets and fill our news media with it," Evans's photography not only offers pointed examples of how advertising blankets American culture, but it also shows how people appropriate specific offerings of advertising with imagination and creativity.

Lincoln Kirstein (1988, 196) insists that Evans's work shows the decay of industrial capitalist society, testifying to "the symptoms of waste and selfishness that caused the ruin." However, it is important to note that Evans's photography also includes an attempt to salvage, for future observers, a record of the beauty still found in society. Fascinated with classical architecture, Evans photographs decorative architectural details of Victorian houses in New England and simple wooden homes, general stores, and gas stations in small southern towns. While he exposes the poverty, dirt, and ruin inherent in many of these buildings, he also offers a glimpse of the functional beauty of commonplace objects. For instance, a 1936 picture of the kitchen wall of a sharecropper's home in Hale County, Alabama, shows a meager array of eating utensils, yet the composition of the image also showcases the ornamental aspect of the forks and spoons and pays homage to these workers' "cultural energy and spirit" (Brierly 1992, 43).

However, people do not play a central role in much of Evans's photography, a fact that prompts some critics to suggest that not only did he breathe life into inanimate objects but that he also seems to care more about those objects than the people who produce and own them. But eventually, as Max Kozloff (1989, 116) explains, "the rightness of this tone gradually sinks in on the viewer, who grasps that Evans aims to describe a broader spectacle, the diffusions of a culture in its material expression" (Kozloff 1989, 116). The dominance of people by inanimate cultural artifacts permeates Evans's photography and not only suggests the myriad ways in which human beings disappear from the artificial images but also how individuals have "abandoned their authority to the fabricated human beings of advertisement posters" (Ward 1985, 128).

Evans's 1936 photograph of a roadside stand near Birmingham, Alabama, offers a lighthearted critique of the domination of advertising in Depression-era society (Figure 7.1). Two young salesmen are dwarfed by the myriad all-encompassing signs, plastered over the country store and promoting a variety of goods and services. While the signs advertise moving services and an assortment of types of fish for sale, the store displays fruit. The signs, which promise reliability, honest weights, and square dealings, dominate the scene, and their promises seem to be reinforced by the boys holding melons. Yet the young merchants seem to play a secondary, almost subservient role in the larger inanimate advertising structure. The large painted fish at the top of the building has far more character development than either of the two boys and may represent a humorous commentary on the intrusion of advertising in American life. However, Evans (1982, 33) notes that the comedy in his work may not be uniformly apparent, and he suggests that some of his attempts to infuse humor into his photographs are missed because of the experiences and attitudes that some readers bring to his images.

Favoring anonymous expression over the truth of portraits, Evans admits that he has no interest in photographing people as individuals and says that human beings "interest me as elements in the total image, as long as they are *anonymous*" (Evans quoted in Mora and Hill 1993, 260). Evans's 1936 photograph of a Birmingham photography shop, depicting 225 small machine-made passport photos,

FIGURE 7.1   *Walker Evans,* Roadside Stand Near Birmingham, Alabama, 1936. *Farm Security Administration—Office of War Information; Photograph Collection, Library of Congress, Prints and Photographs Division.*

carefully arranged in squares of fifteen with the word "STUDIO" emblazoned across them, is but one example of how his work critiques stereotypical notions of portrait photography. The passport photos, identical in size and framing, devoid of artistic sensibility or individual subjectivity, may be seen as "emblems of mechanical stylelessness" (Trachtenberg 1984, 6). For Evans the anonymous subject, created by an anonymous photographer, placed in the context of the cluttered landscape of industrial capitalism, reveals the naked truth about American society. An emphasis on cultural artifacts shows how the American Dream now translates into giving individuals only the choice and arrangement of inanimate, manufactured goods.

Evans photographs the ironic presence of advertising movie posters, billboards, and signs as they insinuate their way into the landscape of American culture. Considering them essential manifestations of the logic of capitalist society, he suggests that even a frayed movie poster contains evidence of a specific historical place and time. For instance, Evans's photograph of a deteriorating minstrel show bill advertising J. C. Lincoln's Sunny South Minstrels is, at first glance, a cartoonlike

FIGURE 7.2   *Walker Evans,* Houses, 1936, Atlanta, Georgia. *Farm Security Administration—Office of War Information; Photograph Collection, Library of Congress, Prints and Photographs Division.*

characterization of African Americans, who are shown hanging out of the windows of a dilapidated house, running after chickens, and pouring water on musicians. Not only does this image illustrate the ludicrous racial stereotyping so prevalent during the Depression as well as the degradation of African Americans, but it also depicts, in the decay of the poster itself, a horrific realization of the agony and violence inherent in American culture. The weather-worn poster depicts half-obliterated faces and disembodied hands that represent the frightening potential of annihilation and viscerally document specific material conditions. The photograph not only represents the history of the poster—what it originally meant to illustrate—but it also indicates the current status of the deteriorating billboard, which focuses on the pain and violence inherent in the image. The minstrel show bill photograph shows that while advertising signs from the 1930s are both familiar and ordinary records of society, when they are ripped out of their usual context, they may also confer essential clues about current issues in society.

A Depression-era structure of feeling emerges from a photograph taken by Evans in 1936. It depicts two symmetrically matching wooden-frame houses on a street in Atlanta, Georgia, each with oval-framed second-story porches (Figure 7.2).

The dreary, faceless houses form a backdrop for the movie billboards, which offer visions of celluloid romance and pleasure. One of the posters advertises Carole Lombard's new film, *Love Before Breakfast,* and shows her gazing at her fans seductively, with an obvious blackened eye. This biting commentary on the contradictions between the American Dream and the actual living conditions of the occupants of these two slightly sinister-looking houses suggests what happens in an impersonal mass society when people are often misrepresented on posters like glamorous film stars.

When confronting this image, viewers may be uncomfortably reminded that beautiful people are often "promoted by the ugliest and crudest of advertising displays" (Ward 1985, 131). Lombard represents luxury and material excess, but the irony of this picture is heightened by her prominent black eye, which mirrors the houses' balconies and may symbolize the actual violence women often endure in oppressive relations. The photograph also includes an advertisement for Anne Shirley in *Chatterbox,* reminding viewers once again of demeaning 1930s stereotypes of women promoted throughout the mass media. Read together, the two posters suggest that while women who talk too much end up with a blackened eye, this violence is necessary to put them in their place so that they are "prepared" to participate in an early-morning interlude.

Crossroads, a store in Sprott, Alabama, provides another example of the pervasiveness of advertising in 1930s American society (Figure 7.3). This image by Evans is one of many of rural post offices, stores, and gas stations. In each case the buildings are simple wooden constructions, decorated with commercial advertisements—most often for Coca-Cola. As places of communication, they illustrate how modern industrial society intersects with its agrarian roots. The barely distinguishable people, shown standing on the porch of the post office, appear as no more than decorations. The emphasis is clearly on the giant Coca-Cola sign, which obscures the building's identity as a post office and serves as an ironic reminder of the major role that the soft drink plays in 1930s southern culture. The image suggests the continued power of advertising and provides "a vision of the commonplace revealing its artlessness as art" (Hulick 1993, 139).

Throughout Evans's work, representations of hand-crafted folk culture clash with images of machine-produced, standardized objects created by the culture industry—witness Evans's (1982, 74) own description of advertising as a "bastard trade." Much of his photography emphasizes the creative visions inherent in the hand-made signs of independent businesspeople, their artistic lettering and primitive imagery expressing their entrepreneurial drive and ingenuity. These signs are representations of a more innocent time that contrasts with an array of mass-produced advertising images which promote the consumption of consumer goods.

The photograph of Lincoln Market, in Winston-Salem, North Carolina, created by Evans in 1935, is an example of the conflict between individual creativity and industrialization (Figure 7.4). A hand-lettered sign on the side of a general store

FIGURE 7.3   *Walker Evans, Crossroads Store, 1935 or 1936, Sprott, Alabama. Farm Security Administration—Office of War Information; Photograph Collection, Library of Congress, Prints and Photographs Division.*

FIGURE 7.4   *Walker Evans,* Winston-Salem, North Carolina, *1935. Farm Security Administration—Office of War Information; Photograph Collection, Library of Congress, Prints and Photographs Division.*

advertises meats, groceries, and delivery services. While this unsophisticated advertising display figures prominently in the photograph, so does the Coca-Cola sign that frames the front door of the establishment and occupies an ownership role in this scene. No matter how much space is given to the independent business venture, it is clear that corporate capitalism prevails.

The general store itself represents a place of social communication, a symbolic public sphere where people may gather to discuss issues of importance to the community. Yet the concerns of Depression-era society are communicated by the prevalence of advertising signs and posters. Both the slickly produced logo and the hand-made market sign may be seen as essential components of public communication in 1930s America. That the signs occupy the entire image and corresponding public space offers a clue to Evans's views on social communication. Echoing other Depression-era critics, Evans suggests that industrialization and its corresponding new media technologies are destroying any real potential for actual communication. Evans's advertising photographs indicate that in modern capitalist society signs, slogans, logos, catch phrases, and visual metaphors may soon replace independent analysis and rational thought.

Throughout his career Evans (1982, 220) continues to "lean toward the enchantment, the visual power, of the aesthetically rejected object," photographing

8

▼ ▼ ▼

Wireless Pleasure: Locating Radio in the American Home

Technology, urbanization, industrialization, and the advent of modern means of electronic communication—these are the dominant themes of the cultural history of the 1930s. The technical and professional advancements in radio, film, and photography, with their reconstruction of information, entertainment, and the reality of everyday life, decisively shaped the social and political environment. It is the performance of radio during this period, however, with its accessibility and national penetration, that looms largest in the transformation of the American experience into a national discourse.

This chapter provides a reading of 1936 family-magazine images to reconstruct an emerging definition of radio and its place in society. It constitutes an attempt to ascertain the social uses of radio—as depicted in magazine advertising texts and images—and the nature of radio as a social and cultural phenomenon in America in the 1930s, when broadcasting had been firmly established as a formidable medium of "mass" communication. For instance, the work of Susan Douglas (1987) explores the social construction of radio in press coverage before the 1930s. Her findings suggest that radio, by creating immense audiences, ushered in a social transformation and fostered class-bound assumptions—in the magazine press, especially—about its promise as a delivery system for high culture. She concludes (1987, 314) that radio "meant progress for all. The technology would bring improvement to many areas of American life, the poor and the rich, the individual and the institution. In these press accounts there was no tension between corporate ambitions and individual desires: they were really the same thing."

This chapter focuses on the construction of radio in magazine advertisements when it had become a major commercial means of public communication and advertisers began to provide a social and economic rationale for the purchase of radio sets. The advertisements were culled from mainstream weekly and monthly magazines, including *Better Homes and Gardens, Collier's, Country Gentleman, Good Housekeeping, House & Gardens, Life,* and the *Saturday Evening Post* to provide insights into the appeals to middle-class Americans. These magazines represent the material and sometimes spiritual needs and desires of a white, middle-class readership through advertisements and editorial matter that contain the rationale for an idealized commercialized life. They are also trusted and therefore credible sources of information about trends in homemaking styles and fashions.

By 1936 the structure of broadcasting in the United States was securely in place. Radio had been harnessed and defined through federal control (Communications Act of 1934), put on a commercial foundation through advertising, and extended and centralized through a comprehensive development of network broadcasting. The result was an organized and supervised assault on the original decentralized practices of local radio by network organizations that changed the character of programming and the type of advertising to accommodate national audiences and advertising clients. In fact, at of the end of 1938, "less than 3 percent of the nation's total nighttime broadcasting power was utilized by stations not affiliated with one or the other of these three [NBC, Blue and Red, and CBS] network companies," according to an FCC annual report (Mosco 1979, 48).

Once it becomes established as a household necessity, radio dominates the social and cultural scene. Gerald Nachman's *Raised on Radio* (1998) provides a vivid account of those early years of radio in the homes of millions of Americans. Unavailable before 1920, radio becomes a craze by 1922, and the sales of radio sets between 1922 and 1927 grow by about 1,400 percent, while the common stock of RCA between 1928 and 1929 rises from about 85 to 549 (Allen 1931, 116–117). In a few years radio had become part of a typical inventory of household goods, particularly in the early 1930s, when the American middle-class family is rather comfortably equipped, according to statistical data. For instance, in characterizing living standards in 1932, Walter Pitkin (1973, 189) concludes that

> a cheap wooden house will contain, among other things, a $500 piano or automatic player piano, a $150 radio, a $50 talking machine, and a $50 icebox (the latter now rapidly displaced by $200 electric refrigerators). There is usually a good bathroom, usually with a shower; and almost always there is central heating, with hot and cold water upstairs and down. All these are bought on installments which run from one to five years.

In fact, the CIT Corporation advocates the purchase of radio sets on the installment plan in 1936. Its budget plan—under the motto "Once a Luxury for the Few—Now a Pleasure to all"—promises to enable "millions of families to enjoy radios, automobiles, refrigerators, and other modern household conveniences which promote health, comfort and happiness" (*Collier's* December 12, 1936, 42).

These changes in lifestyle—including the purchase of new household appliances—rely on advertising and other consumer information. Indeed, a large number of traditional and new media competed for the attention of mass audiences at that time. Americans face not only an increasing volume of Hollywood productions in their local movie houses but also a considerable variety of middle-class magazines that crowd the newsstands, among them the *Saturday Evening Post*, *LIFE*, *Collier's*, and *Reader's Digest*, the last with more than 2 million readers by 1937. There are also weekly news digests in the form of *Time* and *Newsweek*, and *Fortune*, a monthly, in addition to an aggressive daily metropolitan press that faced mounting competition from newsreels, feature films, specialty magazines, and radio.

In a society eager to embrace more efficient ways of ingesting information or even experiencing leisure, however, only radio—and later television—offers a definitive technological answer. In fact, radio took on a major role in the lives of Americans and threatened even the popularity of the movies while cutting into time spent on automobile pleasure rides. The diligent perusal of the daily press or the recreational reading of books, for instance, traditional forms of participation in the production and dissemination of social or political knowledge, are gradually overshadowed by the newly acquired habit of radio-listening. Pitkin (1973, 190) explains these changes as a function of the versatility of the radio, a technology that "offers wider variety at less cost; and, above all, it may be enjoyed at any hour of the day or night." And he speculates in 1932 that "it would surprise nobody to see a radio in every American home by 1935 or thereabouts."

Radio, in turn, quickly understands the people's desire to be entertained, and it capitalizes further on this idea in the late 1920s with the emergence of daytime radio programs that entertain and sell consumer goods at the same time. Known as soap operas, they are broadcast typically from New York or other metropolitan areas and received by tens of millions of people—especially in rural areas or small towns around the country. But the popularity of these daytime dramas, their frequency, and their choice of topics also become threats to certain sections of society. For instance, James Thurber (1972, 163) reports that during the 1930s "radio daytime serials were occasionally sniped at by press and pulpit, and now and then women's clubs adopted halfhearted resolutions, usually unimplemented by research, disapproving of the 'menace of soap opera.'" Nevertheless, soaps have remained a mainstay of American broadcasting right up to the present, in their televised form.

Even music, the dominant factor in early radio, declines by the 1930s to about two-thirds of the daily radio programming, while drama and talk shows become more popular. According to Lichty and Topping (1975, 303), "Three major program types developed in the last half of the 1930s—the suspense-psychological thriller ... , the one-half hour situation comedy drama, and quiz formats with a number of variations."

New program types evolve gradually through the thirties, while news and information programming become more frequent. President Roosevelt's fireside chats made for great radio, as did the live broadcasts of other news, like the abdication speech of King Edward VIII or the Spanish Civil War. An example of the popularity of news programs—which increased from 5 to 20 percent during 1930–1945, according to Harry Wish (1962, 530)—is the success of *The March of Time*. It was a daily—and later weekly (1936–37)—CBS radio program, sponsored by Remington-Rand and *Time,* that provided dramatic versions of news events. Other local stations broadcast variations on the program, which also helped inspire the newsreel version of *The March of Time* in 1935. At the same time news analysts and commentators become household names: Elmer Davis, Raymond Gram Swing, Clifton Utley, Lowell Thomas, H. V. Kaltenborn, and Gabriel Heatter were some of the bigger names in news. The latter regularly calmed his audience with his signature phrase: "There's good news tonight" (Wish 1962, 530).

With a rising public interest in world affairs—particularly in events in Europe—news becomes an important commodity and provides the major stimulus for expanding international coverage. The press, on the other hand, becomes protective of its historical function as news carrier. In fact, a press-radio war ensues that lasts until newspapers realize the value of radio ownership and acquire stations or make agreements with them for the production of news. According to Danna (1975, 347), for instance, in 1936 "Hearst Radio now controls six stations outright; Scripps-Howard owns a station in Cincinnati and both Hearst and Scripps-Howard chains are embarked on active campaigns to build up radio alliances." Only a few years later, the press is firmly entrenched in the broadcasting business, whose growth had dented newspaper circulation and advertising between 1937 and 1940.

This is also the time when the commercial nature of radio is irrevocably established and listeners receive their entertainment wrapped in commercial messages. By 1936 the days are long gone when the acceptability of advertising and sponsorship of programs generated wide concern about exploitation and the public interest. Even after *Printers' Ink,* in 1923, discouraged advertisers from using radio and the American Newspaper Publishers Association reported in 1925 that "radio has not proved itself to be an advertising medium" (Banning 1946, 118, 260), the commercialization of radio continues unabated. In fact, by the late 1920s advertising had successfully merged with programming. In this period "Frank Munn and Virginia Rea appear as 'Paul Oliver' and 'Olive Palmer' for Palmolive soap, Joseph M. White is known ... as the 'silver Masked Tenor' for the sake of B. F. Goodrich Silvertown Cord Tires, and Harry Horlick's gypsy orchestra was sponsored as the *A&P Gypsies*" (Spalding 1975, 227). Time may not have been for sale in the early 1920s, but it had become readily available by the 1930s.

Since listeners pay attention to commercials, advertisers turned to radio, especially for selling consumer goods, which—according to Hettinger (1975, 234)—typically are "small articles of low cost, mass consumption, and a high degree of repeat purchase." They constitute the majority of national network and nonnetwork advertising, with more than 80 percent and about 70 percent of the volume, respectively. Such consumer items are not only affordable, they are also advertised in an easy-to-understand manner to reach most listeners. The latter point is important, since advertising audiences, in general, lack sophistication. They were once characterized (in the late 1920s) as

> $8-, $10-, $12-a-day workers; thirteen- or fourteen-year-old minds scarcely equal to second-year high school. Each gets a book every four months where public libraries reach them; four out of five haven't even this service. And one out of three families have no books in their home.... They all go to the movies every other week; and about one in four listen to the radio perhaps an hour a day.... Writing themselves they use a vocabulary generally fewer than a thousand words although each can understand, in reading, maybe six times that many. In their aggregate action the element of intellect is practically negligible. (Goode and Powel 1970, 97)

These are not the individuals, however, featured in advertisements for radio sets, where a strictly upper middle-class image prevailed in 1936.

Families as the social units of the modern age increasingly become targets of commercial interests with the transformation of various traditional functions in the home—like food processing and individual care, even child-rearing—into industrial concerns, from restaurants and hospitals to kindergartens and schools. The advent of modern technologies had produced the possibilities of a new lifestyle that revolutionized families, and the media furnish examples and incentives through news and advertising, which reinforce each other in the promotion of a modern outlook.

Throughout these years radio plays an important role in the standardization of information and entertainment; for instance, "It created a new kind of national audience for sports events, as well as for a wide variety of music and drama," according to Ostrander (1970, 234), who also concludes that radio has "had the general effect on the national culture of standardizing speech and, with other mass media, synchronizing national interest and taste."

In the case of music, for example, tastes are based on performances of a few outstanding orchestras, while local "live" performances dwindled and local or regional sounds receded to the margins. The result is not only devastating for the profession, as those without radio contracts or employment in radio orchestras become unemployed, but also for the cultural environment, when listening is associated more often with the radio (or phonograph) than with musical presentations in concert halls or roadhouses.

Radio destroys the privacy of the home by introducing the world into the parlors, kitchens, and bedrooms of American families. The appearance of radio sets in the American home changes living habits, disrupting traditional family functions. Individuals are drawn into listening to radio programs, and listening habits split family life. Radio sets become part of living with a modern technology and are part of the regimentation of social life.

Together with film and phonographs—and reinforced by the coverage of society in traditional media, like magazines and newspapers—broadcasting shapes the cultural environment and helps determine advertisements and fashions. In addition, radio replaces gesture with sound, the familiarity of the face with an awareness of the voice, and concrete reality with symbolic context. The result is a new reality, created and reinforced by radio, that relies on the authenticity of sound, the need for repetition, and the rhythm of a phrase.

Radio also connects people with the world and, with the automobile, increased the mobility of what is a young and restless society in the 1930s. For instance, Frederick Lewis Allen (1952, 129) suggests that the "automobile suited the American genius. For that genius was not static but venturesome. Americans felt that a rolling stone gathers experience, adventure, sophistication, and—with luck—new and possibly fruitful opportunities." Radio fits the demands of American ingenuity by reinforcing its yearning for the new and unexplored—in this case the world beyond the reach of the automobile.

But mechanization breeds conformity, and Americans—who dressed in the same attire, drove the same cars over identical highways, and passed commercial strips to reach the same destinations—also listened to the same sound of radio. The media environment—enriched by the arrival of radio—imposed on Americans "the same patterns of emulation: ... making them want to be the same sort of people" (Allen 1952, 223).

Radio is a reliable companion—as it had been throughout the Depression—as motion picture audiences declined, theaters closed, and recreational life took on a collective character that fostered the popularity of spectator sports. The Depression accelerated the consolidation of commerce and industry, and market forces and advertising, in particular, affected the content of radio in the 1930s.

Mass culture emerges despite rising fears of an industrialization of the mind and a debasement of culture, and radio plays its part in the dissemination of ideas—including educational efforts to raise social and cultural consciousness to higher levels of awareness. After all, novels and dramas in 1930s America are rich sources of insights into the lingering American dream amid the agony of the underclass and the failures of democracy. In contrast to the rebellious mood among intellectuals in the 1930s, radio reflects the conservatism of corporate ownership or network affiliation with programming aimed to please sponsors and—only through them—their respective audiences.

The few accounts of radio in the American context are typically marred by an emphasis on content at the expense of form. Examinations of technology in these works often stress chronologies of inventors, institutions, and science while ignoring the social and cultural contexts of the establishment of radio technology. In fact, the material forms of radio, how it was aestheticized, humanized, and sold, are crucial to its success. By 1936 radio had changed from its earlier manifestation as an expensive novel technology for the few to an inexpensive, familiar technology sold to millions. For instance, in 1922 only .2 percent of Americans own radio sets; by 1930 this figure had risen to 46 percent and rocketed to 81 percent by 1940 (Spigel 1992, 29).

Harrold Innis (1951) and Marshall McLuhan (1964) have argued that radio challenged the dominant print culture, which, according to Innis (1951), stresses regionalism and ephemerality. Radio, on the other hand, "introduced a new phase in the history of Western civilization by emphasizing centralization and the necessity of a concern with continuity" (Innis 1951, 60). By 1936 centralization and continuity are epitomized by the domination of national networks, which eradicated an earlier emphasis on local, and oftentimes random, programming. It is the result of national broadcast advertising, which established and maintained the network system. National advertisers sponsor dramatic, news, and musical programming within the context of regular network schedules. Earlier attempts to use radio as a tool of education fell victim to the exploitation of the commercial potential of radio as an advertising medium. Instead, radio challenges the dominance of a print culture within the familiar economic structure of capitalism. Although the early radio industry made profits solely from the sales of sets, by the mid–1930s advertising and sales of broadcast time become the dominant sources of radio-industry profits. In addition—unlike newspapers, magazines, and books—radio is more accessible to the working class since it is less expensive and surmounts the barriers of literacy.

Programming is aimed at the largest possible audience and therefore tends to reflect the lowest common denominator of the "mass" audiences—unlike the more regionally and demographically specific content of newspapers and magazines. Also, with a national network structure, major advertisers could deliver their pitches to a much larger audience and create new consumer markets for their products. As Orvell notes,

> The early years of the 1930s saw the development of a number of new product lines, reflecting not only a flowering of cultural nationalism, but also a simple economic self-interest, for the condition of the economy during the Depression forced on many businesses the task of refashioning goods in the hopes of creating markets where none had previously existed; more simply, not to "modernize" might be to lose the competitive edge in a tight market. (1989, 181)

Before the Depression Herbert Hoover's Bureau of Standards, a division of the Department of Commerce, spearheaded a move to standardize electrical goods and building materials. While this obviously benefited industrial concerns, the cultural impact is no less important. Mass production and its concomitant standardization of material forms ensure that Americans would experience continuity and uniformity on an unprecedented scale and on all levels of their everyday lives. The consumer of the 1930s would experience little diversity in product forms across the country. For example, the 1936 catalog of Sears Roebuck, then celebrating its fiftieth anniversary, was a staple of many American homes. Its pages provided access to a plethora of commodities for all Americans, rural and urban, middle-class and working-class. But beyond the standardization of specific forms such as plumbing fixtures and refrigerators, other pressures to homogenize society were at work.

Large numbers of immigrants had arrived in America during the first decades of the twentieth century, and a massive migration of African Americans to Northern urban centers such as Chicago, Detroit, and New York occurred after World War I. The resulting diversification of the population often meets with resistance, along with the desire by progressive forces to "melt" ethnic and racial groups into a homogenous nation. Broadcasting, by its very existence, promotes such ideas. For instance, Kaempffer (1924, 772) notes in the mid–1920s that "prior to broadcasting, a sense of nationhood, a conception that Americans were all part of one country, was only an abstract idea, often without much force. The millions of towns and houses across America were unrelated and disconnected. But now that atomized state of affairs was changing." Thus, radio ushers in a change from regionally specific communities with specific cultural forms expressed in their broadcasting practices to a homogenous, mass-produced national culture. It is within this larger shift that radio sets are aestheticized, humanized, and sold to American consumers.

Radio, like the phonograph, is both a technological novelty and a commodity to be located within the private sphere of the American home and primarily viewed as a refuge from the industrialized public sphere of commercial production. Radio and phonographs represent the earliest invasions of the private realm by these machines of consciousness. Much resistance to these technologies stemmed from their role as conduits to the public, but Holly Kruse (1993, 11) argues that aesthetic notions were also a concern, particularly with the phonograph. Although radio sets underwent a similar development some time later, she suggests that from "the outset, the phonograph was not only viewed as unsuitable for in-home use because it was a mass amusement, but it was seen, quite simply, as a technological eyesore." And she adds that phonograph manufacturers responded to this resistance by altering the appearance of the phonograph to complement the prevailing aesthetic of the Victorian home. (There is an interesting convergence of shapes and designs between the Victorian home and the Victrola, Victor record label, and later RCA Victor.) Thus phonographs—and later radios—resemble the dark, wooden, and cumbersome accouterments of the middle-class home, serving, in effect, as another piece of furniture to be individualized with a vase of flowers or a statue on top. Spigel remarks that in "this context of modern domesticity, with its emphasis on consumer technologies and family leisure, radio was transformed from a technical gadget into a domestic machine that promised to embellish homes across the nation" (1992, 27).

As the mass production and marketing of radio begins in the early 1920s, radio's design is dominated by a large cabinet that camouflaged the technology. However, by the 1930s changes in industrial design and production begin to affect the appearance of radio. Tied to generic notions of the "machine age" and reflecting the dictates of mass production in the use of plastics and other composite materials, radio sets become smaller, and their form less frequently obscured their purpose. However, this transition does not occur rapidly or comprehensively.

Rather, the shift to newer designs happens gradually, and in 1936 both the established, wood-encased floor models and the newer and smaller "modern" sets were competing for consumers. These two different forms reflect larger tensions between conservative aesthetic notions of the Victorian nineteenth century and the avant-gardism of modernism. For instance, Orvell (1989, 167) argues that "it was symptomatic of the period's ambivalence in the face of radical change that the backward-looking impulse could coexist with an equal and opposite enthusiasm for the machine, as if one could balance the other."

This dichotomy of forms is arguably more pronounced in the private sphere of the home than in public spaces, where modern forms and designs (such as the Chrysler building or 20th Century Limited locomotives) were much in vogue at the time. Furthermore, as the radio set is a conduit to the outside world—particularly the world of entertainment and popular culture—its forms are manifestations of cultural negotiations between tradition and innovation. Thus dour, dark wooden cabinets that cloak the technology inside mitigate what many considered the profligate programming they conveyed. In addition, the material forms of radio in this period reflected—within certain mass-produced limits—the class of consumers (Philco offers models from $20 to $600) and accessibility to electricity in their homes (battery-operated sets were available).

The construction of radio by advertising campaigns in 1936 is based on three themes: technological sophistication, social standing, and the desire for psychic mobility. It was undertaken in the middle-class magazines of the day by almost a dozen manufacturers. Besides the more well-known brands—General Electric, Philco, RCA Victor, Westinghouse, and Zenith—others, such as American-Bosch, Arvin, Atwater-Kent, Fairbanks-Morse, Grunow, and Stromberg-Carlson, contribute significantly to the construction of an American radio public that is white, middle class to upper middle class, and rooted in a culture of traditional tastes.

There is no doubt, according to the magazine advertisements in 1936, that radio had become part of the American scene; the chief questions, however, concerned technical refinements and the potential of acquiring social standing through radio listening. Most of the advertising narratives combine scientific knowledge and aesthetic pleasure, as in Westinghouse's "all the worthwhile developments of modern radio science, built into a really beautiful set" (*Collier's* October 17, 65).

In the 1936 rush for technological innovation as a marketable trait of radio sets, advertisements meet the need for comprehension by humanizing radio technology. For instance, RCA Victor introduces references to the "magic voice" or "magic brain" and "magic eye" of its radio sets (*Saturday Evening Post* October 24, 1936, 75; February 29, 1936, inside cover); others incorporate an "almost human automatic maestro" (*Saturday Evening Post* November 21, 1936, 78), operating with a "focused tone" (*Saturday Evening Post* December 19, 1936, 32), using an "acoustical labyrinth" (*Saturday Evening Post* August 15, 1936, 63), and, with the aid of a "semaphore dial" (*Saturday Evening Post* October 10, 101) or "teledial" (*Saturday Evening Post* December 5, 1936, 99), offering "control-room reception"

138

FIGURE 8.1 *RCA advertisement,* Saturday Evening Post, *1936. Reprinted with the permission of Thomson Consumer Electronics, Inc.*

(*Saturday Evening Post* February 22, 1936, 92) of their "long-distance radio" (*Collier's* October 24, 1936, 48).

Indeed, manufacturers display complete listings of technical innovations; loaded with an expert terminology, they suggest familiarity with the world of radio transmission and reception. For instance, the Zenith Radio Corporation assures its prospective customers that "for 21 years the finest homes in America have been proud of their Zenith" and lists the following features: "Lightning Station Finder, Secret Volume Governor, Foreign Station Locator, Voice and High Fidelity Control, Target Tuning, Acoustic Adapter, Visualized Controls, Headphones for the Hard-of-Hearing, [and] Exclusive Zenith Features Patent-Protected" (*Saturday Evening Post* October 3, 1936, 56).

Each manufacturer insists on the superiority of its product and the standards it sets for the industry. Zenith (*Saturday Evening Post* October 3, 1936, 56), for instance, uses a curious reference to American Indians ("the Indian thought his tent was a palace until he saw the white man's home") to propose that its own standards for a radio set surpassed others. There are frequent invitations to compare the quality of sets in showrooms and to engage in shopping for facts. Otherwise, references to race, ethnicity, or class other than the white, radio-owning upper middle class are absent from the constructed reality of America's radio society in 1936.

Radio listeners, in the fantastic imagery that accompanied the advertisements, are members of a leisure class whose comfort and convenience as audiences are part of the definition of radio. Thus, advertisers went to great lengths to insist on the extreme ease of operation, suggesting, in all likelihood, that the experiences of earlier times with crystal sets and headphones were part of a distant past. But because of these earlier encounters with the do-it-yourself technology of radio, references to technological advancements and technical explanations of such improvements seem appropriate. They help bolster the credibility of the commodity as a scientific product, reinforce the desire for convenience, and envision potential customers as insiders. People's familiarity with radio gives rise to a shared language of pseudoexpertise, the vagueness of which was offset by its concrete conclusions concerning the actual uses of the radio technology. Such references also relate to the idea of progress and the application of superior technological know-how to the uses of radio by listeners.

This technical narrative also reinforces the idea of modernity as a scientifically driven era that rests on the availability of technologies of communication. The potential distancing effects of a scientific language, however, are overcome by personalizing the relationship between radio technology and its users. Addressing the customer directly ("you") and offering a form of "personalized" radio ("your own local station letters flash on when you tune in") suggest individuality and exclusivity (*Saturday Evening Post* August 15, 1936, 40–41). Similarly, Fairbanks-Morse Radios promise that "millions of men—their wives, too—can now be freed from the puzzling complications of short-wave tuning" with its easy and simple "semaphore dial" (*Saturday Evening Post* September 12, 1936, 127). It is equally easy with an RCA Victor—"whether it be battery type or current operated"—for a farm family to "listen to Europe and South America." The fact that "any radio is better with an RCA Antenna System," however, discloses one of the less frequently mentioned aspects of successful radio listening, the need for workable antenna systems (*Country Gentleman* February 1936, 34).

The advertisements' technical narrative about radio often occurs among sets of images of people and their living environments, which indicates an exclusively white, middle- or upper-class clientele. It is a world of well-dressed individuals—often in evening clothes and surrounded by expensive furnishings, including books—that suggests a definite relationship between radio ownership (if not listening) and class. Men and women are typically portrayed in the presence of a radio console, which resembles expensive furniture and blends into their middle- or upper-class environment as a functional yet attractive part of the room. Large radio sets become invisible when a manufacturer like RCA Victor takes pride in the "beautiful piece of cabinet work with hand-rubbed finish" (*Collier's* July 25, 1936, 34). Even Macy's of New York offers "furniture with all the charm of the old world," which contains a "cleverly concealed" radio-phonograph (*House & Gardens* June 1936, 61). In fact, a cartoon in *Life* (October 1936, 15) shows a radio sales floor that looks like a furniture store with a salesman informing his colleague about a waiting couple, "They say they want a radio that looks like a radio."

The presence and placement of radio sets in advertisements are reinforced by articles on interior design in which radio becomes an attribute of a modern household (e.g., *Good Housekeeping* September, October 1936, 56; *Better Homes and Gardens* October 1936, 21). In "Putting the Radio Right in Its Place," *House & Gardens* editors suggest "six ways of placing this indispensable instrument so that it becomes a definite part of your decorative scheme" (January 1936, 30). Radio appealed to the aesthetic pleasures of women, in particular ("Your wife will say it's lovely"), who "like beautiful things," including the radio, which is presented as a "beautiful piece of furniture." In fact, "your wife will like you better if you'll get one of the new Arvins ..." (*Collier's* October 24, 1936, 55).

The social standing of the radio user in advertisements is legitimized and confirmed not only by an inclusionary technological discourse but also by references to a range of entertainers or radio personalities, whose appearance signals an endorsement of sound quality while suggesting the limits of a popular radio culture. Entertainers like Cab Calloway, Rudy Vallee, Guy Lombardo, Paul Whiteman, Bing Crosby, Lionel Barrymore, Shirley Temple, and Burns and Allen are used to promote a culture of solidly middle-class taste that was reflected in network programming. Radio advertisements ignore other types of performers or music and remain particularly network-conscious in their appeal to potential buyers. Since references to programming are rare—with the exception of the Philco advertising campaign—what emerges from the advertisements is a rather limited interest in sharing the range of possibilities offered by information and entertainment radio. Thus, radio may have provided the capability of reaching other places—beyond local stations, for instance—but it remains unclear for what specific reasons. References to metropolitan sites or foreign destinations are without content or context; their presence implies an importance that is hidden from the customer, who either knew or was more easily enticed by technical features. Instead, the focus of the advertising message is on acquisition as association with those already in possession of radio sets.

Participation in the exquisite pleasure of listening—and programming to a lesser extent—remains an upper middle class experience in these advertising constructions of radio listeners; individuals are either confirmed in their status or encouraged to participate in these activities through the acquisition of radio technology. Radio as property assures accessibility, not to status or class per se, but to the (listening) experiences associated with a superior lifestyle. In this sense, radio breaks down social barriers and enables consumers to participate in the pleasures of broadcasting regardless of race, class, or ethnicity.

According to the advertising imagery, radio owners represent urban culture and upper-class tastes. This is an environment of male and female adults who enjoy the luxurious sound of radio; children rarely appear, although women frequently do. They are seen as active listeners and potential customers, especially for smaller radio sets when it becomes fashionable to own multiple sets for different parts of the home. Here the emphasis on the listening pleasures of radio competed with the consumption of radios as convenient technologies around the house, where women and children react approvingly to the purchase of additional radio sets.

Arvin Radios (*Collier's* November 21, 1936, 63) in particular constructs the desirability of multiple sets in a series of conversations among family members ("It was sweet of your daddy to give me this lovely little Arvin"; "That's what Mother said when daddy got the big Arvin downstairs"). These advertisements—which ran for several months in *Collier's*—also suggest that the purchase of radio sets was strictly a man's job, regardless of purpose, and reinforces the traditional decision-making structures in middle-class families.

But it is for Philco—one of the major and more visible radio manufacturers during this period—to reveal the negotiated place of radio technology in the context of the American middle-class home. While the obvious aim of its advertisements is to sell Philco sets to consumers, their cultural contexts and appeals rest on the use of specific broadcasting content and the larger social role of radio in American life.

The Philco advertisements of 1936 stand out for several reasons. They are by far the most prolific (representing 60 of 168 advertisements in this sample) and—with few exceptions—remain unchallenged in their focused representation of radio programming. Nearly all of them emphasize entertainment, even when the visual content and the bulk of the text are devoted to news or international affairs. Also, Philco advertisements are, with few exceptions, the only ones to promote automobile radios. And they occupy full magazine pages. Beyond these shared features, four specific and recurrent themes emerge from these advertisements. They address the private and individualized nature of the radio experience, describe the experience of aural travel to distant locations, list the availability of broadcast entertainment, and represent radio as a democratic and pluralistic medium.

One compelling facet of Philco advertisements is their celebration of the private and individual experience of the radio medium. It occurs explicitly and implicitly and is a crucial part of the assimilation of radio into American culture. Along with the phonograph, radio is one of the earliest media to privatize what were formerly public practices such as sporting events, dramatic performances, and musical concerts. Radio, as a consumer commodity sold to individuals, reinforces individualism and private ownership of property and consumer commodities. For example, Philco connects the appeal of John Philip Sousa and the United States Marine Band to the quality of its sound reproduction, but it also highlights how radio brings formerly public events to the private home. The text notes that radio "brings the Marine Band ... and other great musical organizations into your home with such glorious realism they seem to be marching right out of the Philco Inclined Sounding Board!" (*Saturday Evening Post* January 11, 1936, 3). In a similar fashion, a Philco message that focuses on live musical performances states that "[h]otel and night clubs flood the air with melody ... no cover charge to radio listeners" (*Saturday Evening Post* February 22, 1936, 3). Thus the radio not only brings live, public performances into the privacy of the home, but these events are also free of charge. Another Philco advertisement, appearing in *House and Gardens,* reveals the private nature of the listening experience and details the intense, individualized listening that was beginning to separate people further. It also reveals the compartmentalization of audience members along generational and gender lines within the context of the American middle-class family home.

> Gone are the days when one radio would satisfy the whole family! Too much of interest on the air ... too much conflict of opinion between symphony lovers and swing enthusiasts—between sports fans and the politically-minded. The Ideal House ... provides Philcos enough to cater to the taste of every member of the family. A Philco in the boy's room where adventure serials roll in without disturbing Mother listening to a serious musical program in the library. And a Philco Radio-Phonograph in the game room to bring all that radio offers, plus superb reproduction of recorded music (May 1936, 87).

Beyond insights the text offers about the locations and uses of radio in the home, this advertisement is also noteworthy because, unlike the bulk of the other sixty Philco advertisements examined, it mentions no specific performers or content. Likewise, the visual component consists only of three different radio sets. In a *Collier's* advertisement that emphasizes the work of George Gershwin, Philco further stresses the individual nature of the radio experience. "Philco brings their voices so realistically they seem to be singing for you alone"(February 22, 1936). Elsewhere Philco elucidates the technological features of a high-end radio in a text that notes how the listener can individualize the sound to meet particular personal criteria—the ad claims that this particular radio will "enable the discriminating listener to become his own orchestra conductor ... interpret any selection to suit his own individual taste" (*Good Housekeeping* December 1936, 5). Apparent in this text—as in so many other commercial appeals to potential buyers—is the idea that radio is an individually empowering technology that gives its owner a heretofore unavailable degree of control. A similar approach to individualized listening experiences is evident in Philco Auto Radio advertisements.

In the beginning, radio was a complementary technology to the American automobile rather than a standard feature. Although radio and the automobile were heralded as conquering distance and bridging geographical separation among people, both engendered separation and isolation on a great scale. Philco claims to provide radios for twenty-eight to thirty domestic and foreign automobile manufacturers. While the technologies of cars and radios shared many characteristics in the context of 1930s American culture, their link is largely predicated upon and enhanced by their privatized, individualized nature, which further atomized social life, leading to isolation. Sennett argues,

> Isolation [has] two senses. First, it means that the inhabitants or workers in an urban high-density structure are inhibited from feeling any relationship to the milieu in which the structure is set. Second, it also means that as one can isolate oneself in a private automobile for freedom of movement, one ceases to believe that one's own surroundings have any meaning save as a means toward the end of one's own motion (1974, 14–15).

Linking their products to automotive brands such as DeSoto, Nash, or Plymouth, the Philco advertisements implicitly connect the privatized experiences of both technologies. For instance, a Philco message for Nash notes that "now comes the time when you spend more hours behind the wheel ... get more pleasure from your car. Get the most pleasure by carrying the world of radio with you wherever you go!" (*Saturday Evening Post* May 9, 1936, 2). The emphasis on pleasure and its privatized nature is a key appeal in this and other advertisements, while utilitarian or functional appeals are absent. Technologies are draped completely in notions of individualized entertainment bliss, like "all rides are happier when your DeSoto has a Philco!" (*Saturday Evening Post* August 29, 1936, 2). The obsession for driving and riding in automobiles as a social experience may have inspired Philco to design auto radios that enhanced the listening experiences of passengers and drivers. An advertisement for the Studebaker auto radios asserts, "'Back—Seat' riders in the 1936 Studebakers find new joy in automobile radio! The speaker of [the] custom-built Studebaker-Philco is mounted above the windshield ... assuring perfect radio reception to every passenger" (*Saturday Evening Post* April 11, 1936, 2). Interestingly, the advertisement offers two auto radio models for this Studebaker, "President Control" or "Dictator Control." Although their differences are not detailed beyond a visual representation, their labels seem to reflect the political realities at this time in Germany, Italy, and Spain—or the presidential election year in the United States.

Automobiles and radios are presented as technologies conquering space and distance. For instance, Philco advertises its radio sets as vehicles for aural travel from the comfort of the private home to faraway places. Many of the advertisements feature images of different places and people, while the text reinforces the idea of travel by suggesting what one could hear in those places. To this end, most of Philco's more expensive radio sets feature short-wave bands, and the advertisements emphasize the availability of "foreign" programming. For instance, one text mentions that in addition to domestic programming, Philco radios give the listener "a round-trip ticket to dozens of foreign lands ... to be used whenever you are in the mood" (*Saturday Evening Post* March 21, 1936, 3). Thus, while radio provides the sounds of the world, in the American context it is still individualized. The "Philco Foreign Tuning System"—with a reproduction of the "New Spread Ban Dial" (actual size, according to the text)—devotes three bands to short-wave reception. Along with numeric frequency markers, the dial also indicates locations for specific cities and countries (i.e., Fiji Islands, Moscow, South and Central America). Accordingly, "[t]he 1937 Philco *Foreign Tuning System* brings in many more foreign stations ... and we have made it easy for you to find them." In fact, listening to short-wave broadcasts becomes a regular experience. "Europe ... South America ... Asia ... not as an occasional thrill, but as reliable, enjoyable sources of radio entertainment and education" (*Saturday Evening Post* May 30, 1936, 3).

Philco advertisements feature elaborate visual clues related to their explanations of programming choices. In the case of promoting the availability of short-wave reception, for instance, one sketch contains images of soldiers and politicians in ways that foreshadow the role of several nations in events that would lead to World War II. A line of Italian soldiers, right arms raised in the fascist salute, their mouths open, is positioned above Nazi storm troopers at a rally underneath blowing flags. Opposite stands a lone British guard in front of Big Ben, while the bottom part of the advertisement features a parliamentary body (perhaps the League of Nations assembly) in a semicircular chamber, flanked by what appears to be a marching formation of Soviet troops (judging by the silhouetted architecture in the background). This imagery reflects the salience of these nations in news events and is an indication of the political and military tensions in the world. The accompanying text reinforces—albeit generically—the importance of these states in the shaping of past and future events:

STATESMEN ... WARRIORS ... MEN OF BUSINESS, struggling to hold or to gain "a place in the sun!" ... Berlin! Rome! London! Paris! From their radio stations come the challenging tones of men of might—makers of history. Words that may change the whole course of international affairs ... sped to the four corners of the world by short-wave broadcasting ... the most powerful force for shaping public opinion diplomacy has ever commanded! Who can afford to miss what they say? (*Saturday Evening Post*, January 25, 1936, 3)

FIGURE 8.2 *Philco advertisement,* Saturday Evening Post, *1936. Reprinted with permission from Philips Electronics North America Corporation.*

The advertisement implies that radio—and in particular short-wave radio—is an important source for international news and information. It reinforces the notion of aural travel to foreign places and represents radio as a powerful channel for eavesdropping on the shaping of history.

Entertainment is likewise a destination for radio travel. An advertisement in *Collier's* (February 8, 1936, 6) features Latin-American music this way: "CARTA-GENA ... VALENCIA ... RIOBAMBA ... names as melodious as the music they send winging northward. Mere dots on the map a few years ago ... now familiar, friendly cities ... to which thousands tune regularly for the pulsating rhythms of Latin-American orchestras." Indeed, this Philco advertisement notes that radio made the foreign "dots on the map" "familiar" and "friendly," suggesting that American audiences would not care or even know about such places in the Southern Hemisphere prior to the arrival of radio. This appeal anticipates McLuhan's famous "global village" metaphor by almost thirty years. A small silhouette of South America precedes the textual portion of the advertisement to globally position the reader. This global connection is made explicit in ads in *Collier's*, for instance, where international broadcasts are discussed. This is also the only Philco advertisement to feature nonwhite Americans—specifically a quartet of male African American vocalists and four Native Americans. They were presented together with a guitar-playing cowboy and a big band, perhaps in an attempt to represent the cultural diversity in the United States while alluding to the musical content of such international broadcasts. The text notes that "[a] program originating in the United States will be rebroadcast by stations all over the world. Programs from Buenos Aires ... from the East Indies and from other faraway lands are to follow. Radio knits the world closer in a dramatic gesture" (*Collier's* August 22, 1936, 6).

Although Philco features news and international affairs content in its advertisements, entertainment—and in particular music—is frequently mentioned. In fact, a small visual representation of the radio—a standard feature of most Philco advertisements—is captioned, "A Musical Instrument of Quality." The association with music is direct—a Philco radio was not merely a means of reproduction but an actual instrument linking its operation to notions of individual creativity and control.

At the same time entertainment programming becomes more standardized. Spigel (1992, 29) credits the growing acceptance of radio as a household item to this development: "Program formats had been conventionalized ... so that the public could expect a certain kind of experience when tuning into a specific program type. Radio listening thus became a more familiar and habitual activity, one that seemed more naturally integrated into the rhythms of everyday life."

The entry into the home as an invasion of a private space is reflected in a number of advertisements that address the recognition of radio's potential in the home environment. For instance, an advertisement in *Good Housekeeping* (September 1936, 5) reflects the demographic sensitivity of broadcasters in programming specifically targeted at children—the text reassuringly notes, "[t]he youngest members of the family gather around the radio. It's time for 'The Singing Lady' ... their very own program. 'Little Boy Blue' she sings to a tinkling piano accompaniment ... and Mother can relax for a quarter-hour happy in the knowledge the children will be enthralled by Ireene Wicker's charming voice and story-telling magic." The image of a young girl, leaning forward with her chin cradled in the palms of her hands, reinforces the text. Another advertisement (*Saturday Evening Post* February 22, 1936, 3) pictures a small group of musicians surrounding formally dressed, dancing couples, while the text specifically notes the sensitivity of these entertainers to the accessibility of the home audience: "Ben Bernie wisecracks ... and 'all the lads' go to town. 'May we come in?' asks Seymour Simons ... and plays a rhythmical half-hour. Eddie Duchin ripples through a piano solo ... Benny Goodman demonstrates what swing tempo really means ... Meredith Wilson contributes 'chiffon jazz' from California."

The proximity of the action and the potential of ringside seating for all kinds of events becomes a particularly important issue when sports turned into a national pastime, and radio content capitalizes on the rising demands for coverage. For instance, a *Collier's* advertisement (May 16, 1936, 6) shows two boxers pensively facing each other in the ring. The text imitates an announcer detailing the match: "And there's the gong! Both men leave their corners fast" It continues to play on the realism of the broadcast match: "Hear the thudding impact of fighting-weight gloves landing on bare flesh ... all the color ... glamour ... excitement that surrounds a spectacular ring battle." Placing the listener in the event, the advertisement states, "Philco gives you a ring-side seat right up with the sports writers of the big newspapers," implicitly circumventing the traditional dominance of print media.

Along with sports, dramatic serials and daytime soap operas provide a regular focus for Philco advertisements, offering "moments of romance as you follow the stories of 'Helen Trent' and 'Betty and Bob,'" while providing "cheerful companionship all day long when Philco brings these entertaining visitors to your home!" (*Good Housekeeping* June 1936, 5). The image of a woman wearing an apron and preparing food as she peers at a small radio set accompanies the text and seems to suggest to the target audience, housewives, that radio is complementary to domestic work.

The idea that radio provides entertainment for the American home is supplemented by the notion that radio is necessary for everyone in a pluralistic, democratic society. Thus, Philco advertisements attempted to place radio within the sociopolitical culture of the United States by explicitly and implicitly demonstrating its necessity for the perpetuation of democracy and highlighting the plurality of broadcasting. The 1936 presidential election year was a rich source of explicit political material for Philco advertisements. For instance, in discussing the Republican National Convention, one advertisement (*Saturday Evening Post* April 4, 1936, 3) asks, "Will it be Hoover ... Borah or Knox? Landon ... McNary ... Vandenberg ...

or some dark horses? Admission to the Convention will be at a premium ... but through Philco you can attend every session ... catch all the fervor of nominating speeches ... time the length of each demonstration."

In addition to detailing the specifics of the convention, this Philco text also offers guidance to voters: "Ask your Philco dealer for a copy of the new 'Philco Political Radio Atlas'... just off the press! Full of advance information on both conventions; histories of the major parties; electoral vote maps; radio logs, etc." Likewise, Philco develops a complementary advertisement (*Collier's* April 4, 1936, 6) for the Democratic National Convention, complete with the image of a donkey speaking into a radio microphone. It states, "Philco brings you every thrill-packed moment ... every speech ... every ballot ... every rap of the Chairman's gavel!" and places radio at the crux of the delegates' machinations, while legitimating radio's place in the American political landscape. A third advertisement (*Collier's* October 31, 1936, 6) most clearly identifies radio's crucial informational role in a democracy. Situated within the overall context of the election, this advertisement assigns to radio a critical role in the timely broadcasting of results. A small image of Uncle Sam's profile, head bent downward as if in concentration, right hand cupped behind his ear as if he is listening intently, accompanies the text: "A newsgathering and tabulating organization more elaborate than radio has ever known feeds the networks with returns from coast to coast ... and Philco makes your home the nerve center to which they all report."

Finally, Philco defines radio as a vehicle of free speech. Focusing on a popular radio commentator, Boake Carter, the advertisement states that "no matter how controversial the topic ... no matter whose toes may be trod upon ... he is at liberty to voice his personal opinions and reactions ... Philco's year-round expression of its belief that freedom of speech means freedom of the air as well as of the press." (*Collier's* September 5, 1936, 6) The message is clear: Radio is an empowering technology that reinforces democracy and is protected by the First Amendment.

Other Philco advertisements forge representations of radio as a culturally democratic and pluralistic medium and project with an ethos of participation and accessibility. For instance, an advertisement in the *Saturday Evening Post* (January 11, 1936, 3) notes that in the past "only large cities heard Sousa lead the Marine Band ... " and that "only Washington and the larger cities enjoyed that privilege. There was no radio then to make the whole land one vast auditorium." Implicit in this passage is the presentation of radio as a democratic medium. It brings entertainment as a "privilege" to the homes of radio owners, thus leveling barriers of distance and class. Other Philco advertisements (*Collier's* January 11, 1936, 6) even imply that the ordinary radio listener could become a star on shows, like NBC's *Major Bowe's Amateur Hour*. It describes the program as one "in which contestants compare favorably with professionals. A program that has started many young artists toward radio stardom." Similarly, another advertisement (*Collier's* January 25, 1936, 6) describes one such aspiring star, "a ... girl who has hitch-hiked half way across the continent for this chance faces the microphone.

Truly the wheel of fortune is spinning! Will it be a radio career? Or will a single-stroke on that gong ... bring her air-castles crashing to earth? One real-life drama follows another." The programs portrayed in these Philco advertisements confirm and reinforce the pluralistic nature of radio and its boundless, democratic nature. Radio owners not only had the pleasure of listening to "ordinary" people, but they, too, had the chance to perform on radio.

The pluralistic nature of radio programming is conveyed by an advertisement (*Good Housekeeping* October 1936, 5) that states,

> The National Farm and Home Hour ... has probably done more to improve the relations between farm and city than any other single factor. City women tuning in for the music of Walter Blaufuss and the Homesteaders ... hear discussions of farm problems and activities ... learn about 4-H Clubs, the Future Farmers, harvest festivals ... pick up valuable hints on cooking, preserving, domestic economy.

In this presentation of Philco broadcasting technology, radio is portrayed as a link between farm and city, uniting the diverse American public through pluralistic programming. Philco advertisements represent radio not only as enhancing political democracy but also as reinforcing a democratic and pluralistic culture through entertainment.

Although graphically striking in their use of black-and-white sketches and large formats, Philco advertisements also exhibit great acumen in attempting to adapt radio to the American consumer. Implicitly recognizing and exploiting the cultural landscape of the United States, Philco attempts to sell much more than a mass-produced technology. The success of radio is founded on locating the medium within a culture that values individualism and private consumption and believes in democracy and pluralism. Additionally, the growing American desire for entertainment, news, and information—domestic and foreign—is used and reinforced in these Philco advertisements. Furthermore, an increasing acceptance of radio within the American home was engendering shifts in the culture. The targeting of radio sets—supported by specific programming—at discrete demographic groups such as children and women was complicit in the growing isolation and alienation of American life. While American radio is presented in part as a uniting force, specific commercial practices of broadcasting succeeded in creating a national system of unprecedented sophistication for the sale of consumer products.

The representation of radio in these advertisements promotes the idea that access to the audio world of middle- or upper-class America is within the financial range of many potential customers; radio sets listed from $20 to $750, depending on size and style (about $200 to $7,500 in 1999 dollars). Moreover, with radio there is no need to acquire wealth or move into the fashionable parts of town to participate in the flow of communication that characterizes centers of power and influence; with the purchase of a radio such participation was assured. Radio advertisements constructed a sense of equality that is to be achieved through affordable technology. They say nothing, however, about the monolithic control over program content through networks.

The other appeal of radio is its ability to cater to the desire for physical mobility. Consequently, when advertisements evoke the excitement of tuning in to American metropolitan areas like New York or Chicago, they also stress the availability of short-wave reception by indicating a potentially wide range of foreign stations. Reminiscent of fashionable overseas travel (by high society) to European centers of culture and recreation, these advertisements add a distinct international dimension to radio listening. Radio enables Americans to aurally travel abroad, especially to Europe and Latin America, and to tune in to current cultural and political events. The beginning of the Spanish Civil War, in particular, adds conflict and tension to such excursions via short-wave radio. With radio, immediacy becomes an important feature of modern communication, which enhanced its attraction.

Thus, radio promises mobility to its customers. It offers the potential of upward mobility through access to sophistication and physical or geographical mobility through the use of its short-wave technology.

By 1936 radio becomes an integral part of the American home through negotiations of its economic, technological, and aural nature vis-à-vis the social, cultural, and political characteristics of white, middle-class families. It does not arrive at the door of the American home as an eccentric stranger, but rather as a familiar newcomer bearing fruits that satiate the American palate with novel but not alien tastes. The material form is constructed to complement the home, and the technology is humanized. Radio is modern and technologically advanced yet accessible to the uninitiated. Technological advances are trumpeted as novelties that distinguish brands of sets that are otherwise interchangeable, encouraging purchase of the latest models. Listeners, when they appear in advertisements, are sophisticated members of the middle class or upper class; they underline and perpetuate the progressive nature of the technology and reinforce an ethos of consumption as a vehicle of class advancement. Radio is represented as a means of psychic and aural travel, a way of conquering barriers of national and international geography, providing access to the entertainment and news of the world to all. Likewise, radio emphasizes and reinforces American democracy with its linkage to overt political information and news, and its projection as a conduit for free speech. The emphasis on radio's all-inclusive (but in reality white, middle-class) programming meshed with the republic's belief—but not practice of—cultural pluralism. And, most important, given radio's domestic status, the technology is highlighted as subservient to individualized private use.

The sustained reinforcing of the radio experience through advertising creates a cultural niche for radio in the home and provides unprecedented access to consumers. Industrialization in the technological form of radio brings production to the American home in the form of consumption. It is an event that later comes to fruition with the new medium of television.

9

▼ ▼ ▼

Pierced Memories: On the Rhetoric of a Bayoneted Photograph

As the twentieth century wanes, it is worth remembering that its course—in contrast to earlier centuries—has been chronicled by a visual narrative that relies on the attraction of photographs as means of storing and disseminating information. The use of photographs remains a universal practice, executed in the public sphere by public media as well as in the private realm by private individuals. But regardless of the circumstances, photographs emerge as documents of a lived experience. And their presence in the contemporary cultural milieu of technologically enhanced and commercially driven communication practices has endured nearly unchallenged at the threshold of the twenty-first century.

Photographs are the story-telling companions of time. They direct the gaze of the spectator to ponder the past. Reflecting on our own lives, we often refer to photographs whose presence conditions our recollection of people and events and keeps them alive. Recently I came across a small family album from the 1920s and 1930s that had been left by an aunt who had saved it through times of expulsion, flight, and resettlement in West Germany. It had been severely cut—pierced but not destroyed by the thrust of a bayonet in 1945—when the invading Soviet army overran refugees and ransacked their belongings. Its sudden appearance in my life is a reminder of the power of photographs, the seductive specificity of the dated image, and the collective possibility of an extended visual narrative in considerations of memory. The violent markings of the photo album and its images, however, produce an equally powerful message that jars the memory as they disrupt and distort the photographic chronicle of her life and that of her family and friends. The result is a complex visual experience that addresses the use of images in producing knowledge and making history.

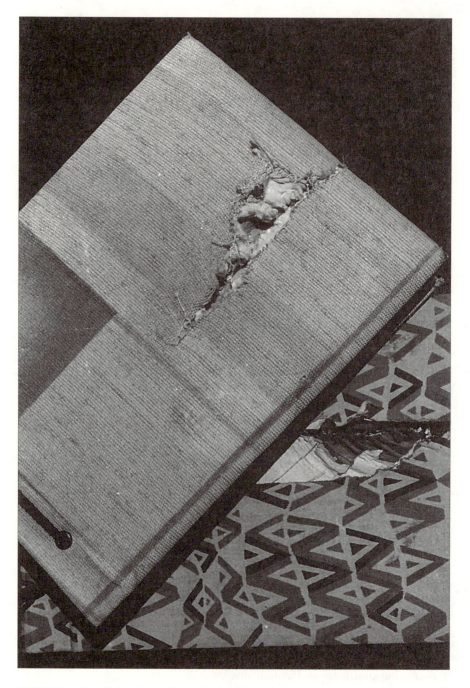

FIGURE 9.1 Untitled. *Hanno Hardt, 1998.*

Photographs are re-collections of the past. This chapter is about photography, memory, and history and addresses the relationship between photographic images and the need to remember; it is based on the notion that seeing is a prelude to historical knowledge and that understanding the past relies on the ability to imagine. At the same time, the role of thought and imagination in the production of society—as reflected in the earlier work of Louis Althusser (1970), Maurice Godelier (1984), and, perhaps more significantly, Cornelius Castoriadis (1975), suggests yet another role for photography in the construction of a social and cultural reality. Photographs in capitalist societies contribute to the production of information and participate in the surveillance of the environment, where their subjective and objective qualities are applied to the private uses of photographic images in the perpetuation of memory.

Photographs are also manifestations of time and records of experience. Consequently, writings on photographic theory are filled with references to representations of the past. Roland Barthes (1981, 76), for instance, writes about the location of photographs in history and confesses that "in Photography I can never deny *that the thing has been there*. There is a superimposition here: of reality and of the past." He also ponders the consequences of photographic imagery that is typically identified with the past and concludes that "in front of a photograph, our consciousness does not necessarily take the path of memory ... but for every photograph existing in the world, the path of certainty: the Photograph's essence is to ratify what it represents" (1981, 85). And what it represents is, at least for Barthes, always what has been rather than what is no longer. Because inevitably "every photograph is a certificate of presence" (1981, 87), photographs anticipate the decisive moment of convergence, when the past meets reality. For Susan Sontag (1973, 15) such a convergence is a reminder that "all photographs are *memento mori*," and she adds that to "take a photograph is to participate in another person's mortality, vulnerability, mutability." Under these circumstances the practice of photography becomes an intensely personal experience that exposes photographer and subject to the fragility of a shared moment and to a realization of life's uncertainties.

Photographs are also cultural products, and others have theorized the photograph in ways that reflect the role and function of photographs as a mode of communication in the cultural and political apparatus. They focus on the ideological in cultural theory in the context of theories of culture and cultural production (Berger 1980; Burgin 1982; Mitchell 1994). Thus, photography as cultural or even political practice constitutes a major terrain of historical inquiry that reinforces its importance in the rise of a contemporary visual culture and in the resulting issues of representation in modern society, including power and access to the means of production.

Photographs are related to notions of image and imagination, which are associated with the idea of memory. The latter has been an object of philosophical and rhetorical study since antiquity, and its use as a medium has been discussed by a number of authors (Casey 1987; Carruther 1990; Krell 1990; Mitchell 1994; Yates 1966). Mitchell (1994, 192) suggests, for instance, that "memory takes the form in classical rhetoric of a dialectic between the same modalities (space and time), the same sensory channels (the visual and aural), and the same codes (image and word) that underlies the narrative/descriptive boundary." He concludes—with Yates (1966)—that memory is an imagetext, a mental storage and retrieval system with intersubjective qualities involving the other as a social or cultural context. Much earlier Henri Bergson had developed a theory of memory in his *Matter and Memory* (1896), proposing that memory constitutes an intersection of mind and matter and displays the seamless succession of past and present. Bound up with his theory of duration, memory guarantees the survival of things remembered, which interact with present things in a continuous exchange of images. Indeed, as Michael Ann Holly (1996, 15) argues concerning artworks, "the continuum between the production of the work and its historical processing negates the distinctiveness of either pole." She recalls Jacques Lacan's observation that "when we look at a work of art, we find the work looking back at us, having anticipated our gaze." Photographs, too, bridge the conditions of their production and subsequent interrogations by history to challenge the physical and psychological orientation of the contemporary reader. But while the gaze may be returned, understanding and interpreting the photograph and its specific historical condition encounter problems of elucidation related to notions of seeing (as opposed to looking) and memory.

Recently, Andrea Liss (1998) has alluded to a crisis of interpretation in postmodern analyses by questioning the contemporary uses of photographs in the representations of Holocaust memory and history. In fact, according to Liss (1998, 1), "Questions of mimesis, strategies of empathy, the truth in fiction, the fiction in truth, and the tension between literalness and metaphor are always at work in documentary photographic representation." Photographs call on the historical consciousness of the reader and challenge the process of interpretation from within a specific historical moment. Consequently, reading a photograph is subject to the existential context in which it appears before the reader and relies on the process of converting memory into present knowledge. It is also hostage to the persuasive power of photography, which conquers the uncharted terrain of memory. Linda Haverty Rugg (1997, 23) proposes that the camera takes on the qualities of the mind; she states that "photography acquires the power to supplant memory, and our image of the mental process of remembering then comes to resemble photography." Her study of autobiographical uses of photography encounters the consistent strength of the metaphor over time as photography emerges as memory and eventually offers "a new arena for visualizing the structure of history" (1997, 25).

The idea of memory is particularly emphasized by social and cultural historians who discuss its role in the construction of history and of the image—or the imagined—as an expression about the past (Benjamin 1969; Samuel 1994; Le Goff

1992). Thus, "Memory is an essential element of ... individual or collective *identity*, the feverish and anxious quest for which is today one of the fundamental activities of individuals and society," according to Le Goff (1992, 98). But there is more than a semantic relationship between image and imagination. Both concepts relate to identity and memory and refer to a process of seeing, recognizing, and identifying; they rely on the eye and the mind to make sense of the world and, ultimately, on the familiar to describe the past.

Photographs attest to the conditions of the past. For instance, Barthes (1981, 89) argues that each photograph "possesses an evidential force, and that its testimony bears not on the object but on time." In fact, "from a phenomenological viewpoint, in the Photograph, the power of authentication exceeds the power of representation." For Victor Burgin (1982, 2), on the other hand, photography is "a practice of signification." The latter resides in society, and its major feature is its contribution to "the production and dissemination of meaning" for specific purposes and at a specific historical moment beyond the narrow range of technical or aesthetic concerns. His work reflects the more recent focus of cultural studies on the notion of meaning and meaning making in society; photography contributes to such practices and becomes a major source of interpreting and understanding the world.

Rhetorical analysis is yet another approach to examining photography; it was introduced as a model of analysis to the study of photographic meaning by Barthes (1977, 32–51), who raises questions about the infusion of meaning into an image and the ways of determining its location. Photographic messages, according to Barthes, are continuous messages, deeply embedded in the cultural fabric of society. Moreover, Allen Sekula (1982, 87) insists that "every photographic message is characterized by a tendentious rhetoric." But he recognizes at the same time that "the most generalised terms of the photographic discourse constitute a denial of the rhetorical function and a validation of the 'truth value' of the myriad propositions made within the system."

More specifically related to the concerns of this essay is Pierre Bourdieu's (1990, 30) work on photography, which refers to the capture of memory and the significance of the family album, in particular. He observes that photographing one's children "is to become the historiographer of their childhood and to prepare as an heirloom for them the image of what they used to be." For Bourdieu the "family album expresses the essence of social memory."

Photographs constitute a major site of theoretical considerations; despite philosophical or ideological differences, various authors confirm the location of photographs between the past and reality and agree on their role in the social and cultural processes of constructing meaning and making sense of one's existence. It is particularly useful, however, to understand the consequences of an "anticipated gaze," which suggests a qualitatively different presence of the photograph, introduces a challenge to the imagination that extends beyond the boundaries of the image, and involves complete immersion in the reading of photographs.

I share the theoretical concerns of these authors and relate the practice of photography and the social uses of the photograph—based on a critical reading of a
found photo album—to the popularity of photographs as expressions of power
and control. After all, photographs are identified with memory and the possibility
of providing a cultural and ideological grounding of experience. Their power derives from their ability to bridge time and space and to respond to the gaze of the
observer with their potential of tapping into memory.

Reading photographs suggests an understanding of communication not only
as the foundation of community but also as the cultural determinant of memory
and history. Indeed, memory and history meet at the site of photography, where
photographs are the text of memories waiting to be deciphered and the representations of historical "truths," revealing "what really happened." Reading photographs implies an acknowledgment of the past; moreover, in contemplating
personal experiences and the ways in which the past has been shaped and reconstructed, photographs help individuals become conscious of themselves as subjects of history. Such consciousness results in reconstructing a sense of belonging
to time and place as well as to the experience of others. And yet, as Alberto
Manguel (1996, 65) once observed about reading, "A text read and remembered
becomes, in that redemptive rereading, like the frozen lake in the poem I memo-
rized so long ago—as solid as land and capable of supporting the reader's cross-
ing, and yet, at the same time, its only existence is in the mind, as precarious and
fleeting as if its letter were written on water." Images are like that. After all, we
offer voice and vocabulary to a reading of pictures, which are burned into our
memory but remain unfixed like colorful dreams.

But photographs also constitute the record of a time; collectively they offer an
eyewitness account of history that reflects an imagined world of relationships
among people and objects. Photographs offer proof of past lives, and they sustain
their power of a personal expression of a time; they breed familiarity and confirm
the social or cultural identity that contributes to a definition of self. Photographs
acquire importance with their ability to capture and preserve the authenticity of a
specific historical moment as they describe various states of being. Their attraction as culture-specific texts, their familiarity as a technology of communication—particularly reflected in family photographs—and their ease of accessibility
explain their popularity.

Photographs possess rhetorical dimensions that relate to informational and
persuasive qualities of a visual narrative, ranging from emotional to intellectual
appeals of representation. They occur in the process of "looking" or "seeing," two
qualitatively different approaches to the reading of photographic messages. As
photographs enter the stream of everyday communication, they become visual
markers of a public discourse that relies on the image as text, on the text as context, and on the context as confirmation of the ideological foundations of community. Photographs are looked at but rarely seen under these circumstances. Indeed, such a use of photographs—and of visual images in general—has become a

common cultural practice that reflects the impact of the visual on the process of textual or verbal communication and that shapes the understanding of people, institutions, and processes. Seeing, on the other hand, refers to an attempt to reconstruct the experience of the photograph by exploring the deep structure of the image; it involves the application of practical knowledge and creative insights and relies on the historical consciousness of the reader.

There is a unique formality about the typical family photograph that speaks directly to the time or distance of the image. Family photographs are signifiers of a collective life; they are evidence of social standing or material wealth, although their real importance lies in their ability to create the experience of a living history. The family photograph offers social and psychological enhancements as it confirms social relations and the personal standing of the individual. In fact, it is a constant reminder of a connectedness—like kinship or friendship—that is essentially human and responds to a universal desire to belong. This is particularly true—and significant—in times of disrupted or disconnected relations among people, including times of war, when isolation and displacement become the rule. In those moments the family photograph provides reassurance; it reconnects individuals and addresses the lost balance between public and private moments by helping the individual recapture a sense of the social self which offers strength in desperate times.

Family photographs, in particular, deliver the text of memories; they refer to the shared experiences of the past, which rely on the proximity between community and communication. Thus, the authority of the family photograph reveals itself to the reader in the process of discovery with its insistence on being a passage into the real social conditions of individuals, their intellectual and material being, and their relations to others. Family photographs provide the opportunity for the reader-as-relative to penetrate the surface of the image and its aesthetic qualities and to enter into the concrete details of previous existences. They always invite looking, but the expectation of seeing lingers on, offering recognition and acknowledgment of kinship.

Not surprisingly, in times of war and physical displacement, photographs are gathered up to find their place in the baggage of a refugee existence, where they reside among the rescued possessions of a disrupted life. Taking a photograph on a journey without return and harboring it through periods of personal hardship and disaster speaks not only to the general appreciation of the visual and its specific task in twentieth-century social life, but it also reinforces the textuality of memory and confirms the need for its physical representation. Photographs as open and yet undeciphered texts invite interpretation, but since they also facilitate instantaneous storage and recall of experience, they represent the inability to forget. Individual memory depends on such an inability, and collective memory builds on it as photographs assist in the process of remembering.

The reappearance of old photographs in the postwar bourgeois milieu of 1945 Europe, for instance, frequently signaled the reconstruction of the past to confirm the concrete historical conditions of a previous life vis-à-vis a hostile and suspicious environment and the failing memories of an aging refugee. This was particularly important for establishing legal claims over property, for instance, but it was equally significant for reasserting the social and economic conditions of a previous way of life. More than fifty years later, family photographs help document the former life of Europe's latest refugees in Kosovo, Bosnia, or Croatia. The need to remember has not changed, and neither has the use of photographs, now typically in color, as portable memories and accessible evidence.

Photographs that endure become the visual building blocks of a biographical narrative; they solicit reflection on relations among individuals, places, and events and aid in the search for a lost identity and in the rehabilitation of a shattered existence. They also reestablish a sense of place and time by revisiting the sites of social and cultural identity and by locating the displaced individual in a specific moment of history.

But they also recall the initial intent of taking photographs and preserving them—as in photo albums, for instance. Photographing family members, specifically, is a process of controlling and directing private memories to certain ends while contributing—collectively and unconsciously—to the construction of a cultural history that privileges the subjective and the idea of individual articulation.

The photo album is an objectification of memory; as a cultural artifact it provides an intense and cumulative visual narrative within specific structural boundaries. These boundaries are dictated by cultural considerations and the creative possibilities of selection and display as well as by the physical limitations of the volume itself. The photo album contains a flow of personal history, typically in chronological order and frequently reinforced by words and dates to fix meanings and to locate the images securely between the growing vagueness of a fading memory and the eternal quest for certainty and historical truths. Series of photographic images are a rich source of biography; they confirm the familiarity of a social milieu and reinforce the feeling of being among family and friends while providing multiple sets of visual evidence and points of factual validation.

By the conditions of its selection and survival, the refugee's photograph represents an often arbitrary choice of evidence; since it is the only tangible sign of a personal presence elsewhere, the photographic image stands for a set of complex relations between the belief in its infinite power of representation and the personal desire to preserve a specific reality. Photographs serve a need for arresting time—for a return to the past, and for resurrecting faces and places—which is never greater than in moments of physical upheaval and psychological crisis that provoke a yearning for a return to permanence and stability. They offer conversations with the details of the captured moment. In fact, their capacity to reveal the details of past lives is only limited by the experience of the reader and the lack of proximity between image and imagination. The lasting photograph transcends the documentary qualities it undoubtedly possesses and emerges as a measure of the depth of memory, which provides comfort and restores self-respect in the face of human disaster. At the same time, the presence of photographs overcomes and eventually defeats other forms of recollection, ranging from the vaguely remembered but lost photographic image to memory itself. The absence of a complete recollection of people or events is replaced by the availability of specific photographic proof that shapes an understanding of the past. Faces and gestures remain in our presence because of photographs, while voices and sounds recede irretrievably into the past, since looking at photographs rarely restores the aural dimension of an individual but confirms the limitations of the photograph as a visual means of preserving the past.

Violence to memory is painful and irreversible. The attempt to destroy the visual links to the past reveals more than the savagery of the attacker; since the act of saving a photograph signifies a strong interest in the textuality of memory and the presence of tradition, the photograph encourages a perception of a powerful source of maintaining and reinforcing a sense of rootedness. The deliberate and blinding stab of the bayonet into the body of the photo album derives from an intense antagonism not only against the physical representation of the enemy but also against the potential of memory and the idea of history as a subjective construction of the past.

In the attempt to destroy memories or eradicate a historical moment, violence stops time and creates a new visual experience. The rough edges of the pierced photographs throughout the album constitute a permanent visual record of yet another, equally real experience that is more abstract, brutal, and direct in its effect on the reader, who is drawn into a text that is immersed in the conditions of war. In fact, the pierced pages and the slashed images of innocent subjects disclose the disappearance of privacy in times of war and alter the popular conception of the album as a coveted private sphere. The slashing of the photographs also acknowledges their power as documentary evidence and the undeniable fact of biography. If war is about death and destruction, it can never succeed, however, in a violent denial of the human spirit, the memories of the past, or the feelings of connectedness to people and places. Since photographs reinforce these human tendencies, mutilating rather than destroying them suggests a strategy of permanent violence based on the knowledge of images and their position as objects of reflection and introspection in the private lives of individuals. Cutting the photographic image is an expression of power relations; it signifies the vulnerability of the victim and the fragility of the photograph itself. Piercing the photograph is also a process of destabilizing memory, resulting—perhaps more importantly—in superimposing a new text, that is, the memory of the act of violence itself. Consequently, photographs and the incision merge irrevocably to reproduce a different memory as history and biography are reconfigured permanently by the thrust of the bayonet.

While injuries to the human body heal—with scars to recall pain and suffering—the blow to the photograph creates a permanent cut without recovery of the object. The wound remains open and projects its violent nature into the memory

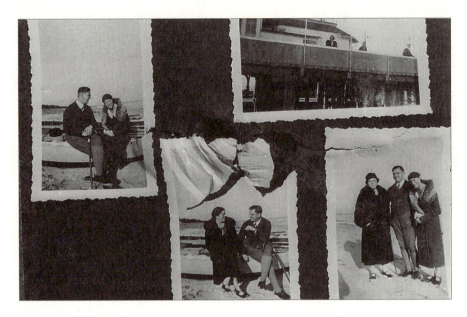

FIGURE 9.2 Untitled. *Hanno Hardt, 1998.*

of the past, disrupting the traditional reading of the photograph. Indeed, the incision creates a physical and psychological distance between image and reader, suggesting a new measure, which privileges the imagery of violence and pushes the photograph-as-experience into a more distant past. The violent cut is also the manifestation of a traumatic experience, the visible result of a physical assault, superimposed upon the imagery of an ordinary life.

Both the slashed photograph and the violated album are signs of a disrupted life and are permanent reminders of a destructive force that separates the image from its historical meaning and incorporates the memory of displacement and destruction into the photo album as a physical representation of history. At the same time, the distance between the inaccessibility of the traumatic experience and the visibility of the defaced photographs raises questions about whether history can ever be comprehensively told by reading the visual evidence.

And yet the cutting of the photograph is a futile attempt to destroy the memory of other times and places and to deny the evidence of biography. The bayonet may have cut through the lives of people, defaced the imagery of past experiences, and destroyed the physical autonomy of private memories, but it could not eradicate history or displace the resilience of memory. On the contrary, the slashed photograph survives in its incompleteness and gives rise to new interpretations and confidence to those in search of understanding their own lives, those who trust that the power of memory and the evidence of history always survive, albeit changed by the concerns of the present.

The saved photograph represents an inevitable compromise between the dangers of forgetting and the promise of recalling the details of a visual encounter with people and places. It must stand for other photographs, innumerable and irreplaceable, that chronicle the lives of individuals. Selected for its documentary value or its emotional appeal—or hastily gathered to maintain a visual link with a private history—the saved photograph reflects the refusal to relinquish the past. Thus, a photograph among the belongings of the refugee provides physical evidence of a place in history, a previous existence, and knowledge of a different way of life; at the same time, it is a sign of individual worth, bourgeois values, and the potential of personal memory.

In the latter sense, the photograph becomes an expression of freedom as its imagery soars above oppression and the threat of destruction, connecting the mind of the reader with the thoughts and actions of earlier times. Photographs are also about worlds of ideas; they relate the intellectual and emotional lives, private values, and public convictions of those looking out at the reader. They are the innocent actors in a profound human drama that spans generations as people and places furnish the text that fuels memory and that constitutes history.

Yet family photographs also have an ideological grounding; they are typically the product of a bourgeois existence, representing the material conditions of life while reinforcing specific values, like the notion of family itself. The production and collection of photographs in this context responds to the desire to reproduce and perpetuate status and power and achieve immortality. The preservation of the photographic image requires modest means, frequently in the form of frames (for public display in the family home) or albums (for private purposes of collection and review). In fact, the photo album becomes a fashionable showcase of family values and accomplishments, however personal, and a chronicle of significant events in the life of the family.

Bourdieu (1990, 30–31) observes that family photographs, arranged chronologically, "evoke and communicate the memory of events which deserve to be preserved because the group sees a factor of unification in the monuments of its past unity or ... because it draws confirmation of its present unity from its past: this is why there is nothing more decent, reassuring, and edifying than the family album." Each of its photographs contributes to the making of a personal history—augmenting the typical series of ritualized poses and studied postures of confidence and good will; the latter complicate the understanding of photographic images when assumptions about the nature of the photograph as visual evidence clash with its actual use as promotion or propaganda.

Consequently, history is but a picture story, carefully composed to fabricate a vision of the family that corresponds to bourgeois ideals. Photographs and their arrangements in albums may reflect personal taste, but they are also the expression of a specific worldview and become objects of empowerment for those depicted as well as for those in control of producing and claiming the album in their possession. Their intent challenges the knowledge and interest of the reader, the ability to relate to the ideological context, and, therefore, the capacity to appreciate the feeling of connectedness as the photographic image begins to resemble life.

The experience of coming across photographs with their wartime markings, finally, is a reminder of the importance of memory. Memory engages experience and constructs a private vision of the world in which the past is continuously forged from the concerns and preoccupations of the present. In fact, when Walter Benjamin (1969, 255) observes that "every image of the past that is not recognized by the present as one of its own concerns threatens to disappear irretrievably," he refers to a crisis of memory and the problem of forgetting. More recently, Paul Virilio (1995, 144–45) addresses the acceleration of historical time and warns that "computing speed is now leading to the possible 'industrialization' of forgetting and lack." Speed kills, and the speed of events destroys historical reality. He concludes that in the near future "we will not only miss history … we will also long to go back to space and times past." Under these circumstances history constitutes a fading response to the search for knowledge and the location of human interests against a rising desire for experiencing the past.

Photographs provide opportunities for disrupting and restructuring history with their appeal to memory; they privilege the subjective, creative power of the personal account against the power of received history. Photographs are the texts of future possibilities as memory engages the image in a dialogue about the past under emotionally—and perhaps politically—charged conditions. Memory assesses and readjusts official history; it may also reduce the acceleration of events by reversing the disconnection of objective appearances from reality.

While film and television epitomize the serialization of images in contemporary culture and contribute to the process of acceleration, photographs represent a different dimension of time. They are much more akin to traditional textual practices with their tolerance for contemplation and speculation—even reconsideration. Photographs, like books or magazines, can be revisited; they are portable records whose accessibility is virtually unlimited in the public sphere. Their use is always private, like the process of reading, and requires intellectual engagement to penetrate the veil of gesture and mime in the age of photography and to appreciate the gaze of the image.

Personal images, like family photographs, offer an emotional and even ideological grounding for memory to remind us of these differences and the need to expand on our inability to forget in order to understand the present. The discovery of a family album—ravaged by the point of a bayonet—stops time and initiates reflections on the conditions of history and the role of photographs in the creation of self-knowledge as memory connects images with time and space to reveal the buried treasures of past experiences. It is a ritual of re-collection as the image returns the gaze of the spectator.

References

▼ ▼ ▼

Chapter 1

Barthes, Roland. 1967. "Le discours d'histoire." Informations sur les Sciences Sociales, 4:65–75.

Culler, Jonathan. 1976. "Literary History, Allegory and Semiology." *New Literary History* 7:2 (Winter), 259–70.

Hardt, Hanno. 1995. "Without the Rank and File: Journalism History, Media Workers, and Problems of Representation." In Hanno Hardt and Bonnie Brennen, eds., *Newsworkers: Towards a History of the Rank and File*. Minneapolis: University of Minnesota Press, 1–29.

Kracauer, Siegfried. 1995. *The Mass Ornament: Weimar Essays*. Edited and translated by Thomas Y. Levin. Cambridge: Harvard University Press.

Lukàcs, Georg. 1981. *Essays on Realism*. Cambridge, MA: MIT Press.

Williams, Raymond. 1977. *Marxism and Literature*. London: Verso.

Chapter 2

America Today: A Book of Hundred Prints. 1936. New York: American Artists' Congress.

Barthes, Roland. 1975. *S/Z*. London: Cape.

Baur, John I. H. 1975 (1960). *Philip Evergood*. New York: Harry N. Abrams.

Bekken, John. 1995. "Newsboys: The Exploitation of 'Little Merchants' by the Newspaper Industry." In Hanno Hardt and Bonnie Brennen, eds., *Newsworkers: Toward a History of the Rank and File*. Minneapolis: University of Minnesota Press, 190–226.

Bogart, Michele H. 1997. *Artists, Advertising, and the Borders of Art*. Chicago: University of Chicago Press.

Brennen, Bonnie. 1993. *"Peasantry of the Press": A History of American Newsworkers from Novels, 1919–1938*. Unpublished dissertation. University of Iowa.

———. 1995. "Cultural Discourse of Journalists. The Material Conditions of Newsroom Labor." In Hanno Hardt and Bonnie Brennen, eds., *Newsworkers: Toward a History of the Rank and File*. Minneapolis: University of Minnesota Press, 75–109.

Brooks, Van Wyck. 1970. "The Culture of Industrialism," in Robert Sklar, ed., *The Plastic Age, 1917–1930*. New York: Braziller, 110–118.

Butler Institute of American Art. 1996. *Visions of America. Urban Realism*. Youngstown, OH: Butler Institute of American Art.

Butor, Michel. 1969. *Les Mots dans la Peinture*. Paris: Editions d'Art Albert Skira.

Calvino, Italo. 1988. *Six Memos for the Next Millennium*. Cambridge: Harvard University Press.

Clark, T. C. 1985. *The Painting of Modern Life*. New York: Knopf.

Debord, Guy. 1992. *Society of the Spectacle and Other Films*. London: Rebel Press.

Edelman, Murray. 1997. *From Art to Politics: How Artistic Creations Shape Political Conceptions*. Chicago: University of Chicago Press.

Ekedal, Ellen and Susan Barnes Robinson. 1986. *The Spirit of the City. American Urban Paintings, Prints, and Drawings, 1900–1952*. Los Angeles: Laband Art Gallery.

Finkelstein, Sidney. 1947. *Art and Society*. New York: International Publishers.

———. 1974. "Art as Humanization." In Maynard Solomon, ed. *Marxism and Art. Essays Classic and Contemporary*. New York: Random House, 277–280.

Flint, Janet. 1980. *Art for All: American Print Publishing Between the Wars*. Washington, D.C.: Smithsonian Institution Press.

Foucault Michel. 1977. *Discipline and Punish: Birth of the Prison*. New York: Pantheon.

Fritzsche, Peter. 1996. *Reading Berlin 1900*. Cambridge: Harvard University Press.

Graphic Works of the American Thirties. A Book of Hundred Prints. 1977. New York: DaCapo Press.

Greenwald, Maurine W. and Margo Anderson, eds. 1996. *Pittsburgh Surveyed: Social Science and Social Reform in the Early Twentieth Century*. Pittsburgh: University of Pittsburgh Press.

Hardt, Hanno and Bonnie Brennen, eds. 1995. *Newsworkers: Toward a History of the Rank and File*. Minneapolis: University of Minnesota Press.

Hardt, Hanno. 1979. *Social Theories of the Press: Early German and American Perspectives*. Beverly Hills: Sage.

Harrison, Charles and Paul Wood, eds. 1992. *Art in Theory, 1900–1990: An Anthology of Changing Ideas*. Oxford: Blackwell.

Hauser, Arnold. 1951. *The Social History of Art*. 4 vols. New York: Vintage.

Hicks, Granville et al., eds. 1935. *Proletarian Literature in the United States: An Anthology*. New York: International Publishers.

Jay, Martin. 1988. "Scopic Regimes of Modernity." In Hal Foster, ed., *Vision and Visualty: Discussions in Contemporary Culture 2*. Seattle, WA: Bay Press, 3–23.

Jenks, Chris. 1995. "The Centrality of the Eye in Western Culture: An Introduction." In Chris Jenks, ed., *Visual Culture*. London: Routledge, 1–25.

Kainen, Jacob. 1972. "The Graphic Arts Division of the Federal Art Project." In Francis V. O'Connor, ed., *The New Deal Art Projects: An Anthology of Memoirs*. Washington, D. C.: Smithonian Institution Press.

Kraeft, June and Norman Kraeft. 1984. *Great American Prints. 1900–1950*. New York: Dover.

Merleau-Ponty, Maurice. 1962. *Phenomenology of Perception*. London: Routledge & Kegan Paul.

Morse, Peter. 1969. *John Sloan's Prints: A Catalogue Raisonné*. New Haven: Yale University Press.

Mott, Frank Luther. 1950. *American Journalism. A History of Newspapers in the United States Through 260 Years: 1690 to 1950*. New York: Macmillan.

North, Joseph, ed. 1969. *New Masses: An Anthology of the Rebel Thirties*. New York: International Publishers.

Paret, Peter. 1997. *Imagined Battles: Reflections of War in European Art.* Chapel Hill: University of North Carolina Press.

Park, Marlene and Gerald E. Markowitz. 1977. *New Deal for Art.* Hamilton, NY: Gallery Association of New York State.

Read, Herbert. 1966. *Art and Society.* New York: Schocken.

Schapiro, Meyer. 1992. "The Social Bases of Art." (originally published in 1936) In Charles Harrison and Paul Wood, eds., *Art in Theory, 1900–1990: An Anthology of Changing Ideas.* Oxford: Blackwell, 510.

Soyer, Ralph. 1967. *Self-Revealment.* New York: Maecenas Press.

Susman, Warren, ed. 1973. *Culture and Commitment: 1929–1945.* New York: Braziller.

Terdiman, Richard. 1985. *Discourse/Counter-Discourse: The Theory and Practice of Symbolic Resistance in Nineteenth-Century France.* Ithaca, NY: Cornell University Press.

Whiting, Cecile. 1989. *Antifascism in American Art.* New Haven: Yale University Press.

Wolf, Janet. 1991. *The Social Production of Art.* New York: New York University Press.

The Artists and Their Works in this Essay Are Listed in Alphabetical Order

Bacon, Peggy. *Crosspatch (The Titan).* Lithograph. 1929. In Kraeft & Kraeft, 1984, 6.

Cikovsky, Nicolai. *On the East River.* Lithograph. Mid-1930s. In Kraeft & Kraeft, 1984, 26.

Citron, Minna Wright. *An Honest Living.* Etching. 1934. In Ekedal & Robinson, 1986, 15.

Evergood, Philip Howard Francis. *Still Life.* Lithograph. 1944. In Kraeft and Kraeft, 1984, 46; *Street Corner.* Oil on canvas. 1936. In Baur, 1975, 44; *The Forgotten Man.* Ca. 1949. Oil. In Baur, 1960, 66.

Haupers, Clement. *Metro 1st Class.* Etching. 1928. In Kraeft & Kraeft, 1984, 59.

Lewis, Martin. *Cathedral Steps.* Drypoint. 1931. In Ekedal and Robinson, 1986, 38; *Subway Steps.* Drypoint. 1930. In Kraeft and Kraeft, 1984, 91.

Locke, Charles. *The Evening Paper.* Lithograph. Ca. 1925. In Ekedal & Robinson, 1986, 39.

Marsh, Reginald. *Hauptmann Must Die.* Egg Tempera. 1935. In Butler, 1996, 81; *2nd Avenue El.* Etching. 1929. In Kraeft and Kraeft, 1984, 97; *Why not Use the El?* Egg Tempera. 1930. In Butler, 1996, 41.

Mastro-Valerio, Alessandro. *Morning Paper.* Mezzotint. 1941. In Kraeft & Kraeft, 1984, 98.

Sloan, John. *Nude and Newspaper.* Etching. 1933. In Morse, 1969, 307; *Sunbathers on the Roof.* Etching. 1941. In Kraeft & Kraeft, 1984, 121; *The Woman's Page.* Etching. 1905. In Morse, 1969, 141.

Soyer, Isaac. *Cafeteria.* Oil on canvas. 1930. In Butler, 1996, 70.

Soyer, Raphael. *Window Shopper.* Oil on canvas. 1938. In Butler, 1996, 76.

CHAPTER 3

Althusser, Louis. 1971. Lenin and Philosophy and Other Essays. New York: Monthly ReviewPress.

Brik, Osip. 1992. "From Picture to Calico-Print." In Charles Harrison and Paul Wood, eds., *Art in Theory, 1900–1990.* London: Blackwell, 324–328.

———. 1992. "Photography versus Painting." In Charles Harrison and Paul Wood, eds., *Art in Theory, 1900–1990.* London: Blackwell, 454–457.

Buhle, Paul. 1987. *Marxism in the USA: From 1870 to the Present Day.* London: Verso.

Bukharin, Nicolai. 1969. *Historical Materialism: A System of Sociology.* Ann Arbor: University of Michigan Press.

Elliott, David, ed. 1979. *Alexander Rodchenko.* Oxford: Museum of Modern Art.

Hopkins, Mark W. 1974. "Media, Party, and Society in Russia." In Alan Wells, ed., *Mass Communications: A World View.* Palo Alto, CA: National Press Book, 42–72.

Lenin, V. I. 1961. *Collected Works.* 45 volumes. Moscow: Progress Publishers. (Selections on the press are reprinted in M. Saifulin, ed. 1972. *Lenin About the Press.* Prague: International Organization of Journalists.)

Michelson, Annette, ed. 1984. *Kino-Eye: The Writings of Dziga Vertov.* Berkeley: University of California Press.

Lukàcs, Georg. 1980. *Essays on Realism.* Cambridge, MA: MIT Press.

Oktober. 1992. "Declaration." In Charles Harrison and Paul Wood, eds. *Art in Theory, 1900–1990.* London: Blackwell, 465–467.

Rodchenko, Aleksandr. 1928. " Newspaper," a photo essay. *30 Dnei* 12, 49–63.

———. 1929. "TASS is Speaking," a photo essay. *30 Dnei* 11, 12–19.

Saianskii, Leonid. 1928. "Newspaper." *30 Dnei* 12, 49–63.

Tretyakov, Sergei. 1992. "We Raise the Alarm." In Charles Harrison and Paul Wood, eds., *Art in Theory, 1900–1990.* London: Blackwell, 459–462.

Trotsky, Leon. 1992. "Literature and Revolution" (excerpts). In Charles Harrison and Paul Wood, eds., *Art in Theory, 1900–1990.* London: Blackwell, 427–432.

Tupitsyn, Margarita. 1996. *The Soviet Photograph, 1924–1937.* New Haven: Yale University Press.

CHAPTER 4

Barthes, Roland. 1981. Camera Lucida. Reflections on Photography. New York: Hill and Wang.

Barthes, Roland. 1983. *Mythologies.* St. Albans, U.K.: Granada.

Benjamin, Walter. 1977. "Kleine Geschichte der Fotografie." In *Das Kunstwerk im Zeitalter seiner technischen Reproduzierbarkeit.* Frankfurt: Edition Suhrkamp, 45–64.

———. 1986. "The Author as Producer." In Peter Demetz, ed., *Walter Benjamin: Reflections. Essays, Aphorisms, Autobiographical Writings.* New York: Schocken, 220–238.

Brecht, Bertolt. 1975. "An der Schwelle des zweiten Jahrzehnts." In Heinz Willmann, *Geschichte der Arbeiter-Illustrierten Zeitung, 1921–1938.* Berlin: Dietz, 125.

de Mendelssohn, Peter. 1959. *Zeitungsstadt Berlin. Menschen und Mächte in der Geschichte der deutschen Presse.* Berlin: Ullstein.

Eisenstaedt, Alfred. 1969. *The Eye of Eisenstaedt, Life Photographer.* London: Thames and Hudson.

Eskildsen, Ute. 1978. "Photography and the Neue Sachlichkeit Movement." In David Mellor, ed., *Germany: The New Photography, 1927–33.* London: Arts Council of Great Britain.

FAZIT: Ein Querschnitt durch die deutsche Publizistik. 1929. Berlin: Neuer Deutscher Verlag.

Gay, Peter. 1968. *Weimar Culture: The Outsider as Insider.* New York: Harper and Row.

Gidal, Tim N. 1972. *Deutschland—Beginn des modernen Photojournalismus.* Luzern: Bucher.

Grunberger, Richard. 1971. *The 12-Year Reich. A Social History of Nazi Germany. 1933–45.* New York: Holt, Rinehart and Winston.

Hale, Oron J. 1964. *The Captive Press in the Third Reich*. Princeton: Princeton University Press.

Hardt, Hanno. 1989. "Pictures for the Masses: Photography and the Rise of Popular Magazines in Weimar Germany." *Journal of Communication Inquiry* 13:1 (Winter), 7–29.

_____. 1992 "Social Uses of Radio in Germany: An American Perspective, 1924–30." *Journal of Communication Inquiry* 16:2 (Summer), 7–20.

Heidegger, Martin. 1974. "The Age of the World Picture." In *The Question Concerning Technology*. New York: Harper & Row, 134–64.

_____. 1962 (1927). *Being and Time*. New York: Harper and Row.

Hicks, Wilson. 1952. *Words and Pictures*. New York: Arno Press.

Hoernle, Edwin. 1978. "The Working Man's Eye." In David Mellor, ed., *Germany. The New Photography. 1927–33*. London: Arts Council of Great Britain, 47–49.

Hofmannsthal, Hugo von. 1921. "Der Ersatz für die Träume." In *Das Tagebuch* 2, 685–87.

Horkheimer, Max and Theodor W. Adorno. 1972. *Dialectic of Enlightenment*. New York: Herder and Herder.

Kerbs, Diethart, Walter Uka and Brigitte Walz-Richter. 1983. *Die Gleichschaltung der Bilder. Zur Geschichte der Pressefotografie, 1930–36*. Berlin: Fröhlich & Kaufman.

Khan-Magomedov, Selim O. 1987. *Rodchenko: The Complete Work*. Edited by Vieri Quilici. Cambridge: MIT Press.

Kisch, Egon Erwin. 1972 (1925). "Foreword" in *Der Rasende Reporter. Hetzjagd durch die Zeit. Wagnisse in aller Welt. Kriminalistisches Reisebuch*. Vol. 5. In B. Uhse and G. Kisch, eds., *Gesammelte Werke in Einzelausgaben*. 8 vols. Berlin: Aufbau.

Korff, Kurt. 1994. "Die Illustrierte Zeitschrift." In Anton Kaes, Martin Jay, and Edward Dimendberg, eds., *The Weimar Republic Sourcebook*. Berkeley: University of California Press, 646–647.

Kracauer, Siegfried. 1977. *Das Ornament der Masse*. Frankfurt: Suhrkamp.

_____. 1995. *The Mass Ornament: Weimar Essays*. Cambridge: Harvard University Press.

Lania, Leo. 1926. "Reportage als Soziale Funktion." In *Die Literarische Welt* 2:26, 5.

Laqueur, Walter. 1974. *Weimar, a Cultural History, 1918–33*. New York: Putnam.

Lorant, Stefan. 1983. Interview with Stefan Lorant. Lenox, MA, May.

Lorsy, Ernst. 1994. "Die Stunde des Kaugummis." In Anton Kaes, Martin Jay, and Edward Dimendberg, eds., *The Weimar Republic Sourcebook*. Berkeley: University of California Press, 662–663.

Lukàcs, Georg. 1980. "Reportage or Portrayal?" In *Essays on Realism*. Cambridge: MIT Press, 1980, 45–75.

Man, Felix. 1984. *Man with Camera. Photographs from Seven Decades*. New York: Schocken.

Mellor, David. 1978. "London-Berlin-London: A Cultural History. The Reception and Influence of the New German Photography in Britain 1927–33." In David Mellor, ed., *Germany: The New German Photography 1927–1933*. London: Arts Council of Great Britain, 113–130.

Michelson, Annette, ed. 1984. *Kino-Eye: The Writings of Dziga Vertov*. Berkeley: University of California Press.

Mills, C. Wright. 1956. *The Power Elite*. New York: Oxford University Press.

Molderings, Herbert. 1978. "Urbanism and Technological Utopianism." In David Mellor, ed., *Germany: The New German Photography 1927–1933*. London: Arts Council of Great Britain, 87–94.

Mörchen, H. 1983. "Reportage und Dokumentarliteratur." In A. von Bormann und H. A. Glaser, eds., *Deutsche Literatur: Eine Sozialgeschichte.* Band 9: *Weimarer Republik–Drittes Reich–Avantgardismus–Parteilichkeit–Exil. 1918–1945.* Reinbek/Hamburg: Rowohlt, 180–188.

Riehl, Wilhelm H. 1990. *The Natural History of the German People.* Edited and translated by David J. Diephouse. Lewiston, NY: Edwin Mellen Press.

Roland, Günter. 1977. *Fotografie als Waffe. Geschichte der sozialdokumentarischen Fotografie.* Hamburg: VSA.

Saunders, Thomas J. 1994. *Hollywood in Berlin: American Cinema and Weimar Germany.* Berkeley: University of California Press.

Smith, C. Zoe. 1986a. "Fritz Goro: Emigre Photojournalist." *American Journalism* 3:4, 206–221.

_____. 1986b. "Black Star Picture Agency: Life's European Connection." *Journalism History* 13:1 (Spring), 19–24.

Sontag, Susan. 1977. *On Photography.* New York: Farrar, Straus and Giroux.

Stenbock-Fermor, Grad Alexander. 1931. *Deutschland von Unten. Reisen durch die Proletarische Provinz, 1930.* Stuttgart: J. Engelhorns.

Tucholsky, Kurt and John Heartfield. 1929. *Deutschland, Deutschland Über Alles.* Berlin: Neuer Deutscher Verlag.

Will, Wilfried van der and Rob Burns. eds. 1982. *Arbeiterkulturbewegung in der Weimarer Republik. Eine historisch-theoretische Analyse der kulturellen Bestrebungen der sozial-demokratisch organisierten Arbeiterschaft.* Frankfurt: Ullstein.

Willett, John. 1978. *Art and Politics in the Weimar Period.* New York: Pantheon.

Wulf, Joseph, ed. 1966. *Presse und Rundfunk im Dritten Reich. Eine Dokumentation.* Hamburg: rororo edition.

Zeitungs-Verlag. 1928a. "Die kulturelle Bedeutung des Zeitungsbildes." *Zeitungs-Verlag: Fachblatt für das gesamte Zeitungswesen* 29: March 31, 637–640.

_____. 1928c. "Der Presse-Photograph." *Zeitungs-Verlag: Fachblatt für das gesamte Zeitungswesen* 18: May 5, 901–904.

_____. 1932. "Die Bilderfrage und die Tageszeitungen." *Zeitungs-Verlag: Fachblatt für das gesamte Zeitungswesen* 31: July 30, 528.

_____. 1928b. "Ein neuer journalistischer Berufszweig: der Bildredakteur." *Zeitungs-Verlag: Fachblatt für das gesamte Zeitungswesen* 30: July 28, 1617.

_____. 1930. "Die Verflachung der Bildberichterstattung." *Zeitungs-Verlag: Fachblatt für das gesamte Zeitungswesen* 29: July 19, 1181–84.

_____. 1931. "Bildsünden der deutschen Presse." *Zeitungs-Verlag: Fachblatt für das gesamte Zeitungswesen* 32: February 7, 99–100.

Zeman, Z.A.B. 1973. *Nazi Propaganda.* London: Oxford University Press.

CHAPTER 5

Herzog, Herta. 1955. "Why Did People Believe in the 'Invasion from Mars'?" In Paul Lazarsfeld and Morris S. Rosenberg, eds., The Language of Social Research. Glencoe: The Free Press, 420–428.

Hornblow, Arthur. 1925. "Will Radio Hurt the Theatre?" In *Theatre Magazine* 41:3 (March), 7.

The American Review of Reviews. 1923. "'Listening In,' Our New National Pastime." LXVII: 1 (January), 52.

Kracauer, Siegfried. 1977. *Das Ornament der Masse: Essays*. Frankfurt: Suhrkamp.

Lerg, Winfried. 1970. *Die Entstehung des Rundfunks in Deutschland*. Frankfurt: Josef Knecht.

——. 1980. *Rundfunkpolitik in der Weimarer Republik*. München: *Deutscher Taschenbuchverlag*.

The New York Times. 1923. "Berlin to Broadcast a Speech by Marx." December 23, 3.

——. 1924a. "Berlin Broadcast Daily Food Prices." February 15, 4.

——. 1924b. "Butt in On German Anthem." February 16, 7.

——. 1924c. "Would Bar Our Radio Sets." April 7, 15.

——. 1924d. "Radio Barred in German Campaign." December 1, 12.

——. 1924e. "Radio School in Leipzig." December 21, 24.

——. 1924f. "Radio School in Leipzig." December 21, 24.

——. 1924g. "500,000 German Radio Fans." December 25, 20.

——. 1925a. "German Authors Bar Radio." February 25, 4.

——. 1925b. "Hauptmann and Hoffmannsthal Win Suits Over Broadcasting." March 13, 1.

——. 1925c. "Seek Berlin Radio Peace." August 9, 16.

——. 1925d. "Socialist Fight to Oust Luther." October 30, 2.

——. 1926a. "Broadcasting of Reichstag Debate Urged by Many Radio Fans in Berlin Petition." November 13, 6.

——. 1926b. "Germans Ask Radio Advertising Cut." December 19, 3.

——. 1929a. "Berlin School Has 34 Radio Sets." April 10, 22.

——. 1929b. "To Try Broadcast Here From Germany." August 9, 19.

——. 1929c. "To Try Broadcast Here from Germany." August 9, 19.

——. 1929d. "To Try Broadcast Here From Germany." August 9, 19.

——. 1929e. "Exchanging Radio Programs." August 10, 12.

——. 1929f. "Act to Get German Air Programs Here." August 25, 1.

——. 1930a. "Berlin to Hear Schurmann." January 11, 6.

——. 1930b. "Radio News Rights Denied." May 1, 7.

——. 1930c. "Soviet Radio Talks Resented in Berlin." July 11, 10.

——. 1930d. "Right Way Combat Soviet with Static." July 15, 7.

——. 1930e. "Einstein Sees Radio as Aid to Democracy." August 23, 1.

——. 1930f. "Murder Play on German Radio." September 27, 18.

——. 1930g. "Hindenburg May Overcome Prejudice to Microphone." November 23, 3.

CHAPTER 6

Adams, Samuel H. 1921. Success. Boston: Houghton Mifflin.

Adorno, Theodor W. 1989. "The Culture Industry Reconsidered." In Eric Bronner and Douglas MacKay Kellner, eds., *Critical Theory and Society: A Reader*. London: Routledge, 128–135.

Aiken, Conrad. "Expatriates." *New York Herald Tribune Books*. October 31, 1926, 4.

Anderson, Phil L. 1934. *Court House Square*. Minneapolis: Augsburg.

Anderson, Sherwood. "Dreiser." *Saturday Review of Literature* 2 (January 9, 1926), 475.

Andrus, Louise. 1937. *Though Time Be Fleet.* New York: Lothrop, Lee & Shepard.

Arnold, Elliott. 1934. *Two Loves.* New York: Greenberg.

Baker, Ernest A., and James Packman, eds. 1967. *A Guide to the Best Fiction.* New York: Barnes & Noble.

Beach, Joseph Warren. 1932. *The Twentieth Century Novel. Studies in Technique.* New York: Appleton-Century.

Becker, May Lamberton. "Books for Boys and Girls." *New York Herald Tribune Books.* September 20, 1936a, 12.

_____. "Books for Young People." *New York Herald Tribune Books.* October 11, 1936b, 8.

Bell, Lisle. "New Popular Novels: Though Time Be Brief." *New York Herald Tribune Books.* April 25, 1937, 16.

Belsey, Catherine. 1987. *Critical Practice.* London: Methuen.

Benchley, Robert C. February 1921. "Heroes of Realism." *The Bookman* 52:6, 559–60.

Benefield, Barry. 1925. *The Chicken Wagon Family.* New York: Grosset & Dunlap.

Bent, Silas. "A Sheltered Son of the Press." *The Nation.* January 4, 1928, 20–21.

_____. 1932. *Buchanan of the Press.* New York: Vanguard.

Berger, Josef (Jeremiah Digges). 1938. *Copy Boy.* Philadelphia: Macrae Smith.

Berry, Thomas Elliott. 1970. *The Newspaper in the American Novel 1900–1969.* Metuchen, NJ: Scarecrow.

Bookman. "Realism and Fancy." 62:2 (October 1925), 206.

_____. "Trumpet in the Dust." 71:4 (July 1930), 474.

_____. "Hot News." 73:6 (August 1931), vi.

Boston Evening Transcript. "Unconscious Crusader. A Novel of Life in the World of Journalism." August 28, 1920a, 4.

_____. "The Moon Calf." December 1, 1920b, 11.

_____. "Deadlines." January 13, 1923, 4.

_____. "The Copy Shop." May 29, 1925a, 4.

_____. "Manhattan Transfer: The Tawdry and Grim Parade of New York Life." December 30, 1925b, 6.

_____. "The Sun Also Rises." November 6, 1926, 2.

_____. "Splendor. Ben Ames Williams's Story of a Boston Newspaper Man." December 7, 1927, 5.

_____. "Scoop." February 15, 1930a, 5.

_____. "Ink: A Fearless Newspaper Editor in a Western Town." June 28, 1930b, 2.

_____. "Hot News." July 29, 1931, 2.

_____. "Reach for the Moon: The San Francisco Earthquake the Center of a Novel." November 3, 1934, 3.

Boyd, Ernest. "Readers and Writers." *The Independent* 117:3990 (November 20, 1926), 594.

Brecht, Bertolt. 1977. "Bertolt Brecht Against Georg Lukàcs." In Ronald Taylor, ed., *Aesthetics and Politics.* London: Verso, 68–85.

Brickell, Herschel. "Mad Manhattan Sits For Sordid Portrait." *Literary Review of the New York Evening Post.* November 28, 1925, 5.

Brier, Royce. 1934. *Reach for the Moon.* New York: Appleton-Century.

Brush, Katharine. 1930. *Young Man of Manhattan.* New York: Grosset & Dunlap.

Bugbee, Emma. 1936/1940. *Peggy Covers the News.* New York: Dodd, Mead.

_____. 1937. *Peggy Covers Washington.* New York: Dodd, Mead.

_____. 1939. *Peggy Covers London.* New York: Dodd, Mead.

_____. 1941. *Peggy Covers the Clipper, a Story of a Young Newspaper Woman.* New York: Dodd, Mead.

_____. 1945. *Peggy Goes Overseas.* New York: Dodd, Mead.

Butcher, Fanny. "Here's Story of News People, So Many Plan. But Katharine Brush Has Done Job Well." *Chicago Daily Tribune.* January 11, 1930, 11.

Cail, Harold L. "Editorial Room Romance." *Portland Evening News.* January 7, 1930, 5.

Charnley, Mitchel V. "In the News." *Saturday Review of Literature* 10 (December 9, 1933), 342.

Chase, Cleveland B. "Out of Little, Much." *Saturday Review of Literature* 3 (December 11, 1926), 420.

Christian Science Monitor. "The Man Who Never Got Started." June 22, 1938, 11.

Claudy, Carl H. 1930. *The Girl Reporter.* Boston: Little, Brown.

Colum, Mary M. "Literature and Journalism." *The Freeman* 4 (November 30, 1921), 281–82.

Cook, Dorothy E., and Isabel S. Monroe, eds. 1942. *Fiction Catalog 1941 Edition.* New York: Wilson.

Crawford, John W. "The Greatness of Hurstwood in Dreiser's Latest Character." *New York World.* January 10, 1926, 6m.

Davis, Clyde Brion. 1938. *The Great American Novel.* New York: Farrar & Rinehart.

Dean, Graham. 1933. *Jim of the Press.* New York: Doubleday, Doran.

Dell, Floyd. 1921. *The Moon Calf.* New York: Knopf.

Dial. January 1937. "Briefer Mention." 82, 73.

Dos Passos, John. 1925. *Manhattan Transfer.* Boston: Houghton Mifflin.

Douglas, Lloyd C. 1932. *Forgive Us Our Tresspasses.* Boston: Houghton Mifflin.

Dreiser, Theodore. 1925. *An American Tragedy.* New York: Penguin.

_____. 1931. *Tragic America.* New York: Horace Liveright.

Duffus, Robert L. "Dreiser's Undisciplined Power. His New Novel Contains a Haunting Study of Crime and Punishment." *New York Times Book Review.* January 10, 1926, 1, 6.

Edgett, Edwin Francis. "A Californian in Manhattan Jungles." *Boston Evening Transcript.* October 19, 1921, 6.

_____. "Theodore Dreiser Writes Another Novel. He Again Pursues the Will o' the Wisp of Realism in a Story That Takes His Hero Down Into the Depths of Crime." *Boston Evening Transcript.* January 29, 1926, 3.

Fadiman, Clifton. "Books." *New Yorker* 14 (June 4, 1938), 60–61.

Field, Louise Maunsell. "Novels of the Current Season." *The Bookman* 66:5 (January 1928), 591.

Flexner, James Thomas. "Tortured by Dreams." *New York Herald Tribune Books.* April 13, 1930, 23.

Fowler, Gene. 1930. *Trumpet in the Dust.* New York: Liveright.

Gauvreau, Emile Henry. 1931. *Hot News.* New York: Macaulay.

Gavit, John Palmer. "A Newspaper Story." *The Literary Review.* October 19, 1921, 115.

Geller, James J. "Tabloid Dirt." *New York Herald Tribune Books.* July 12, 1931, 10.

Goldberg, Issac. "The Depths of Realism. 'Eric Dorn' the Ultimate Rule of Modern Fiction." *Boston Evening Transcript.* October 19, 1921, 6.

Gorman, Herbert S. "Hemingway Keeps His Promise." *New York World.* November 14, 1926, 10m.

Hackett, Francis. "Erik Dorn." *The New Republic* 28 (November 14, 1926), 24–25.

Haddock, Hugh V. 1937. *City Desk*. New York: Speller.

Hardt, Hanno. 1992. *Critical Communication Studies: Communication, History, and Theory in America*. London: Routledge.

Harper, Moses. "Fiction Notes." *The New Republic* (December 16, 1925), 118–19.

Hart, James S., and Garrett D. Byrnes. 1930. *Scoop*. Boston: Little, Brown.

Hawkes, Terence. "Blood and Bone." *Times Literary Supplement*. October 19–25, 1990, 1131.

Hecht, Ben. 1963. *Erik Dorn*. Chicago: University of Chicago Press.

Hemingway, Ernest. 1926. *The Sun Also Rises*. New York: Macmillan.

Hopkins, Mary Alden. "A Boy Who Dreamed." *The Publishers' Weekly* 98 (December 18, 1920), 1885.

Hungerford, Edward. 1925. *The Copy Shop*. New York: Putnam.

Irwin, Will. "In a San Francisco Newspaper Office." *New York Herald Tribune Books*. October 14, 1934, 7.

Jameson, Fredric. 1981. *The Political Unconscious: Narrative as a Socially Symbolic Act*. New York: Cornell University Press.

Joel, George. "Trumpet in the Dust." *New York World*. May 4, 1930, 11m.

Kaul, A.J. 1981. "Ben Hecht." In James J. Martine, ed., *Dictionary of Literary Biography*, Volume 9, *American Novelists, 1919–1945*. Detroit: Bruccoli, Clark, 116–124.

Kazin, Alfred. "The Man Who Was Going to Write a Novel. The Simple and Terrifying Story of a Bored Husband and Plodding Newspaperman." *New York Herald Tribune Books*. June 5, 1938, 3.

_____. 1962. "What's Wrong With Culture." In *Contemporaries*, 427–431. Boston: Little, Brown.

Kelland, Clarence Budington. 1923. *Contraband*. New York: Harper.

Knowles, A.S. Jr. 1981. "John Dos Passos." In James J. Martine, ed., *Dictionary of Literary Biography*, Volume 9, *American Novelists, 1919–1945*.. Detroit: Bruccoli, Clark, 217–236.

Levin, Meyer. 1929. *Reporter*. New York: John Day.

_____. 1950. *In Search: An Autobiography*. New York: Horizon.

Lewis, Edwin Herbert. 1924. *Sallie's Newspaper*. Chicago: Hyman-McGee.

Lewis, Sinclair. "Manhattan at Last!" *Saturday Review of Literature* 2 (December 5, 1925), 361.

Lowenthal, Leo. 1984a. "Preface." In *Literature and Mass Culture: Communication in Society*, Vol. 1, ix-xiv. New Brunswick, NJ: Transaction.

_____. 1984b. "On Sociology of Literature (1932)." In *Literature and Mass Culture: Communication in Society*, Vol. 1, 243–255. New Brunswick: Transaction.

_____. 1987. "Scholarly Biography." In Martin Jay, ed., *An Unmastered Past*. Berkeley: University of California Press, 163–182.

Macy, John. "A Mad World." *Literary Review of the New York Evening Post*. August 20, 1921, 3.

Mallette, Gertrude Ethel. 1937. *Private Props*. New York: Doubleday, Doran.

Martine, James J., ed. 1981. *Dictionary of Literary Biography*, Volume 9, *American Novelists, 1919–1945, Part 1: Louis Adamic—Vardis Fisher*. Detroit: Bruccoli, Clark.

Mellett, John C. 1930. *Ink*. Indianapolis: Bobbs-Merrill.

Meltzer, Milton. 1969. *Brother, Can You Spare a Dime? The Great Depression 1929–1933*. New York: Knopf.

Morley, Christopher. "Homer Zigler Goes Home." *Saturday Review of Literature* 18 (June 4, 1938), 5.

Morris, Lawrence S. "Warfare in Man and Among Men." *The New Republic* 49 (December 22, 1926), 142–43.

Mosco, Vincent, and Janet Wasko. 1983. *The Critical Communications Review. Volume 1: Labor, the Working Class, and the Media.* Norwood, N.J.: Ablex.

Nagel, James. 1981. "Ernest Hemingway." In James J. Martine, ed., *Dictionary of Literary Biography,* Volume 9, *American Novelists, 1919–1945,* 100–120. Detroit: Bruccoli, Clark.

Nation. "Moon-Calif on the Mississippi." December 8, 1920, 670.

New Republic. "Moon-Calf." December 8, 1928, 49.

_____. "Topical Novels." August 26, 1931, 53.

New York Evening Press. "Gentlemen of the Press." February 13, 1930, 11m.

New York Herald Tribune Books. "Merton of Park Row." March 15, 1925, 11.

_____. "Buchanan of 'The Press.'" October 16, 1932, 9.

_____. "Gathering the News." November 14, 1937, 28.

The New York Times. "Theodore Dreiser Dies at Age of 74." December 29, 1945, 1, 14.

_____. "Ben A. Williams, 63, Novelist, Is Dead." February 5, 1953, 23.

_____. "Samuel Hopkins Adams Is Dead; Novelist and Biographer Was 87." November 17, 1958, 31.

_____. "Clarence Budington Kelland, Prolific Author, Is Dead at 82." February 19, 1964, 39.

The New York Times Book Review. "Unconscious Crusader." June 20, 1920a, 25, 329.

_____. "Latest Works of Fiction." December 12, 1920b, 20.

_____. "Erik Dorn." December 12, 1920b, 12, 18.

_____. "Success." November 6, 1921b, 16, 30.

_____. 7 "Deadlines." January 1923, 17.

_____. "A Batch of Theories." August 17, 1924, 9.

_____. "Old Newspaper Days." March 22, 1925, 9.

_____. "Marital Tragedy." October 31, 1926, 7.

_____. "A Newspaper Story." November 20, 1927, 6.

_____. "A Roving Reporter." March 30, 1930a, 21–22.

_____. "Trumpet in the Dust and Other Works." May 11, 1930b, 8.

_____. "Exposing Tabloidia." July 5, 1931, 7.

_____. "A Star Reporter." October 23, 1932, 7.

_____. "A Newspaper Novel." May 27,1934a, 7, 18.

_____. "Newspaper Romance." June 3, 1934b, 7.

_____. "Latest Works of Fiction." November 11, 1934c, 26.

_____. "The New Books for Boys and Girls." December 6, 1936, 14.

_____. "The Woman's Angle." April 25, 1937a, 23.

_____. "Newspaper Work." December 5, 1937b, 12.

New York World. "Young Man of Manhattan." January 6, 1930, 15.

Outlook. "New Novels with a Special Interest." November 23, 1921, 129, 486.

_____. "Splendor." November 23, 1921, 147, 507.

Powell, Dawn. "Novels and Novellas." *The New Republic* 95 (May 25, 1938), 82.

Rascoe, Burton. "An American Epithetician." *The Bookman* 54:2 (October 1921), 164–66.

_____. "Romance and Result of Newspaper Work." *New York Tribune.* January 14, 1923, 17.

Rideout, Walter B. 1992. *The Radical Novel in the United States 1900–1954: Some Interrelations of Literature and Society.* New York: Columbia University Press.

Ross, Mary. "Beads in a Box." *New York Herald Tribune Books.* December 27, 1925, 1–2.
_____. "The Bookshelf." *Atlantic Monthly* 145 (March 1930), 22.
Ross, Virgilia Peterson. "The Literary Racket." *New York Herald Tribune Books.* January 5, 1930, 5.
Saturday Review of Literature. "The Copy Shop." March 28, 1925, 635.
_____. "Scoop." March 8, 1930, 6, 809.
_____. "In Tabloidia." March 8, 1930, 8, 57.
Schriftgiesser, Karl. "A Young Newspaper Man of Manhattan." *Boston Evening Transcript.* December 28, 1929, 8.
Seldes, George. 1938. *Lords of the Press.* New York: Julian Messner.
Seldes, Gilbert. "Arriviste and Aristocrat." *The Dial* 71 (November 1921), 597–600.
Sherman, Stuart. "Mr. Dreiser in Tragic Realism." *New York Herald Tribune Books.* January 3, 1926, 1–3.
Smith, Henry Justin. 1923. *Deadlines.* Chicago: Covici-McGee.
_____. 1933. *Young Phillips, Reporter.* New York: Harcourt Brace.
Springfield Republican. "A Newspaper Story." April 18, 1920, 13a.
_____. "Two Knights of the Yellow Press: Samuel Hopkins Adams's 'Success' Pictures Journalism Cynically." November 20, 1921, 11a.
_____. "Deadlines: Life and Spirit of American Newspaper Office." January 7, 1923, 7a.
_____. "Romantic Newspaper Yarn. Hero of 'The Copy Shop' Survives the Usual Experiences." April 12, 1925, 7a.
_____. "Seeking Sensations: 'The Sun Also Rises' Pictures Anglo-Saxon Expatriates." November 28, 1926, 7f.
Stuart, Henry Longan. "John Dos Passos Notes the Tragic Trivia of New York." *New York Times Book Review.* November 29, 1925, 5, 14.
Tate, Allen. "Hard Boiled." *The Nation* 123:3206 (December 15, 1926), 642–43.
Tebbel, John. 1978. *A History of Book Publishing in the United States.* Volume III. *The Golden Age between Two Wars, 1920–1940.* New York: R.R. Bowker.
Tracy, Don. 1934. *Round Trip.* New York: Vanguard.
Van Gelder, Robert. 1937/1946. *Front Page Story.* New York: Dodd, Mead.
_____. "A Bitter Comedy of Frustration, Clyde Brion Davis Portrays a Newspaper Man Who Hoped Someday to Write a Great Novel." *New York Times Book Review.* June 5, 1938, 6.
Walker, Stanley. "Getting Out a Newspaper." *New York Herald Tribune Books.* November 13, 1938, 28.
Weinberg, Steve. 1991. "Novels with Journalists as Characters." Unpublished raw data. Columbia, MO.
Whitman, Alden. "Floyd Dell, Novelist of 1920s And 'Village' Figure, Is Dead." *New York Times.* July 30, 1969, 39.
Williams, Ben Ames. 1928. *Splendor.* New York: Dutton.
Williams, Raymond. 1981. *Politics and Letters: Interviews with New Left Review.* London: Verso.
_____. 1990. *What I Came to Say.* Edited by Neil Belton, Francis Mulhern, and Jenny Taylor. London: Hutchinson Radius.
Williams, Sidney. 1920. *An Unconscious Crusader.* Boston: Small, Maynard.
Yaakov, Juliette, and John Greenfelt, eds. 1991. *Fiction Catalog.* 12th Edition. New York: Wilson.

CHAPTER 7

Andrews, Lew. "Walker Evans: American Photographs: The Sequential Arrangement." History of Photography 18:3 (Fall 1964), 264–271.

Brierly, Dean. "Walker Evans: The Shock of Recognition." *Camera & Darkroom* 14:8 (August 1, 1992), 40–47, 56.

Baudelaire, Charles. 1980. "The Modern Public and Photography." In *Classic Essays on Photography*. Edited by Alan Trachtenberg. New Haven, CT: Leete's Island Books, 83–89.

Carey, James. 1989. "Advertising: An Institutional Approach." In Roxanne Hovland and Gary Wilcox, eds., *Advertising in Society: Classic and Contemporary Readings on Advertising's Role in Society*. Lincolnwood, IL: NTC Business Books, 11–26.

Evans, Walker. 1980. "The Reappearance of Photography." In Alan Trachtenberg, ed., *Classic Essays on Photography*. New Haven, CT: Leete's Island Books, 185–188.

_____. 1982. *Walker Evans at Work*. New York: Harper & Row.

Ewen, Stuart. 1976. *Captains of Consciousness: Advertising and the Social Roots of the Consumer Culture*. New York: McGraw-Hill.

Fox, Stephen. 1997. *The Mirror Makers: A History of American Advertising and Its Creators*. Urbana: University of Illinois Press.

Giles, Mora, and John T. Hill. 1993. *Walker Evans. The Hungry Eye*. New York: Abrams.

Goodrum, Charles, and Helen Dalrymple. 1990. *Advertising in America: The First 200 Years*. New York: Abrams.

Hulick, Diana Emery. "Walker Evans & Folk Art." *History of Photography* 17:2 (Summer 1993), 139–144.

Kirstein, Lincoln. 1988. "Photographs of America: Walker Evans." In *Walker Evans, American Photographs*. Fiftieth Anniversary Edition. New York: Museum of Modern Art, 189–198.

Kozloff, Max. "Signs of Light: Walker Evans' American Photographs. *Artforum* 27:8 (April 1, 1989), 114–118.

Orvell, Miles. "Walker Evans and James Agee: the Legacy." *History of Photography*, 17:2 (Summer 1993), 166–171.

Purvis, Alston W. "The Extra-Ordinary Signs of Walker Evans." *Print* 47:5 (Sept. 1, 1993), 52–61.

Rabinowitz, Paula. "Voyeurism and Class Consciousness: James Agee and Walker Evans, *Let Us Now Praise Famous Men*." *Cultural Critique* 21 (Spring 1992), 143–170.

Rathbone, Belinda. 1995. *Walker Evans: A Biography*. Boston: Houghton Mifflin.

Schudson, Michael. 1986. *Advertising, the Uneasy Persuasion: Its Dubious Impact on American Society*. New York: Basic Books.

Takata, Ken. "Toward an Elegance of Movement—Walker Evans and Robert Frank Revisited." *Journal of American Culture* 12:1 (Spring 1989), 55–64.

Trachtenberg, Alan. 1984. "Walker Evans's America. A Documentary Invention. In David Featherstone, ed., *Observations*. Friends of Photography, Untitled 3, 56–66.

_____. 1989. *Reading American Photographs. Images as History: Mathew Brady to Walker Evans*. New York: Hill & Wang.

Ward, J. A. 1985. *American Silences: The Realism of James Agee, Walker Evans, and Edward Hopper*. Baton Rouge: Louisiana State University Press.

Ware, Robert. "Walker Evans: Impersonality and Metaphor." *History of Photography* 17:2 (Summer 1993), 147–151.

Raymond Williams. 1961. *The Long Revolution*. London: Chatto & Windus.

_____. 1977. *Marxism and Literature*: Oxford: Oxford University Press.

_____. 1980. "Advertising: the Magic System." In *Problems in Materialism and Culture*. London: Verso, 170–195.

_____. 1983. *Writing in Society*. London: Verso.

CHAPTER 8

Allen, Frederick Lewis. 1931. Only Yesterday. New York: Harper.

Allen, Frederick Lewis. 1952. *The Big Change. America Transforms Itself, 1900–1950*. New York: Harper.

Banning, William Peck. 1946. *Commercial Broadcasting Pioneer. The WEAF Experiment, 1922–1926*. Cambridge: Harvard University Press.

Better Homes and Gardens. October 1936.

Collier's. 1936. January 11, 25; February 8, 22; April 4; May 15; July 25; August 22; September 5; October 31; November 21; December 12.

Country Gentleman. February 1936.

Danna, Sammy R. 1975. "The Press-Radio War." In Lawrence W. Lichty and Malachi C. Topping, eds., *American Broadcasting. A Sourcebook on the History of Radio and Television*. New York: Hastings House, 344–50.

Douglas, Susan J. 1987. *Inventing American Broadcasting 1899–1922*. Baltimore: The Johns Hopkins University Press.

Good Housekeeping. 1936. June, September, and October.

Goode, Kenneth M. and Harford Powel, Jr. 1970. "What About Advertising?" In Robert Sklar, ed., *The Plastic Age, 1917–1930*. New York: George Braziller, 87–97.

Hettinger, Herman S. 1975. "Some Fundamental Aspects of Radio Broadcasting Economics." In Lawrence W. Lichty and Malachi C. Topping, eds., *American Broadcasting. A Sourcebook on the History of Radio and Television*. New York: Hastings House, 230–36.

House & Gardens. 1936 January, May, and June.

Innis, Harold. 1951. *The Bias of Communication*. Toronto: University of Toronto Press.

Kaempffert, Waldemar. 1924. "The Social Destiny of Radio." In *Forum*, 71 (June), 771–772.

Kruse, Holly. 1993. "Early Audio Technology and Domestic Space." In *Stanford Humanities Review* 3:2, 1–14.

Life. October 1936.

McLuhan, Marshall. 1964. *Understanding Media: The Extension of Man*. New York: Signet.

Mosco, Vincent. 1979. *Broadcasting in the United States. Innovative Challenge and Organizational Control*. Norwood, NJ: Ablex.

Nachman, Gerald. 1998. *Raised on Radio*. New York: Pantheon.

Orvell, Miles. 1989. *The Real Thing: Imitation and Authenticity in American Culture, 1880–1940*. Chapel Hill: University of North Carolina Press.

Ostrander, Gilman M. 1970. *American Civilization in the First Machine Age, 1890–1940*. New York: Harper Torchbooks.

Pitkin, Walter B. 1972. "The American: How He Lives." In Warren Susman, ed., *Culture and Commitment, 1929–1945*. New York: George Braziller, 188–192 (originally published in 1932).

Saturday Evening Post. 1936. January 11, 25; February 22, 29; March 21; April 4, 11; May 9, 30; August 15, 29; September 12; October 3, 10, 24; November 21; December 5, 9.

Sennett, Richard. 1974. *The Fall of Public Man.* New York: Vintage.

Spalding, John W. 1975. "1928: Radio Becomes a Mass Advertising Medium." In Lawrence W. Lichty and Malachi C. Topping, eds., *American Broadcasting. A Sourcebook on the History of Radio and Television.* New York: Hastings House, 219–28.

Spigel, Lynn. 1992. *Make Room for TV: Television and the Family Ideal in Postwar America.* Chicago: University of Chicago Press.

Thurber, James. 1972. "The Soap Opera." In Warren Susman, ed., *Culture and Commitment, 1929–1945.* New York: George Braziller, 151–169 (originally published in 1948).

Wish, Harry. 1962. *Society and Thought in Modern America.* New York: David McKay.

CHAPTER 9

Althusser, Louis. 1970. "Ideology and Ideological State Apparatuses." In Lenin and Philosophy. London: Verso, 121–173.

Barthes, Roland. 1981. *Camera Lucida. Reflections on Photography.* New York: Hill and Wang.

_____. 1977. "Rhetoric of the Image." In *Image—Music—Text.* New York: Hill and Wang, 32–51.

Benjamin, Walter. 1969. "Theses on the Philosophy of History." In Hannah Arendt, ed., *Illuminations.* London: Cape, 253–264.

Berger, John. 1980. *About Looking.* New York: Pantheon Books.

Bergson, Henri. 1896. *Matter and Memory.* London: George Allen & Unwin.

Bourdieu, Pierre. 1990. *Photography: A Middle-Brow Art.* Stanford: Stanford University Press.

Burgin, Victor, ed. 1982. *Thinking Photography.* London: McMillan.

Carruther, Mary. 1990. *The Book of Memory. A Study of Memory in Medieval Culture.* Cambridge: Cambridge University Press.

Casey, Edward. 1987. *Remembering: A Phenomenological Study.* Bloomington: Indiana University Press.

Castoriadis, Cornelius. 1975. *The Imaginary Institution of Society.* Cambridge: Polity Press.

Godelier, Maurice. 1984. *The Mental and the Material.* London: Verso.

Holly, Michael Ann. 1996. *Past Looking: Historical Imagination and the Rhetoric of the Image.* Ithaca: Cornell University Press.

Krell, David Farrell. 1990. *Of Memory, Reminiscence, and Writing.* Bloomington: Indiana University Press.

Le Goff, Jacques. 1992. *History and Memory.* New York: Columbia University Press.

Liss, Andrea. 1998. *Trespassing Through Shadows: Memory, Photography and the Holocaust.* Minneapolis: University of Minnesota Press.

Manguel, Alberto. 1996. *A History of Reading.* New York: Viking.

Mitchell, W. J. T. 1994. *Picture Theory: Essays on Verbal and Visual Representation.* Chicago: University of Chicago Press.

Rugg, Linda Haverty. 1997. *Picturing Ourselves: Photography and Autobiography.* Chicago: University of Chicago Press.

Samuel, Raphael. 1994. *Theatres of Memory*. Vol. 1. *Past and Present in Contemporary Society*. London: Verso.

Sekula, Allan. 1982. "On the Invention of Photographic Meaning." In Victor Burgin, ed., *Thinking Photography*. London: Macmillan, 84–109.

Sontag, Susan. 1973. *On Photography*. New York: Farrar, Straus and Giroux.

Tagg, John. 1988. *The Burden of Representation: Essays on Photographies and Histories*. Amherst: University of Massachusetts Press.

Virilio, Paul. 1995. *The Art of the Motor*. Minneapolis: University of Minnesota Press.

Yates, Frances. 1966. *The Art of Memory*. Chicago: University of Chicago Press.

Index

▼ ▼ ▼